yonder

yonder

a place in **montana**

JOHN HEMINWAY

ADVENTURE PRESS

NATIONAL GEOGRAPHIC
WASHINGTON, D. C.

Published by the National Geographic Society
1145 17th Street N.W., Washington, D.C. 20036

First Printing, September 2000

Interior Design by Kathleen Cole
Printed in U.S.A.

for Kathryn

Montana is different from most other states because it embodies a simple, compelling idea. The idea is: open space, sparsely populated.

The idea assumes its own life if we situate ourselves at the heart of this aloneness. When each of us first sets foot in Montana, it would appear we can do what we like with the void. We can fill it, we can exploit it, we can restore it, we can leave it alone.

Elbow room combined with personal freedom leads to dangerous enticements. When land woos us with the power of creation, it confers on us a mighty burden. Overnight, we must make a choice that will render us either hero, rogue, ally, adversary, custodian, or crook.

A story of Montana must always be about people, for they are central to the land. No book that tackles this astonishing region of the Northern Rockies dares leave them out.

Mine is thus a small story, overwhelmed by one intoxicating idea.

CONTENTS

The three of us drove slowly, watching the valley change from open ranchland to aspen grove. The river, gouged deep into the floodplain floor, was rarely visible, but when we stopped, switched off, rolled down windows, it conveyed itself to us through the hush of chill March air as a series of mutters and growls.

From our first view of the West Boulder Valley, we felt ourselves Magellans, pioneers of a new firmament. Here was a river, a valley, and a landscape distinctly desolate, yet sculpted on a scale that accommodated humanity. I was certain I'd never seen such a mix anywhere else on earth.

Admittedly, we were in a mood for revelations. For two years, my sister, Hilary, and I had taken to inspecting Montana river systems in the hope of finding a small cabin for our family to buy. We were looking for a fishing camp, a mountain place still beyond the reach of developers. It would become perfect complement to the family ranch to the east, also in Montana. There there were no rivers, the only moisture being that which we teased from deep in the earth with a succession of windmills.

The West Boulder River seemed offbeat, a dead-end drainage that even a friend, the state's most successful real estate broker, hadn't bothered to visit. But something from his description stuck. "Just follow the river south," he explained by phone, "until you pass the Road Kill Café, hang right onto a sort of gravel road. There's probably a left involved, but you'll have to figure that out yourselves. In time...maybe ten miles...the road'll take you into what they call 'the hippie commune.'"

Hippies. The prized ranch of the West Boulder Valley, he explained, had been adopted in the early seventies by a group of highly educated, underfinanced dropouts bent on escape from the East. "Fuzzy-headedness," he proclaimed. They'd made a down payment on this ranch for the purpose of having a place to build guitars, weave baskets, throw pots, play music, and live free—that is, if they could meet the payments.

But something, according to the broker, had gone wrong. Now, hardly 15 years since the commune's inception, a number of these latter-day pioneers were bailing out, putting their land up for sale. "Might be an opportunity."

Who knows, we thought as we crossed the cattle guard to the mysterious enclave. We studied the aspen groves and the base of limestone cliffs, overlain by cloud. No yurts in sight. No smell of pot. Just a sign: "Welcome to the West Boulder Reserve. Private land. Please stay on road for next 2 and a half miles." Shortly we came to a cluster of log buildings. A slender woman, her brown hair braided down her back, was planting asparagus under a transparent geodesic dome. When I stumbled out of the pickup, she didn't look my way; even when I leaned over the fence to talk, she made no move to approach. "Beautiful place," I began.

"Uh-huh." Her eyes shifted to the black earth. I was bothering her.

"You here for the long haul—what with the asparagus and all?"

"Yup."

I studied the modest log house and thought it couldn't be more than one large room and a sleeping loft. I wondered if they depended on videotapes. "Gets lonely in winter?"

"Do you want to speak to Chan?" she interrupted, heading off for one of the sheds. We heard the low singsong of their voices and soon her partner, also unsmiling, appeared. He too wasn't dressed like a Montanan; no "howdies," no small talk. His hat advertised a lumberyard, and his boots were steel plated. He looked at us wordlessly. It was clear the burden of conversation lay on me.

"We're just driving through and wondered whether there might be land for sale."

I could see Chan was working Copenhagen across his gums. "Yeah," he said after a pause. "Number of places." Without a word he left us, and for a while I doubted he would return. But in time he was back, a plat map under his arm. He unfurled it against the fence and put a dot on the place where we stood—the place he dubbed "the reserve guesthouse and caretaker cabin," adding that he was "the caretaker." North and south, to the east of the river, on the slopes of cloud-covered slopes were three sites, all for sale. The fourth, described by the map as the "Bar 20," lay to the west of the river. With deadpan delivery, he warned us about the bridge: "Might be a little iffy for your pickup." We said our good-byes, settled ourselves back in the truck and drove away, all the time pondering the couple's "un-Montanan" reserve.

Throughout the afternoon my friend, my sister, and I walked hills, studying the map and locating ourselves on its isobars. It was a wildly beautiful collection of hours—a scramble among rock, through chokecherry, across snow, lingering at the base of big-branched firs. For a second, standing on a potential homesite, the overcast parted and high, jagged spires of rock emerged at the end of the valley. The Alps, I thought, trying to focus my eyes to the gleam of silvered snow.

Until late afternoon, the West Boulder Valley had been for us a fine Sunday diversion. We sat in the pickup, munching sandwiches, and let the valley inch under our skins. Now the hour late, light flat, wind cutting, we chose to dedicate our last few minutes to the improbably named Bar 20. We drove down a track which approached the river diagonally. To either side, we saw log buildings, painted muddy orange, their windows boarded. Beside the river bottom lay two barns, all sagging roofs and tar paper. At the bridge, our way was barred by a chain. We set out on foot; beneath us timbers creaked as we gazed upon the river.

The West Boulder ran slow and thick as if it had just emerged from ice. The river bottom shone through the current as pure as air; it was all pebble, stone, boulder, rounded through eons of miscarried travel from high mountains north to the Yellowstone River, east and south to the Gulf of Mexico. A water ouzel burst from its shelter under the bridge and skittered across the river to perch on an exposed boulder. A pair of mergansers fleeted past, rounded the bend, and vanished in rising mist. Ravens cried out and an eagle, probably a golden, circled beneath a glowering ceiling of troubled cloud.

On the far side, we cut through the aspen to enter a clearing. Facing us was the Bar 20—a low-slung log building, its roof overarched by Douglas firs. A pole fence enclosed the house, cabin, shed, brittle honeysuckle, and lilac bush—these seemingly the only human touches immune from neglect. We looked through the windows of the house, but drop cloths concealed the interior. The main building appeared to have been built erratically, room by room. Not the work of an architect, the building's structure seemed to squirm haphazardly across terrain, each addition a momentary impulse. It recalled to me a collection of railway cars, shunted onto a siding and abandoned.

Shingles had blown from the roof across the patchy lawn; the building's porches sagged, and a mountain chickadee lay dead beneath a crudely installed picture window. The Bar 20 was certainly no trophy home; it boasted no cathedral ceiling, no great room, no hot tub, and the marauding aspens denied what every house should have—a breathtaking view. The Bar 20 seemed so inconspicuous in fact—a mere brushstroke of rural engineering—I wondered why cartographers had chosen to list it on topographical maps. Viewed from the air, I knew its dark logs and weathered roof would be subtle to the point of invisibility. Any sensible person seeing it for the first time would have walked away.

But for me, the Bar 20 was perfection. I instantly recognized it as our imagined cabin, and I felt my heart racing with a premonition of my future. Serenely situated within its own habitat, the building appeared to be the transition zone from clearing to grove. It lent the impression that Douglas firs had fallen down, then rearranged themselves to create a shelter especially comfortable for Douglas firs. Unlike so many new homes, the Bar 20 was no affront to nature; it seemed to have an affinity with limestone cliffs, aspens, and the river. Age had made it a feature of the drainage. Should the West Boulder rise and flow around its footings, making it an island or a headland, it little mattered: the Bar 20 would accommodate itself to nature's whim and, somehow, survive to become an ark.

I didn't leap to the conclusion, "We must have it." I wasn't even certain I liked it. Instead I was consumed by a sense of familiarity, a gnawing, perhaps atavistic memory of both clearing and cabin. The Bar 20 didn't communicate itself as a chocolate-box log house—cozy little daffodil place reeking of woodsmoke and hot biscuits; it was, if anything, imperfect, perhaps downright homely, yet in me it seemed instantly to fill a gaping hollow, to fulfill unspecified, ineluctable yearnings. I impulsively thought: This is where I ought to be.

"What do you think?" I asked my sister, knowing from the hush, she was equally stunned, even though our tastes often ran counter. But she had already advanced beyond "wows," turning instead to practical matters. When we retraced our steps to the bridge, I watched her pause to look over her shoulder until the dusk had turned the Bar 20 into one continuous shadow. From the flicker in her eyes it was clear she already had begun decorating.

We returned to our family ranch in darkness. After we drove through Big Timber and reached cruise speed on the interstate, I let Hilary do the talking: "It's going to take lots of work.... You know if they cover the windows, the inside must be a mess.... But I can see there's one long room which will be perfect.... Probably three bedrooms sharing one bath in the worst place imaginable. We'll probably have to add bathrooms. And the kitchen: we'll be lucky if it's anything better than a wood stove."

"Let's keep it simple," I interjected. "You know, it's only a cabin, and we'll only use it for fishing. It's not that I want to hang out year round with a lot of basket weavers, talking about where to build the bomb shelter."

By morning we started making calls and by noon we had identified the owner of the Bar 20 and contacted Jim, our real estate guru, to retain him as our agent. Two days later, we began negotiations. Soon we learned the Bar 20 had been on the market for well over a year—good news since it implied our offer would attract the owner's attention, but worrisome since it suggested a problem known to everyone but ourselves.

A week later, we still were ignorant of the Bar 20's secret. Worst, the owner, Eugene Magat, was adamant we meet his price. After another week and a battery of telephone calls, he had budged a mere fraction from where he began.

Four months later, on July 17, 1987, an indulgent father, my sister, and I would sign the deed on the Bar 20. Two of us had visited it once, none of us had ever seen the interior, nor walked its contiguous 16 acres. Moreover, we began hearing that the 1300 acre "commune" to which it was associated was a place with a "checkered history" and that other plots of land were somehow so encumbered they couldn't be sold. All we knew for certain was that we had paid top dollar for a site whose only redeeming feature was what I can lamely describe as good vibes.

At first, the purchase of the Bar 20 was viewed as just a land transaction. Little did I suspect that, by acquiring the Bar 20, we had embarked on a remarkable family expedition into the American West.

CHAPTER 1

A Talisman

From the beginning, I had a hunch the Bar 20 was destiny, a place that, for yet undisclosed reasons, had been waiting for us. As we prepared for ownership with earnest money, title insurance, and contracts, I was at work in a world removed from logs, mare's tails, and meanders. It was then I developed the affectation of saying I had to go East for a day job to afford to be a Montana rancher. "Just as well you're far," commented the realtor, for he believed it would appear unseemly for me to be seen snooping around the Bar 20 until the owners had an opportunity to clear out.

During the wait I traveled extensively, completing work on a science series to be aired on PBS in the fall. No matter how grim a motel I awoke to each morning, I found comfort in knowing the Bar 20 would soon become our family "hill station." Innocently, I believed we could improve it. I studied its photographs, captured on that gray March day. The roof would have to be replaced, no doubt about it. Maybe fencing, as well. I cocked my head, closed my eyes, and tried to imagine the house elbowed by stands of aspen in full leaf. Meanwhile my sister, having found a layout of the interior, was developing her "design strategy."

The current owners, it appeared, had been using the large room as a recreational hall. It was dominated by a Ping-Pong table in the middle and a deer head above the mantel. "They'll have to go," Hilary informed me by phone.

My sister has inherited the family decorating gene. Ever since she was a teenager, she has been driven to make habitats habitable and to find charm and comfort in unfamiliar places. Hers is a gift that has launched a successful career as interior designer. It also has informed her relationship with her two brothers ("I can't believe you're still wearing plaids and stripes." "Oh my God, when are you ever going to get rid of this clutter?"). During the spring, she dedicated her free time to the Bar 20. She sent me swatches of material as a possible theme for its living room, and soon rustic furniture, some from the Adirondacks, began arriving in vans at my eastern home. Before long, my cellar was full. What had been proposed as a "small cabin on a river," now had became a major undertaking.

We Americans, I've found, are often gulled into the doctrine of Now. For us the past might as well be a curiosity, an artifact that's usually flawed. For us there's no more important epoch than the present. We moderns require contemporary surrounds. Deferred maintenance, so the argument goes, is clear proof of history's irresponsibility. "Look at those weather-wasted logs," someone might exclaim. "The telltale indicator of transience, the baggage of others' failed lives."

For so many of us nomads, houses are but temporary encampments on the trail of profession, passion, and necessity. They and all their associations must regularly be abandoned so one can be available to reinvent oneself. I have heard of a nabob with many houses, one on an island in a Montana lake. For the last seven years he has underwritten a full-time crew, building his island fortress for his exclusive use. So far the tycoon hasn't lived in the house. In fact, it's doubtful he ever will, for now he says he has lost interest in the whole project and wants to move on.

A dwelling may represent nothing more than a passing fancy, a fleet mood, a whim for those who see life not as narrative of internal growth but as an explosive series of structural changes. America is, after all, the land for new beginnings.

One popular solution to antiquity in smart Western places like Aspen and, increasingly, along blue ribbon rivers of Montana is the "million dollar knock-down"—whereby a perfectly sound house of a certain age is leveled so a larger, modern expression of its owner's personality can emerge upon its ruins. Old houses are often too small; only a new home, laid out by a name architect, accessorized by a savvy designer, can customize one's very particular claim to success.

I don't exclude myself entirely from this pretense of ownership. My family's approach has been perhaps a slight variant of the theme. A decade earlier, we had adopted Montana as our personal frontier, yet we didn't look upon the hardscrabble Bull Mountain Ranch as trophy—there were so many other ranches that dwarfed us in size and grandeur. Our intention at the Bar 20 was to build not a stately home but to preserve an old place's integrity, however fugitive. We had fallen under the spell of a river and a set of buildings: We were smitten by its logs.

Still, there's no point in overstating intentions. We knew antiquity had its place. Change would have to be central to our tenure. The place had gracelessly succumbed to a 1960s aesthetic. The game room would be reconfigured, windows upgraded, kitchen appliances chucked out, all to be replaced by the latest devices, the whole structure scrubbed clean, its past reduced to a witticism so our lives could begin on a proper footing. In the end, the Bar 20 would reflect us in every way, even though it was created for someone else—whomever that was.

On July 17, 1987, in a lawyer's office, we closed on the Bar 20. It wasn't necessary for any of us to be there. That day, with my sister, I drove down the West Boulder Valley to pay our first and final respects to the seller, settle on a few items of furniture if there was anything, and find out if we had indeed acquired a lemon.

In July the valley was transformed: meadows were awash in coneflowers, Indian paintbrush, lupine, and brittle shards of June's balsam root. High on the edges of pastures, mule deer shifted between the shadows of firs, and on meadows by the river bottom, white-tailed deer skittered in an out of willows. The sky was marine blue with high, wispy clouds that, trailing tails, raced eastward. When we turned onto the final stretch of West Boulder Road, we stopped the pickup, hearts racing as we saw at last, at the end of the valley, the snow-capped peaks that had teased us during a break in March weather. "So far," my sister said, "our hunch was 100 percent correct." We drove across the bridge and noted it sagged only slightly from our weight. The river no longer chortled. It roared. We drove between a stand of cottonwoods and firs, rounded a bend, entered the clearing, and parked in front of the cabin. The Bar 20 was smaller, more awkward than I recalled. Outside the fence, grass, turning yellow with summer, stood high, while within, there were signs the owner and a handmower had attempted to bring order to a maverick lawn.

Eugene Magat came to the door. I suspected he was in his 60s: I was struck instantly by his precise manner, bordering on fastidiousness. He introduced us to his wife, who then retired to the gloom of the house. Later, I had the impression she went from window to window, observing our every move. All the while, Mr. Magat moved around the grounds efficiently, as if he had planned this route well in advance. When he spoke I detected a deliberate way with words: perhaps English was not his first language.

He was determined to take me first to the back of the house, across a drainage ditch, then into secondary cover on a path slick from running water. Five minutes later we arrived at a copse, edged by wild rose; here, with wet feet, I saw a spring bubbling from the limestone cliff. Now I understood our mission. Mr. Magat explained he had built this spring box to capture water gushing from the cliff. Clearly, its square frame filled him with pride, even though the tin was now pocked with holes. He said not a word to allow the keenness of this engineering feat to overwhelm the discomfort of wet feet. Soon we retraced our steps, following the pipe's course to the foot of the cliff and again across the ditch. He paused, this time to point out the watercress, growing like weeds wherever water flowed. He said not a word but pursed his lips to effect a kiss. Later he said, "You'll also become addicted to the water. Very pure. Full of minerals. It'll make you very regular." I now made up my mind Eugene Magat was a Frenchman.

While we were doing the tour of the grounds, my sister had been inspecting the house—a delicate maneuver because Mrs. Magat purposefully didn't want to talk.

The rooms were dark and the furnishings, many now boxed, were a jumble of unrelated collectibles. The couches and the piano, Mr. Magat indicated, would stay—if we wished to pay for them; so too the 1950s bicycle for which his daughter had set the price at $25. But two pieces of Mission furniture that had caught my sister's eye were not available, even though they had belonged to the Bar 20 when the Magats acquired it. "My wife wouldn't allow it," Mr. Magat said, shrugging his shoulders with Gallic resignation.

Soon, it became clear the courtly Mr. Magat had sold us the Bar 20 over the protests of daughter and, possibly, wife. In fact, in all likelihood we had interrupted a frosty exchange between the couple. I later learned Mrs. Magat had dedicated her career to education; and now, in retrospect, I recall the look of a disapproving pedagogue—the pinch of disdain—as she removed herself to the shadows of the house. For her, we were children, raised permissively by our parents. Meanwhile a well-rehearsed Mr. Magat treated us analytically—players, perhaps, in his estate-planning strategy.

Like us, the Magats were easterners; they had lived first in Delaware, later in Vermont, finally in North Carolina. Eugene, an engineer, had dedicated most of his life to the DuPont Company. When we walked the Bar 20 property line, he hinted darkly he had been central to a great discovery there. I was later to learn he had helped create Kevlar, a reinforcing fiber, used most notably in the manufacture of bulletproof vests.

At DuPont, one day in the early seventies, a colleague approached with an out-of-the-blue question: "Do you want to buy land in Montana?" Apparently, this friend's son had entered into a contract with others to subdivide a Rocky Mountain ranch—a goal that couldn't be achieved unless the remaining plots were sold.

A month later, the two Magats, en route to visit a daughter at school in Missoula, stopped at the ranch on impulse. They walked the West Boulder Reserve and found the land so bewitching, they bought a plot of land on the spot. It circled an inholding—a log cabin which had become the spoils of an acrimonious divorce. This, too, they acquired. "It was amazing. Within a month of our first footstep on Montana soil, we owned land and a house—all for a modest outlay." No doubt, bulletproof vests had helped make the purchase possible.

Now, on this crisp July day, I could see it was time to leave. After nearly 17 years of ownership of this remote cabin, Mrs. Magat was palpably uncomfortable in the company of strangers, even though she and her husband stood to make a healthy profit on their investment. Her husband appeared torn between courtesy and family peace. As agreed, in about a day, once they had packed their belongings, they would hitch a lift into Big Timber. There they would catch the Greyhound bound for Billings, thence to fly east, one imagines, forever. Tomorrow the Bar 20 would, officially, be ours. But at this moment the Magats' discomfort was real. The wife abruptly disappeared into the house, leaving her husband to endure good-byes.

My sister gave me the nod to leave. I thought: They're balmy to sell this gem, in exchange for some planned community back East. Blue sky and cloud wrack, snap in the air, and a gentle breeze off the high glacier: an awkward chill crept over us as we shifted weight on the lawn, trying to effect a graceful departure. I turned to the pickup, coughed, cleared my throat, looked back, and said, "Thank you for letting us acquire this lovely place." Mr. Magat didn't seem especially affected by my attempt at empathy. He cleared his throat and turned to get something, perhaps imaginary, in the house. Soon, he returned with some papers. "Here," he said. "They're yours, if you wish." I glanced at them: three pages of legal foolscap, sentences condensed to phrases. "Good luck," he said, looking away. Soon he had joined his wife in the house. Through the picture window, I saw he had placed his arm around her waist and they were watching us.

Twelve years later in a phone call to Eugene Magat, living in a North Carolina lake community he and his wife had acquired with the proceeds from the Bar 20, I confirmed my suspicions of that July afternoon. These days, his French accent is more apparent, his words studied and clipped as if he suffers from an ennui of language. "We loved Montana," he said after a pause. "We thought we were going to retire there. But something happened...I'm not sure what. Sometimes we think we shouldn't have sold the Bar 20 to you...." Again, he offered a hurried good-bye. Before I had a chance to reply, the line went dead.

The three sheaves of paper Eugene Magat handed me in 1987 contained few complete sentences. The notes were headed "Brewer" and, on another page, "Early History." It began, "First homestead, filed by a woman in 1910 in Pruitt Park...bought by Helen Fargo Arnold."

If these three pages were the history of the Bar 20, they mystified more than clarified. They included many names, all unrecognizable, and absolutely no chronology. In carefully rounded lettering, they bruited of a "failed dude ranch," of "crooked deals," of (an illegible) someone who "lived at the Bar 20 Ranch, while (someone else, unnamed) lived with servants in cabin across river." For days I carried a copy of the notes with me. I read them feverishly, trying to make myself comfortable with a sequence of ownership. What began as a challenge became my talisman. We had paid for title and had earned, as bonus, a set of clues to a mystery we couldn't comprehend.

These rough notes became my road map to the history of a place. They have guided me to a succession of owners, each of whom left behind the patina of a life. How many generations of predecessors might I encounter? What could I learn in this mountain valley about others' hopes, dreams, accidents? And how, in the end, would long-ago narratives inform me about my own motivation, success, failure, future?

CHAPTER 2

Hippies

I inherited an elegant volume that is my family genealogy. Dedicated in 1930 to her late husband, my great-grandmother commissioned it for her progeny. While its binding is a work of art, its contents seem thin. Apart from dates of births, age at death, the transfer of land in counties named York, Cumberland, and Charlotte, I'm not certain what I've gained from it. Pity it stops short of explaining the guts of these peoples' lives—whether they were happy and fulfilled, if they were marked by character flaws that might inform me of my own. Heroes? Cowards? Euphoric? Melancholic? Such traits would be more valuable to me than a name and a set of dates. I also wish the volume didn't assume all history begins when an antecedent reaches North American shores. I'd be thrilled if it could determine what my family was up to during the Black Death, if we came, 1,000 years before, from Mesopotamia, whether 40,000 years ago we might have enjoyed a concealed liaison with a Neandertal, thus to account for long arms, pointed chins, and brow ridges. I'd also like to find out when my family left Africa and why. *Johnson and Allied Families* clearly, for me, falls short. So, I suspect, shall most genealogical research, unless one plans to exhume graves and conduct sophisticated DNA probes.

Perhaps there may be other clues in the search for identity left unexamined. I'm thinking especially of places. Is it presumptuous to assume that like-minded people gravitate to the same corner of this planet? Would it be a stretch to imagine our genetics might predispose us to a locale? If so, one might possibly discover commonalities between a former resident and ourselves, clues about shared behavior as well as premonitions of the future.

At the beginning, even with the three pages of foolscap in my back pocket, I had only a fleeting curiosity about Bar 20 history. Then, I was entirely consumed by its future, but when the ardor for redesign had faded, I began sensing the presence of ghosts in the logs. I took to pondering whether, somehow, past might be revealing of the buildings' roots.

Whatever ineffable quality had wooed my family here might well have attracted others on similar grounds. Might the allure of the Bar 20 be cross-generational? Who were all those others who shared our passion for this corner of the wilderness? Why did they come? What lives had they lived? Why did they leave?

I needed to understand the cycle of enchantment that has been sweeping an innocuous Montana valley.

The day after we closed on the real estate purchase, we returned to a deserted Bar 20. True to our financial arrangement with the Magats, over-stuffed couches, piano, and bicycle had been left behind. So too, much to my sister's dismay, the deer-head mount. In time she would find a place for it, not over a mantel but in the kitchen, sporting a chef's *toque blanche* from the Road Kill Café. Without furniture, our eyes spotted dust balls, quick on the wind, worrying the corners of the rooms. There were gaps in the chinking, holes in the ceiling, a heavy layer of discolored lacquer on the floor, and in the kitchen, a smell of rancid cooking oil. Everywhere, the cumulative effects of absentee love.

Where I was astonished at neglect, my sister saw opportunity. The contractor had been engaged and the two toured the house with pad and pencil. There were no beds, only one bathroom, itself defective. I spotted scratches on the floor where furniture had been shifted, dead miller moths around the windows, and in the dining room, central to the house, a desolate mood of transience. I wasn't yet prepared to camp out at the Bar 20.

Instead, I drove four miles to the fork of the West Boulder Road. Here an imposing gate led to a dude ranch, owned by two wonderful hosts, Renny and Tracey Burke. Their struggling business was strictly word of mouth; and this month, their clientele must not have been thinking of the West, for Renny was fixing the fence and the rooms were all empty. Disguising their desperation, they appeared happy to let me have one of the cabins for about the price I'd pay for a motel room. The West Boulder Ranch became my temporary headquarters.

A week later the commune conducted its annual meeting. I attended in hopes of meeting a few of the hippies and, maybe, of learning how life was lived in our valley. The meeting got under way early on a brilliant Saturday morning in the guesthouse next to the caretaker's cabin. This was a log structure resembling the Bar 20, formed by several log structures linked akimbo. The kitchen appliances and Formica counters, celebrating the 1950s, had to be negotiated before reaching the living room, where the furniture was arranged as if for a séance.

I awkwardly introduced myself to the others. There were 20 in all and, while a few had built houses on their reserve plots, most were absentee owners, exercising their rights to the reserve by staying once a year at the guesthouse. I suspected all of them would view a newcomer with suspicion. I sat down and studied them one by one: no tie-dyed shirts, one set of Birkenstock sandals, one ponytail. All the others appeared, at first blush, a routine mix of humanity. The presiding leader was a Billings anesthesiologist. Someone described, in whispers, the lanky giant sitting next to him: an oceanographer from Rhode Island, his wife a novelist. Another introduced herself as the wife of a psychiatrist. By far the most curious were the reserve's "founding fathers"—one who called himself a "substitute teacher" and another, simply, "potter"—both with striking good looks and a deftness with words.

From the start, the one who billed himself as a substitute teacher appeared to dissent with the other reserve members, as a matter of policy. Where they wished to build a fence, he advocated tearing it down; when they urged rewarding the caretakers for a job well done, he favored having them summarily fired, their positions retired forever. For some, his outbursts seemed a matter of habit and they treated him with no more than thinly veiled ennui. For others, his rancor seemed a personal affront. By mid-afternoon, after little progress, one member could no longer disguise his impatience and the meeting appeared on the verge of becoming a melee, the president attempting to maintain order by changing the subject. Unfortunately, he chose to raise the delicate issue of finances. Each year, I would discover, landholders were assessed a fee to defray taxes, caretakers' starvation wages, and all the other incidentals related to the operation of 1,350 acres of Montana ranchland. In all, the annual budget barely bruised $20,000, with each shareholder's burden under $1,000. The matter now before the membership was whether the annual "call" should be further reduced and the West Boulder Reserve operate "in the red," or whether it should be raised in the interests of sound financial management. I knew which of the two courses seemed sensible, but even with a cool mountain wind, the air within the log cabin was an inferno. "Cut," cried almost all the other members and, even I, still shy, found myself drawn by the tide of consensus. To my utter astonishment, a motion that sanctioned bankruptcy was thus passed.

As soon as the substitute teacher had scored his one victory, the air cooled. And with this change in the temperature, the anesthesiologist adjourned the meeting and the members drifted away, the prospect of battle postponed for another year. "Happens every year," commented one, feeling the healing wind. "This organization thrives on disputes. And it's been that way since it was founded in the early seventies."

In late afternoon, still aquiver from the tension of the meeting, I retired to the barren Bar 20. I was now certain I had joined an association of lunatics. And through this dysfunctional alchemy, I qualified as one myself. So strange was the experience, I vowed one day to find out as much as I could about this reserve, its outlandish beginnings, and the strange bedfellows this breathtaking corner of Montana had embraced.

In time, I sought out Rick Spellman, the substitute teacher. He explained that in 1970 and 1971 a group of friends used to gather most afternoons at a Washington guitar shop, owned by Steve Spellman, Rick's brother. Few members of this gathering—Joe McMichaels, Mark Strange, and his girlfriend, Laura Worth—were inclined to steady jobs, sharing a mutual disdain for bosses, schedules, and most societal obligations. They required little money for their lives were simple. "I'll give you a personal example," Rick volunteered: "In those days, I was in the habit of just getting by.... I was used to living rough. One time my girlfriend and I stayed for two months in our VW camper, parked illegally in an indoor-parking garage in San Francisco. I kept a culture of yogurt going. Combine that with the oranges falling off the trees in Marin County and you'd have yourself breakfast. Then when we got a lot of notes saying we'd be charged for occupying the garage, we moved to Seal Rock, a national park where camping was forbidden, but who knew, for every morning when the rangers came along, we'd have cleaned it up so no one could tell we camped there. Without doubt it was the finest real estate in San Francisco. Later when the weather cooled, we drifted down to the Baja Peninsula."

Money, wages, and landlords, these friends believed, were at the root of a national malaise, especially around Washington. "It was a pit," recalled one, "with daily riots, people unhappy, Nixon still in office, and the executive police force being used as a kind of personal Presidential bodyguard to do police action on the streets of Washington... Big peace demonstrations were everyday occurrences, and folks were getting rounded up and stuffed into the D.C. stadium.... Leaving Washington seemed, at that time, a fabulous idea."

This band of guitar-shop regulars all yearned for an American utopia, far from the city. In the early seventies, they began to hunt for a sanctuary, first stop West Virginia. They found it "full of coal dust, rotted-out cars, and happy rednecks that didn't like hippies." Montana, little known and appropriately remote, seemed more promising. Joe McMichaels, a partner in the guitar shop, flew there and, in a rented car, scavenged the southern corners of the state, near Yellowstone National Park. Not knowing where to begin, he drove mile after mile until he happened upon an interesting side road. One turned out to be "breathtaking." Not much better than a dirt track, it connected two exquisite drainages, skirted snow-capped massifs, cut across wildflower meadows, and, on the brow of one hill, presented a panorama as grandiose, as stark as Tibet's. For several miles there didn't appear one blemish. McMichaels drove until he spotted a sign, any sign. It read: "63." He followed the arrow until he reached a dude ranch. Its owner stood outside, looking quizzical. Solemnly, she listened to his request and suggested he explore the next drainage, some 13 miles distant. There, she thought, there might be land for sale.

The West Boulder Valley indeed overwhelmed McMichaels. The 1,350-acre ranch that was for sale appeared to possess all the characteristics the band of modern Thoreaus needed to be free. It commanded mountain views, two and a half miles of river, rolling meadows, tent sites on every one, and because it was situated on a dead-end road, sublime privacy. The perfect antidote to Washington. But how would this confederacy of impoverished dreamers meet the asking price of $300,000? McMichaels stewed over the dilemma. Before he found the answer, the question proved academic: Harry Brewer, a stove-up cowboy, the ranch's owner, called him to say a committed buyer had been found. Joe McMichaels, having discovered utopia, returned to Washington, frustrated the West Boulder property had been sold out from under him.

A week later, Brewer called the guitar shop to report he and his wife, Mabel, had rejected the other buyer's offer. It had been from a developer who confessed he intended to build 400 one-acre cluster units on the 1,350-acre ranch. Brewer suspected any idea as "cracked" as theirs would end in ruin. He had no intention of holding a mortgage on a piece of land so catastrophically impoverished by modular homes. Instead, he would now make the property available to the "boys." "Take it or leave it."

"That's when we did the big tour," recalls the potter, John Worth. He and the others flew to Montana to inspect the ranch. "Harry was totally polite and wonderful. He drove us over his enormous acreage and actually put us up for the two weeks we needed to figure out how to buy this place when there was no money to buy it with... Our group came and went. I'm sure to Harry's great dismay and puzzlement, nothing really happened even though he was willing to drop the price to $280,000."

At the time, Harry Brewer lived in what has now evolved into the reserve guesthouse. Emphysema had slowed him, and a suspicious impairment of the inner ear had deprived this legendary horseman of his balance. Now, his family, with his wife's urging, was forcing him—perhaps against his will—to sell the ranch he loved so much. While he waited, equivocally, for a buyer, ranch fence posts rotted, shed roofs sagged, corral posts teetered, and "cows wandered from one end of the ranch to the other, living the ideal life." When Brewer's wife moved to town in anticipation of the Sale, Harry lived rough in the drafty cabin, relying solely on milk-house heaters for warmth during winter gales. He stoically told county snowplowers not to bother plowing his road. He'd rather be cut off from the world.

"Harry Brewer had a reputation of being very grumpy when he wanted to be grumpy," recalls John Worth, "very charming when he wanted to be charming...and the people from around here were saying they basically couldn't figure him out one way or the other—sometimes incredibly sweet, other times mean and short-tempered.... He would always be nice to us when we first met him—'Hello, glad to meet you'—but when he saw us through the window as we passed, he'd supposedly say to Mabel, 'Goddamn hippies.'"

Suddenly there seemed to be an unexpected windfall; the money impasse appeared breached, thanks to a wealthy grandmother lured from her home in Texas. She had fallen in love with the ranch and, in front of his house, gave Harry Brewer her verbal commitment she would purchase the West Boulder Ranch. But a few days later, once all had returned home, smiling, she withdrew the offer.

Now the stakes were even higher: to welsh on Harry Brewer would have put the entire dream in jeopardy. No one in the West went back on a handshake.

"It was so hard not to fall in love with the land," recalls Rick Spellman who had allied himself to his brother, on the reserve founding fathers. "I didn't feel I could make it better. No. I just wanted to be **with** it." The problem was how to pay the price for such perfection.

The McMichaelses' mother, Virginia, was impressed into service. Employed as an executive assistant in a Washington law firm, she one day screwed up her courage to ask her boss, chief counsel for the Mortgage Bankers' Association, whether he would give her boys a moment of his time. Sam Neel, now retired and in his late 80s, recalls he saw them right away. Handsome through command, his impressive height now leavened by a stoop, he still exhibits a mental courtliness as he pieces together fragments from his storied career. Whenever he wants to make a true and decisive point, he quiets all conversation with a blast of throat-clearing. "They wanted," he recalls, "to establish an organization in which they and their friends could live under primitive conditions, where they could find peace and quiet, where they could do the kind of work they wanted to do with their hands. For this to happen, the boys had to find 20 people who could afford $5,000 apiece for the down payment, and $1,200 a year from then onward for ten years."

Neel remembers how difficult it was then to raise such a sum, even with a stack of brochures and members willing to mount presentations throughout Washington and Maryland. Ten days before the expiration of the option with Harry Brewer, the subscription list was short five investors. It appeared the ranch might be lost. Whimsically, Sam Neel agreed to take one of the shares. He then called his friend, Jim Rouse, of the Rouse Company, the fountainhead developer in and around Baltimore. In turn, Rouse asked one of his associates to join the group. He later showed the prospectus to the architect Frank Gehry, then at work on a Rouse Company project. Before long, 19 of the 20 shares had been spoken for. It would be enough.

When the West Boulder Reserve Association held its first board meeting, even before the contract had been signed by Harry and Mabel Brewer, there was no question the confederation of buyers were strange bedfellows. At least five were self-described hippies, two oceanographers, a Foggy Bottom attorney, a principal in a Fortune 500 company, and a renowned California architect. Two brothers were married to two sisters; another member was married to the third sister. Various parents had been roped into meeting their children's responsibilities by becoming members themselves. The Spellmans' mother, a congresswoman from Maryland, was dragooned into recording minutes. Most landowners, assembling in Laurel, Maryland, on January 21, 1973, had, in fact, never yet visited Montana. The meeting commenced at nine in the morning and ended at six in the evening. Commissions like the Water and Sanitation Committee were formed. Other members were charged with looking into appropriate corporate structures. Some declared themselves "perpetual members" of the planning board. While, according to one witness, "nothing got decided...and all was chaos," the mood was decidedly bright, enthusiasm palpable, and the future, in Montana at least, secure. The meeting adjourned with a Montana slide show and a buffet supper "enjoyed by all."

Shortly afterward, the deed with the Brewers was signed. When he read the small print, Harry discovered he had not sold his ranch to seven hippies. Behind his back, as an affront to his hospitality, they had increased the number to 20. Unwittingly, he had transferred the family ranch into a dreaded subdivision—just the kind, in fact, he and Mabel had sworn never to allow. Rick Spellman recalls: "He thought he had been swindled and I can understand why. Maybe we weren't all that forthcoming as we should have been."

The potter, John Worth, is even more laconic: "Harry felt he was betrayed, that he had been lied to...." It led to "some hard feelings and some notable run-ins later.... He was really pissed these guys from the East had done him out of his ranch."

But what did it matter? Two square miles of land in the West Boulder Valley was theirs. Zion had been secured. Now no one would ever have to worry about authority, at least not on what would be called the West Boulder Reserve.

One of these early reserve shareholders recalled his excitement with the process. In the late seventies, Bryan Lascaris (not his real name) attended a family reunion in Ocean City, Maryland. There he overheard a conversation between two of his cousins, one married to one of the reserve founders. She and others were raving about the land they owned in Montana. They despaired that one of them needed quick cash and was willing to sell a share. The eavesdropping Bryan, an ebullient computer "techie," had just signed a two-year contract to work in Saudi Arabia. He had no obligations. He owned no land, had few belongings. Even though he couldn't imagine two square miles of faraway Montana, and in fact had never even seen a photograph of the place, the descriptions of the ranch were hypnotic. "It really infected me," he remembers. "I knew I'd be making a a good deal of money in Saudi Arabia.... They asked me 'Are you serious?' and I said, 'I think I am.'"

Bryan shook hands, left for the Kingdom, and thereafter, each month religiously sent home a portion of his paycheck. The work in Saudi Arabia was grim, especially since his boss was difficult. "Had I not had this obligation to pay my share of the reserve, I might have cut short my contract and left. It wasn't pleasant, but I held out."

In December 1982, Bryan made his final payment. "It was my 30th birthday and the end of my contract. I decided to celebrate." Bryan bought a first-class ticket, flew all over Europe, stopping in towns like Frankfurt and Amsterdam to celebrate his birthday and his ownership of the yet-to-be-seen Montana land. By the time he reached London, after two weeks of solid carousing, Bryan Lascaris was seriously drunk. Booked on Concorde, he arrived at the lounge with the support of a friend. His jeans were torn, his sweater rank, and, behind his ears, there were party streamers. On the flight, more champagne. And when he arrived in Washington, he made his way to a favored bar for the final romp. "Everyone was there and I could hardly stand up, and Steve walks in. In his hand, he had a piece of paper wound up—a brown piece of paper with a ribbon on it, and he walks up to me and hands it over and says, "Here it is, here's what you've been waiting for...the deed to the ranch."

Since then, Bryan has visited the West Boulder Valley only a few times. He hasn't yet built a home and isn't certain he ever will. What he likes is to know he owns a sliver of Montana. Every trip to the reserve is like a beginning, a replay of that first arrival. "It always seems an awfully long way to go on a dirt road. But when I make the last turn and I see those snow-covered mountains overlooking the valley, I think to myself, "My God, am I really part of this?"

CHAPTER 3

A Whisper of Cox

Long before I'd ever been to Montana, I knew I missed it. An America that was free, wild, and uncluttered, it seemed as close to the Third World as one could get without crossing an international frontier.

I reached Montana circuitously. Way back in the seventies, I had attempted to reengineer my life. I was then based in London, making films in remote fastnesses, especially Africa, the land that had stolen my young heart.

Ever since I went there as a schoolboy, age 16, this continent, bracing for winds of change, had aroused longings for essentials. Sub-Saharan Africa was an extravagant landscape in which I would be but a speck. Gradually, this privileged city boy came unbuttoned on the savanna. It was here, discovering my own worth in the out of doors, I felt at home, alive, unencumbered. Sometimes I lived with nomad peoples, sandal trudging with them all day in pursuit of wary game or fetid water hole, then sleeping between sweet smoky blankets at night. When the light played out a hair before seven each evening, I might take a slug of the only liquid left—hot whiskey—to mix with corn meal mush, as we sat on the ground beside an acaccia fire while a lion roared just beyond our thorn boma. Dirty, dessicated, reduced to elemental languages, here I found out who I was—and that somebody had nothing to do with New York City.

Even hubs like Nairobi suited me. Bursting with inefficiency, corrupted by the crazy quilt of unimaginable wealth and unspeakable poverty, this frontier town was the beginning of most every traveler's tale. At noon in Nairobi it wasn't uncommon to stand at the Long Bar with a friend, packing a revolver on his belt, while by the curb his staff guarded the Land Rover, double-parked in the hot sun, the horns of a trophy buffalo festering under a tarp. Laws were inexpert; friendships, contact sports. In the swirl between mayhem and solitude, I witnessed Third World development as a madcap enterprise—comedy of misjudgments punctuated by unlikely victories. Africa was outrageously honest: a world where the racial divide was altogether forthright, human barriers virtually nonexistent. Here I became what I couldn't be at home, and for years I thought little of my roots. I had fallen for Africa so hard, my heart raced every time—no matter where I heard her name.

Making films in the back of beyond trained me to be lucky. Things always went wrong in Africa, but we usually found a way of fixing them, and when we did, these hiccups became the escapades that seemed to guarantee perpetual youth. There was another benefit: when I returned to Europe and America, the films we brought back to audiences found heady viewing. They documented subjects as random as ancient trade routes, human evolution, colonial self-importance, and the life cycle of the shoebill stork.

I wished I could have lived in Africa. I tried once to buy land on an island off the coast of Kenya, but the enterprise came to naught. Another time, I flipped over a ranch near Lake Naivasha, but wise friends discouraged me from making a bid. In Africa, title deeds were often murky, and white people, even though they were readily granted privileges like "jumping the queue" at the bank, were second-class citizens in land contests whenever one went up against the omnipotent politician.

One day in the early seventies, I awoke in London, a grown-up. I looked into the interminable haze over rooftops and thought: No matter how much I aspired to Africa, it didn't aspire to me. Here I was, an American, knowing more about a land doomed to conflict and despair than about my own home, a place of undeniable promise. Why was I making life so difficult for myself? Why did I know nothing of my own roots? Was I doomed to be an exile?

Something else troubled me: food. Much of the world I had come to know, once a breadbasket, was now panhandling for staples. I had seen firsthand the plight of the Ethiopians—children more rib cage than flesh; old women pecking for hours in the dust for a grain of wheat. Food shortages, I believed, would one day be at the heart of global mayhem, and America, the world's cornucopia, might become a lure to all the dislocated. Many years later, I was reminded of this dream when we dedicated 160 acres of Bull Mountain pasture to grain. We took a gamble on winter wheat and for nine months we remained uncertain whether our dry land would produce anything at all. By July, the field looked more promising than I thought we deserved. One day late in the month, a mammoth combine harvester and its team of seasonal harvesters arrived and made good on our gamble. In ten months we had produced enough wheat to make three quarters of a million loaves of bread. While, in the end, the venture proved to be a loss, I took satisfaction in the knowledge we had done our small share to fill the world's belly.

In the 1970s I was definitively an idealist: I felt an urge to turn theory into action. I left my job and, after a farewell trek through Africa, returned to New York, the city of my birth, to plot how I could participate in a new agrarian renaissance. For two years I continued to make films, but whenever work was scarce, I set off to explore my native land, first in New England, then the Midwest and Colorado, each time hoping to find a ranch that would satisfy my African aesthetic. By the time I reached Wyoming, I knew I was getting warm. I had heard much of Montana and its ballyhooed big sky, but I hesitated going straight there. I believed I needed to earn it by the long opiate of a transcontinental drive.

And when, finally, I reached Montana, there was instant recognition. I entered the state obliquely, driving from Cody, Wyoming, to Billings, Montana. The moment hills gave way to plains and then eroded into river drainages, I felt the hair on the back of my neck rise. Montana was not the Serengeti, but it, too, seemed to be about human desolation, animal magnetism, unrecorded history. On dusty roads, passing strangers waved and pronghorn antelopes fled, just like Grant's gazelles. Within a week, I had begun to nod at old acquaintances. In two weeks I shared their complaints about the cattle market, and in a month I knew how to wear my cowboy hat so I no longer looked like a music hall parody of the cowboy. Just as in Africa, there was a rhythm to the day: it began with birdsong and ended in blackness as thick as chocolate. While I hadn't literally come home, I felt *at home*.

For the next two years, my family and I saw lots of ranches before settling on one we could afford. Located in badlands north of Billings, a genteel cow town, it can be reached by driving first through strip malls, trailer chaos, odiferous feedlots before you are free to launch yourself onto the great, uninhabited shortgrass prairie of Montana. After much wheat and cattle, you reach broken woodlands and flat hills (named "mountains" because that's how they appeared to 19th-century flatlanders). Along old sandstone benches and dry creek lies the ranch—big squares of territory, each a 640-acre section that climbs flatfooted through timber up to a plateau. Remove all those trees and the land resembles Africa—cliff, canyon wall, and bunchgrass.

It was here on the Bull Mountain Ranch that I learned about Montana and began to care for it. Perversely, the more committed I became, the fiercer the setbacks: fire and flood, hail and hoppers. And, throughout, the cattle market languished. So it had been in Africa: open your heart and be violated.

Somehow, with all these reverses, I wanted more. My sister and father agreed. By 1988, the year we acquired the Bar 20, Montana had become my drug. I had always aspired that the ranch would be a commercial success. But cattle ranching is thankless, the price of beef paid to the producer never sufficient to cover the cost of production.

At least this great tract of land would inspire my nephew and niece. Here, working each summer, they might learn a few lessons. We'd all ride horses, gather cattle, drill seed, bale hay.

It was a pipe dream, never to be realized. The prospect of remoteness was not as tempting for them as it was for me. Summer after summer, they took jobs elsewhere, in places where kids their age outnumbered everyone.

Perhaps I needed greater incentive to lure them to Montana—a place where, say, I might teach them to fish. The road that leads to our new property, the Bar 20, within three miles dead-ends at a spot where foot trails access 14 million acres of mountain, river, glacier, forest, and glade in national forest, wilderness, and national park. Raw nature, increasingly under siege, was still undefiled around the Bar 20. What luxury, especially for a child!

During my first Bar 20 year, foremost on my mind was a goal of making it a singularly private family retreat. Over the winter carpenters, under the command of Chuck Defendorf, a friend of the commune's caretaker, tackled the structure's most glaring problems. We acquired a new shingled roof, an enlarged, friendlier kitchen, floors were stripped and lightened, logs chinked.

Chuck was small, wire-haired, possessed of a sardonic sense of humor. He was at his best when left unsupervised. He worked for us on a New Age schedule—over weekends, sometimes at night, occasionally on projects we had never formally approved but which he knew we needed. A bridge was built over the creek behind the house—all kept a dark secret until one cold winter day. He took us out back and showed it to us: his winter's folly—all aspen twig and sagging board. On that same visit, I noticed, beside the river, bent saplings supporting a blanket. Later, I was to learn it was a sweat lodge to which he, his girlfriend, and co-workers repaired after the workday. Once, driving home late, I saw them, cleansed by heat and smoke, running naked in the light of the moon to the ice-clogged river.

In January, the Bar 20 disgorged a small secret, thanks to Chuck. He and his team had been battling snowdrifts each day to commute from Livingston to the West Boulder. In January, during the relative warmth of a chinook, Chuck decided to tackle one of the outbuildings—the shed which then provided storage for one bicycle. At one end of this shed, there was an enclosed room, destined, in time, to become my office. In its midst there was a clunky concrete footing—at one time, no doubt, mount for a generator. Buried outside was the generator's fuel source, a crude drum, its contents now turned to gunk. Long before the rural electrification programs of Franklin Roosevelt's administration, this generator must have been the sole source of lighting and power for the Bar 20. Years before my arrival, it had been removed. Only the ankle-cracking mount remained behind.

"Worst than a Superfund site," Chuck groused on the phone as we debated whether or not to rent a front-end loader for the tank's removal. A day later, he called to say he had delayed that plan because the ground was frozen. Instead, he had begun work on the interior. "The walls—if they're not particleboard, they're Sheetrock. Today, I began tearing it off. Pretty soon I got the idea—because everything was taped with black—this place, long ago, was a photographer's darkroom, so, what the hell, I kept ripping and, lo and behold, a couple of business cards fell out. Thought you might be interested. I'm sending them on."

Four days later, Chuck's letter and enclosures arrived. One was the business card of G. E. McKay, manager of the Northern Hotel in Billings ("Good gas & oil will take you to the Northern...excellent café with soft water..."). The other was a press card certifying a certain Stanley Cox to be "a registered staff photographer of the Free-lance Photographers Guild and authorized to take pictures for publications." It expired September 15, 1938, and it featured a faded signature.

Why was a hotel manager so important to someone back in the thirties? Who was Stanley Cox and where were his photographs? I grew excited with the prospect of discovering a cache of pictures that might explain the looks of the Bar 20 during its glory days. Who were these people and how had they lived their lives?

By June the following year, Chuck notified us to say the Bar 20 would, more or less, be livable in two weeks. I called Haven Marsh, the irrepressible manager of our cattle ranch, to ask whether he knew a young kid interested in picking up a little money by driving our furniture in a U-Haul truck 2,400 miles from the East to the Bar 20.

"Yup," he replied instantly. "I know just the kid. Me."

When he and his wife, Deanna, delivered the furniture after a three-and-half-day cross-country sprint, my sister was poised, pad in hand, to put everything in its ordained site. A friend and I had flown to help with the placement, but we soon discovered we were superfluous. The moment we off-loaded the collection onto the lawn, we found it prudent to stay out of my sister's way. She had an exacting vision where every end table and chair was to be located; it seemed dangerous to interrupt.

My sister's monomaniac work was instant success. Light began to pour into the dark house. A superfluous screen porch was now connected to the living room. Both rooms she filled with furniture that made the ranch appear to have belonged to our family for the better part of a century. With Hilary's deft touch, the kitchen now attracted everyone. No more dank and gloom. While still spare, the Bar 20 had been reborn.

In 1988, for the 22 miles of road to the closest grocery store, there were no more than seven houses to be seen. One of the last, before coasting into the town of Livingston, belonged to the furniture maker Don Hindman. Don was now retired and said to be clinically blind, yet his reputation as one of the foremost artisans in the workshops of Thomas Molesworth remained his badge of honor. Molesworth, a product of the Chicago Arts and Crafts Movement of the 1920s, had settled in Cody, Wyoming, to make rustic pole furniture for ranches. His chairs and couches were distinctive: massive burls and bright leather upholstery, inlaid with stylish cowboys and bucking horses. Today, at auction, they are sold for large sums of money.

One afternoon I screwed up enough courage to call on Don Hindman. I wanted to locate examples of his work. The old man met me at the door and appeared to consider unannounced visits altogether normal. He explained things weren't as neat as they used to be since his wife died. He sat me down in his dark living room, smelling of tobacco and senescence. I told him we had bought the old Bar 20. He nodded politely, not hearing a thing. Soon I turned the conversation around to him. He coughed and rubbed his knees. "Do you still make furniture?" I asked.

"Bit. Some days I can hardly get out of bed I hurt so bad, so the furniture usually takes a long time." He was sitting on a log-and-leather couch, rubbed to a glow. His eyes, focused on the gloom of the distant kitchen, were trying to discern a memory. "Few years ago the Chevy heiress...you heard of her?"

I nodded, lying.

"Well, as I say, just the other day, she comes here and she says, 'I want a couch and I want two chairs and I want a coffee table and...' Well, before you know it, she'd ordered over 10 pieces and she takes out a big book and writes me a check for the whole damned lot. Well, I look at the check and I says, 'See here, I'll accept this check on one condition.'"

"'What's that?'" she asks.

"'Well,' I says, 'If ever, if ever you call to ask me if the furniture's ready, the whole deal's off and I keep the check.'"

"What did she say to that?" I asked, astounded.

"Dammit," Don replied. "She accepted, of course." He sat for a while in silence. Finally, he added: "The furniture should be ready in a week."

I could see he was hurting so I attempted words that might relieve some pain. "Mr. Hindman," I said at last. "Please don't take this badly, but if ever you'd think of selling the furniture you have in this house, I wish you'd let me know. You know, that couch and those bureaus and that chair...."

I had gone too far. I knew I had spoken too soon.

Don Hindman wasn't at all bothered by my forthrightness. He looked around the room at each piece, then turned to study me. "How much?"

I was dazed. I had no idea of the furniture's value. I cleared my throat and rattled off a number, without a clue whether it would be insulting nor excessive. Suddenly, I had turned a social call into a business.

"Ok," he said. As I wrote out the check, he interrupted: "When you want them?"

Now I could redeem myself. "You keep them," I said. "Have them for as long as you want and when you're done, I'll take them. Maybe in a year or two—whenever you've found replacements."

"How about this afternoon?"

Three hours later, back at the Bar 20, I heard a vehicle hit the wooden support of our bridge. I ran fast. Don Hindman was at the controls of a new red pickup. Even half-blind, he had successfully negotiated the road, but the bridge was another proposition. His front bumper was damaged and his pickup leaned akimbo toward the river. I tried dissuading him from another run at the bridge, but he wasn't listening.

"I can do it." I stood back on the bridge and watched him race at it, just missing the edge. He had achieved the impossible. Now I ran before him until he had parked in front of the Bar 20. He paused to study the building and, for a while, wouldn't leave the driver's seat. I couldn't be certain what he was seeing. Finally, he opened the door, edged onto the ground, and braced himself against the front bumper.

"I'll tell you something," he said, catching his breath. "I built most of this place."

"Naw," I replied, imitating his style.

"I did. I built it for Stan Cox. Damn him."

I remembered the press card behind the Sheetrock in the shed.

"What year did you build this? I asked, not certain where to begin.

"Aaaw, it must have been in the early thirties. Lived here one whole winter, cut the timber myself and jacked it down the hill. Hell of a cold time."

"And who was Stan Cox?" I pursued.

"Stan Cox," he began, almost wistfully. "Stan Cox—he was a guy with a lot of dreams. That's all I remember. It was a long, long time ago."

I unloaded the furniture and then he drove away. It seemed he had told me all he wanted.

CHAPTER 4

Transitions

From that day in 1988, when we moved into the Bar 20, life in the West Boulder Valley proved as unexpected as Africa. On a late spring visit, we glimpsed a mountain lion ghosting up the hill behind the house. In summer, Chui, my golden retriever, spent fruitless hours, lying in wait for nonchalant deer who dared breach her personal space around the house. Late in August, black bear, having polished off grubs and berries in the mountains, then had the effrontery to treat our chokecherries as their own. Chui would sound the first alarm—a distinctive bark reserved exclusively for bear. The ruckus never failed to orbit me out of my desk at a gallop. Sometimes Chui succeeded in scattering them; more often the sows and cubs climbed into the fir trees, which then seesawed precariously above the house, driving Chui into further hysterics. She would only relax the maniacal baying if she were hand-dragged into the house. As long as I was about, bear and youngster stayed tree-bound, but the moment I turned my back, they'd shimmy to the ground and bound into the gloom of the forest.

In 1988, my father, back East, began to slow and his children worried.

I sensed the bears viewed Chui and me as nothing more than a nuisance. They fled from habit, not need. Once, struggling with something or other at the word processor, I distractedly looked out of my office window. There, peering inches from my face, was a yearling cub. I whooped. It bolted. Another time, on horseback, I lost all cool when I rode under a tree into which a bear had retired for the afternoon. As Coop and I innocently passed beneath the tree, the bear let out a throaty hiss—a sound that I discovered horses don't like. For a good minute, Coop let loose with a world-class display of bucking. Now, every time I ride beneath Douglas firs at the end of summer, I check for fur.

For a time, grizzlies were said to be on the increase in our country. Yellowstone Park officials, we were told, had released "problem bears" in the nearby national forest. One had been seen at trailhead, another about a mile within the forest. In those first years at the Bar 20, whenever we hiked into the wilderness area for picnics in the meadows, three miles from trailhead, we took packer Larry Lahren's advice—and kept Chui on a leash. While black bears ran from her, grizzlies were said to chase dogs, following them at a run. Once on a hike with a friend to Lost Lake, her Jack Russell and Chui tested the theory on another species.

They had bounded ahead of us down the trail and were out of sight for several minutes. Suddenly they materialized, bolting toward us, as if shot from a cannon. A large moose was chasing them and when they reached us, he was nearly upon them. The sight of us, however, brought him to a halt. Breathing heavily, his midnight eyes unblinking, he studied every one of our twitches. After another long moment, he shook his rack, turned his head, and high-stepped back down the path. For the rest of the afternoon, the dogs never left our side.

My father, our silent partner, loved hearing these stories. Whenever one of us returned from the West, he sat us down for a cocktail to hear the latest. The wilder the experience, the more carefully he listened. Yes, one of these days he would see the Bar 20 for himself.

Wildlife was at the heart of my happiness being at the Bar 20. Here I felt I was living a timeless existence—all thanks to the vision of long-ago hippies.

Occasionally, as I rode onto the bench behind the old Bar 20, feeling my heart beat wildly at the sight of wildflowers, river, and snow on the mountains, I wondered if, in fact, every landowner's aim is the same. Rick Spellman once told me his "dream was to get out from under the landlord." Mine was not altogether different. Here I wasn't policed, spied upon, harried, nor, apart from the telephone, troubled by the outside world. While there were always deadlines lurking afar, here I could work my own schedule, choose my insect hatch, don waders, and lose myself in the shimmer of a hopeful afternoon.

I told my father about the hippies and what little I knew of the other owners in the reserve. He was curious about the ranch's past. He thought there might be an outside chance he would recognize a name.

Just after the reserve was created in 1971, Rick Spellman and others, I learned, became disillusioned. Rick had been appointed reserve caretaker and was living in the cabin where I encountered Chan and Carla the day I first set foot in the valley in 1987. It was then half the size, with plumbing limited to a distant outhouse. Spellman's approach to management was "low impact," a direction not always shared by others.

Spellman's critics rallied around a letter dated February 7, 1975, written by reserve member Eric Schneider, an oceanographer then living in Rhode Island. He complained, "There appears to be a total lack of management of the property.... My father and friends who have visited [it] during the last year, have reported that sections...seem to be going downhill very rapidly.... The time is long past...we can continue to operate on a loose concept of mutual trust" over "two square miles of beautiful and valuable property."

"I allow that the ranch was not in good shape," says Rick Spellman today, but he believes there was integrity in letting it appear shoddy. "The lawnmower was the push variety. I owned my own chain saw. My Volkswagen was the only ranch vehicle." Rick had vowed he and his friends would hardly leave a footprint on the West Boulder Reserve, and he went to extremes to hold to this principle.

One time Rick struck up a friendship with a couple of other laid-back folks living in a nearby valley. Eric and Anne Oksendahl were working as ranch hands and Anne was about to give birth. Determined to have the baby delivered in the country, she approached Big Timber's resident obstetrician with a big smile. He shook his head. He only delivered babies in hospital settings.

Anne persisted. She ran into Rick one day and explained how she had been rejected by the region's only obstetrician. She described her dream of a wilderness birth. Rick was happy to oblige. He introduced her to just the right person—a reserve landholder, a retired doctor. While the doctor had allowed his license to expire, he was delighted to help. Rick's unplumbed cabin, the reserve caretaker house, would be the perfect delivery room.

The birth was premature so Rick rushed into Big Timber to retrieve medical instruments, which the doctor had absentmindedly left behind. When he returned, the baby was nearly born. She was a healthy girl and the Oksendahl's called her Prairie. The doctor's fee was a case of homemade pickles.

I called my father and asked him to come out, to see the place for himself. He was noncommittal.

In those early days, few non-hippie members visited the reserve. Most were content with photographs of their holdings. One exception was real estate development executive Aubrey Gorman, who once booked the guesthouse for a week. "My wife and I," he remembers, "we got here, and it was just the biggest mess you ever saw in your life. I mean there was a bunch of cats in it. In the middle of the night in the back bedroom, one leaped off an armoire right onto the middle of my wife's back, while she was asleep.... Everybody was sort of running in and out of here, getting their mail, and cooking, and getting stuff out of the refrigerator. It was like a community house.... The kitchen floor had...a 30-degree angle.... The living room ceiling was just exposed beams.... [There was] every kind of bug and varmint in here you could think of and no...way to keep them out. The yard was a mess—ranch stuff and weeds all over the place.... I'm sure the fences weren't much better.

"[Then] we see out in this field... the manager's tail stickin' up in the air, and a shovel. And he picks his head up out of the hole as we were coming by and says, "Well, you've got one flush [left] in the toilet....

"But, anyway, we loved it...the fishing was fun, and I just thought it a great place."

One early share owner didn't share Aubrey Gorman's enthusiasm. According to John Worth, the potter, the first time this reserve member and his wife stayed in the guesthouse, he became seriously troubled by resident fauna. He felt not just the valley but the guesthouse itself was possessed of wild animals, all a threat to human life. This fellow "held the distinction," remembers Worth, "of shooting mice with a .22 pistol from inside the guesthouse." When someone said to his wife, "It sure is a beautiful valley," she replied, "Not to my way of thinking." Within a year they had sold out, never to risk a return.

"I left the job [of caretaking]," recalls Rick Spellman. "I didn't like being...an employee yet trying to be equal with other members." He was replaced by Paul Dix, an Environmental Protection Agency photographer then living in Narragansett, Rhode Island. Dix took the job unseen, at starvation wages, and then drove his wife and young son across the continent to the West Boulder Valley with just enough cash for a one-way trip. The Dixes arrived one evening in spring, with the ground covered in snow and roads mired in mud. Since no one had bothered giving them directions to their house, they wandered the reserve, crossed the bridge, and, imagining the Bar 20 a satisfactory residence, broke in. The minute they spotted the name "Magat" everywhere, Paul Dix yelled "'Whoops,' and beat a hasty retreat to the appropriate reserve headquarters." Here the Dixes settled in, without formal goals or responsibilities. Everywhere they looked across the reserve, fences, roads, and improvements were seriously run-down. Dix was horrified by the deterioration, and the absence of operating funds to reverse it. "Fortunately," he said, "we loved the place the minute we saw it."

One serious problem to haunt the Dixes during their few years in the valley was the personal arrangement of a recent member who viewed the reserve as business venture. When others weren't looking, he used the reserve guesthouse as base camp for his professional hunting trips. Here he invited his clients to stay before and after elk hunts into the national forest. Reserve covenants and bylaws were then in their infancy; and while this member's activities clearly violated the spirit of the reserve, no one other than the caretaker was around with enough will to enforce it.

The recently arrived Paul Dix had the ill-fated task of dealing with the problem. "At the beginning I thought he was this great guy...really interesting, but he had quite a line." Dix maintained that he was of dubious integrity, possibly "a chronic liar and...a sociopath...[with] a habit of having all his houses burn down [for the insurance payments]." One day, in fact, "his truck burned up, right in front of the guesthouse.... I went over to try to put it out, but he wasn't interested.... I was afraid it was going to take the reserve buildings with it."

Once the violations became known, the member vanished. So, too, did Paul Dix. Caretakers soon came and went in tight rotation. Many of the reserve's founding fathers also abandoned the enterprise. Chief among the departures were the McMichael brothers, whose vision had been critical to the founding of the reserve. For many, the ownership of land and the cost of maintaining it from afar was unwieldy and prohibitive. Others found their plan for a peaceful commune a child's fantasy. Still, their hard work, vision, and the care of lawyer Sam Neel generated a set of covenants that, in time, became enforceable and, unwittingly, a ground-breaking model for other Western conservation communities.

The reserve covenants specify the land is to be left wild, that each lot, ranging from 15 to 20 acres, is to accommodate no more than one house, its size, color, and landscaping to be approved by the Planning Committee. The balance of the land not owned by individual members, is held in common by all. No one has yet found a better use for the land than traditional cattle ranching. Each year the reserve is leased to neighbors as summer range for cows and calves. Ranching remains the only commercial enterprise permitted on these more than 1,300 acres.

I told my father about the reserve. He nodded agreeably. "How is the fishing?" he wanted to know.

Now, nearly 30 years old, reserve covenants are still being fine-tuned. Not everyone has been happy with them. One time a potential buyer took one look, met a few members, and left, declaring: "You guys like playing God." Another time a recent arrival from New Jersey decided to build a trophy house in violation of the spirit of the reserve. The reserve's leaders weren't diligent as the house rose, one story after another—perfect for Bergin County, an anomaly on a lonely Montana river. The edifice was painted macho brown and its new, house-proud owners were so contemptuous of Western way they took to cutting their neighbor's water pipe. He, a congenial sort, repaired it haplessly, until after it had been cut for the fourth time, he decided to give up on the reserve. Now, having vindicated themselves in this sorry little battle with a neighbor, the New Jersey empire-builder and his dutiful wife suddenly lost interest in Montana. Some say he needed the money for another project that had taken his fancy. Some say the couple now could no longer justify the sight of the house. They sold it, abandoned its furnishings, and left furtively.

The Bar 20, located dead center in the reserve was, I discovered, exceptional because the ownership of land on which it was built preceded reserve jurisdiction. Our plot was called an "in-holding." While we also owned contiguous reserve lots, the uninhabited cabins nearby—the ones I passed every day on the far side of the river—appeared to enjoy the same in-holding status. They also resembled the Bar 20.

The two small log cabins, close to the river like the Bar 20, had suffered neglect. With the foolscap pages left me by Eugene Magat, I tracked down the owner in Arizona and called. Within a week we had agreed to a price. A month later we closed. The property amounted to about an acre of real estate plus "improvements" in dire need of attention. Years before, the old man said, they had been the Bar 20's bunk and tack houses.

I called my father about the new additions. He found it incomprehensible we needed more land.

The verb "grandfather" arose several times during our cabin transaction. It applied, in our case, to the historic privilege that allows existing buildings to remain put—within the floodplain of a wild river. Had the land been a vacant lot, the Environmental Protection Agency would have denied us building rights. But the EPA could not change history. We felt privileged to be here and instantly changed the color of the houses to render them invisible.

Another in-holding in the vicinity also appeared to have been part of the Bar 20 complex. It too lay on the far side of the river and consisted of one large and one small log cabin at the brow of the track leading to the Bar 20. Sited beside Grouse Creek, which began as a spring and ended in the West Boulder, it, also, I learned, played a role in Bar 20 history. No neighbors, however, knew the details. I called the owner, a Mrs. Payne, living near Denver. She was willing to sell Grouse Creek House and we settled, without fanfare, on a price. The negotiations took a few minutes, and, within a month, the old Bar 20, whatever it had been, was now, more or less, reassembled.

The Grouse House exterior was the pallor of jaundice. Its screen porch was condemned by plywood and its kitchen hadn't been touched since the 1930s. On the floors, there was a carpet of miller moth wings and mice droppings. On her first visit, my sister closed her eyes to contemplate what it might become. We were, admittedly, infatuated by its stylish, pavilion design—two wings, one large living room with fireplace, walk-in closets—all sited around a flagstone courtyard. It implied the house had been built according to an

Eastern aesthetic. We pondered the possibilities of its mysterious past and, once again, assigned Chuck and his team the winter task of restoring another Bar 20 building.

For a few of the Bar 20 acquisitions, our silent partner was our father. Only someone as indulgent as him would have dared take a chance on two children with whom he not always agreed. Once I brought him pictures. He liked the size and heft of the river. My sister described design plans. He said, "Uh-hum." We outlined the cost of rehabilitation. He cleared his throat and said "Uh-hum" yet again. Then he sent a check to cover some of these costs. That was it, he explained: "I've done my bit."

In August he calls. No preamble: "September 15," is all he says. He and his new wife will fly to Billings. There they will stay a night at the ranch.

The road into the Bull Mountains is dusty, and when my father reaches the ranch house, he seems uncertain. He adjusts a chair next to me on the deck and we both stare into the sage and twilight. I tell him of tomorrow's plans—the West Boulder, the Bar 20, maybe a few casts before dinner. He stares so intently I can't be certain he's listening. He lights a cigarette, sips his vodka, puckers his lips at the jolt, then studies the dark meadow surrounding the schoolhouse, the tall bull pines clinging to the rims, the flag hanging limp in the last heat of day. I am certain he hasn't listened to me. "Uh-hum," he says.

The next day we leave the ranch at noon and drive slowly toward the west. Somehow, I need to gain my father's absolution for this Western dream, but I don't think he understands my drift. He seems distracted by the violence of the landscapes: silhouettes of the Beartooth and Absaroka Mountains to our left and the Crazy Mountains, just off the right. We leave the interstate at Big Timber, and his first words in two hours are to inquire about the Grand Hotel. My sister and my brother's wife have preceded us to prepare the Bar 20 for his first visit. My brother, our stepmother, my father, and I are alone in this car.

Conversation has been stalled for the last two hours. My brother, also visiting the Bar 20 for the first time, appears skeptical. Clearly, I must audition for him as for my father. I feel myself a two-bit actor before a hostile audience.

We drive south, following the Boulder. Along the way, the sight of this lavish river curling and boiling beneath bridges and beside hay meadows excites my father. "Shouldn't we have bought here?" he asks. "Isn't this the better river?"

I change subjects, instead trying to get a laugh out of him about the Road Kill Café, our local gin mill. He reads something else into the story. When we pass it, a quonset hut with a sign, he tells me to stop. "I'm getting nervous about the Bar 20," he explains.

He and his wife sit beneath the Rainier Beer sign at the bar, both puckering their lips with their first Montana gimlet. Meanwhile, his two boys wage war against each other at the pool table. Rivalry, older than childhood, sweeps over me. I play to win, determined to gain one advantage on a day when everything else seems cast in doubt. In silence, my father watches the two of us, never squandering an inequitable look on either. He is masterly in closing the shutters, especially against his own family. But the stale smoke, Merle Haggard on the jukebox, the blousy bar maid has an effect. He absorbs the scene and I watch a smile pool across his face. With that, my brother sinks the eight ball and wins the game.

We drive the final leg with the sun low, a bonfire of color caught in the dust and the meadows milling with mule deer. At last we pass the reserve sign and turn onto the river. I can see my father wants to postpone the reckoning. A few hundred yards short of the Bar 20, on the bridge, he signals to stop to check out the river. He smells it first, then puckers his lips as he did with the gimlet. He stares at the river without a word. "Not bad," he says softly—the signal for me to continue.

With fall already in the air, as we enter the Bar 20 cabin, I make for the fireplace. I think I will let the old man be, with just my sister to pursue him with explanations. I light the fire, absentmindedly not checking the flue. Immediately the room fills with smoke.

While it distresses me, the smoke doesn't seem to bother our father, his eyes streaming, like mine. I had planned this visit as if it were a piece of theater. Now we can barely see five feet in either room. I open windows onto the screened porch, and there he goes, sitting in the cool evening with the sound of the purring river. With his wife elsewhere, he lights a cigarette, takes the drink I've made, and begins to look at ease—the first time, it would seem, over the last 24 hours. During our drive I had noticed he seemed in pain, that all these years of hard living, after our mother's death some 30 years before, had taken their toll. Now he brightens; the long trip to the Bar 20 behind him. "It's beautiful," he says. "You've done a wonderful job." He sips the drink I'd made him. "I think it will be fine."

For two days we fish together, first on the West Boulder and later, floating the Yellowstone with guide Steve Pauli. During the following year, he will tell his friends about these days, about the brown trout and the whitefish and "our place on the river." Prior to his visit, the Bar 20 had belonged to his kid's, now it had become "ours."

My father's visit to the West Boulder may well have been the highlight of his year. At Christmas we were together again and of all the presents I remember the best was a fishing rod. He had bought it for Annabel, his granddaughter, my sister's daughter, age 5. She was nonplussed by the possibilities. He, in turn, was imagining the future and a little girl learning to fish, perhaps under his tutelage. None of us had seen our father in such high spirits. We thought he had turned the corner.

I was then preparing for a new television project, which within a month would take me to a remote island in the South Atlantic. On the first day of the new year, my father called and, after some small talk, said he had "news." Back in November, he explained, he had been diagnosed with cancer. He had waited until now to tell his children because "I didn't want to spoil anyone's Christmas.... They tell me it's incurable, but I'm going to fight it."

My father did fight it and by July, with my urging, he decided he was well enough for a return to the Bar 20. I booked his flight for the 6th of August. On the 4th, his wife called to say he was in no condition to fly. From her unsettled tone of voice, I knew she was in deadly earnest. I caught a flight to New York and went straight to my father. His face was gray and had settled onto the bone. He had difficulty rising from his chair. He never mentioned the setback. Instead he suggested we dine.

In the restaurant, he had much to say. At first he talked of World War II, his landing at Utah Beach and the invasion by the allied forces of France and Belgium. He had never before recounted his war years (all I knew of them was what I learned from his friends). I listened awestruck. A man who could only talk of himself with disparagement, tonight he employed a few uncharacteristic moral flourishes. He spoke of how, in a small village in the Ardennes, he and his company had once uncovered a quisling. It was, in fact, the mayor— a man who had betrayed others to save himself. The fat little bureaucrat, having confided everything to the Germans, my father learned, was the first to welcome the invading American forces. My father, the captain, thereupon made an example of the mayor—slapped him in irons and paraded him through the high street of his Belgian hometown.

That was it—what my father had been meaning to tell me.

I was dazzled. The telling of the tale was so unlikely. I studied him as he sat, mysteriously impassive, pretending, for our sake, to be hungry. His war story was, I decided, his gift, more important than the Bar 20. He wanted me to have something I might otherwise have lost. Now he was tired.

The evening was his last tale, our final dinner, and, as it were, the beginning of the end.

The next day he collapsed. The ambulance took him to the hospital where, over the ensuing week, we all filed in for daily visits. Sometimes he was with us, other times we sat beside him, listening to his sudden breath and watching for flickers in his now gray eyes.

On my last visit, he seemed greatly improved. I asked whether he might enjoy a last expedition to the Bar 20 once he was released from hospital. "Yes," he said, nodding, but we both knew it would never be. I held his hand—the first time since I was a child—and he asked me for news of "our place." I rambled about this and that, how I had recently been fishing with hoppers. I never noticed when he closed his eyes, and I never knew whether it was to dream of Montana or remember the war or just to let the hush of darkness settle everything. I pressed firmly over the delicate bones of his hand and marveled at how he always did things better than I.

After a time, when he felt I was preparing to leave, he opened his eyes, now so dry he couldn't blink. He looked piercingly at me and whispered something. I leaned over and asked him to repeat it. He whispered again.

He said what I had been waiting to hear all these years.

CHAPTER 5

Cruising Montana

I'm in a cemetery that hardly anyone visits. It's no distance from the junction of the Missouri and Yellowstone Rivers, virtually on the North Dakota–Montana state line. Heavy clouds, bluffing rain scuttle east on a cold wind. Good to be alone at Fort Buford: whitewashed pine markers glory in perfect symmetry as far as a picket fence. I study the inscriptions, covering the years 1866 to 1881, and note death visited our frontier warriors in many disguises—consumption, cholera, Indians, road agents, accidental shootings, and, on more than one tombstone, inebriation. Here on wooden headboards, no gentility.

Duma, my black Lab, and Chui, mother superior of all golden retrievers, are also enjoying sacred ground. Right now, Chui is spoiling for a run-in with a Richardson's ground squirrel, while Duma has taken a ferocious interest in a hole in the dry ground. I wander over for a look: at its bottom, there's something round and white, like old ivory. Mushroom? No. Root? Nope. I blink. One more minute and Duma will retrieve Sergeant Jeremiah Burroughs's skull. I usher both dogs, tails wagging, out of the graveyard and return to cover the soldier's remains.

I'm three days out of New York. In six days I'll be back at the Bar 20 for another spring. So far, a commonplace trip. In western Pennsylvania, I nearly fell asleep at the wheel. On the Chicago fly-way, I was caught in two hours of morning rush and there were cloudbursts near Janesville, Wisconsin. But once I crossed the Missouri at Fargo, I came alive. I laughed at Western kitsch like the giant fiberglass buffalo by the side of the road. Just before Williston, on the western edge of North Dakota, I opened the window to smell sage. Once again, I'm in the West, home of my American heart.

On the Montana–North Dakota line, I slow my pace. Before me: the perfect road trip hoves in sight. My two companions, dedicated to motels with shag rugs, foil bags of chicken-fried steak, and the distant blur of prong-horns are no longer acting caged. I can stop almost anywhere, open the door and watch them hurl themselves against the horizon. If we drive straight from here southwest to connect with I-94, we'd be at Bull Mountain Ranch within eight hours, the Bar 20 within eleven. But this time, that won't do. I want to understand this Montana thing, every single back road of it. Sticking to secondary, if not tertiary, roads, we'll begin on the flattest of land, and, after passing through an "empty quarter," will dramatically end our trip in the Rockies.

At least in my mind, this cross-country journey begins at Fort Union, a few miles from Fort Buford. Here the dogs stay confined to the car as I wander the stockade enclosure of this restored trading post. Between 1829 and 1867 Fort Union was dedicated to fur trading. Here, at the junction of the Missouri and Yellowstone Rivers, many Western myths were born. Ever since Captains Meriwether Lewis and William Clark passed this way in 1805, this spot, the nexus of rivers, caught outsiders' fancy. When the fort was erected, a vast array of traders, especially Indians, including the feared Blackfoot, converged here. Fort Union also attracted artists and their patrons: in 1832, George Catlin, explorer Prince Maximilian of Wied-Neuwied and his Swiss artist, Karl Bodmer. Later, John James Audubon bivouacked at Fort Union, rebuking Bodmer's work as being "in bad taste."

On this cold and dusty day, I walk Fort Union's restored ramparts to consider its fleet dream. During the fort's heyday, its agent, the "bourgeois" was king. He served as judge, general, and CEO of a vast Western enterprise influencing the lives of at least five Indian tribes. At the center of the fort is a white clapboard frame house, surmounted by a widow's walk. Here he lived. Neither pompous nor austere—with the sensibility of New England coziness and thrift, his dwelling exudes democracy—a place where Indian, trader, artist, thief might once have been welcome. What began as a civil idea—a place where many races met—ended just after the Civil War in an atmosphere of mutual distrust, the U.S. Army systematically foisting upon Indians blankets laced with smallpox. This site, once a shrine to trade, was overtaken like so many other institutions of the time by paranoia, greed, hate.

Fort Union ended its days indecisively. It reflects an era when, throughout the Northern Plains, Indians had become marginalized. A few years after Fort Union was decommissioned, the Crow Nation around the Bar 20 was shifted eastward so white folks (like me) could enjoy what had been their ancestral land. Everywhere, an ugly tale. Yet this is the stuff on which legends of the West have been crafted. I ask the national park's ranger, behind the kiosk in the bourgeois' house, whether Fort Union is a popular destination for tourists. He's downright jubilant: "Today we had 16 visitors. We're doing well."

Few travelers venture across this quadrant of the Northern Plains. From nearby Sidney, its lights dimmed this Sunday, I drive on Route 200 due west for one hour, no other car visible. The country is remarkably dry for this time of year; on the radio I hear nothing but farming woes; the May rains have all but failed. As many as ten counties have declared themselves disaster zones.

Steering this straight two-lane road is much like aviation. Without the nuisance of a speed limit, I fly—airborne after each rise, with four-point landings onto rolling valleys. The road is but a stripe of paint between plow ridges. Meanwhile the blue Suburban, two of its occupants fast asleep, traces the orb of earth. I play Thornton Wilder's *The Bridge of San Luis Rey* and hear

Sam Waterston tell of long-ago happenings in Peru. Now, while I contemplate the cosmic nature of chance, I experience a languorous carpet ride, the ground nuzzling me as if it were the soft underbelly of a very large organism, I at its teat. At 95 miles an hour—no lefts or rights, few landmarks, hardly a tree, just ups and downs. At times I become oblivious to speed and consider opening the door to step into the deathly metaphysics of the Great Plains.

In time, I stop, attracted by an oil well. The dogs stir, elated by the prospect of a romp; the solitary well, pumping metronomically on autopilot, rewards me with this notice: "Caution H_2S possible releases." Below me, a town so polite it has no outskirts, just a speed limit, church, log building, school, cinder track, and a sign saying "Welcome to Lambert: Home of the Mighty Lions."

Eastern Montana is basketball country. It's the singular activity that, in these parts, sets youngsters free from the torpor of the landscape, gives old folk the prospect of long drives on winter evenings and invests each town, each cluster of grain elevator, Long Branch Bar, auto body shop, with an identity. Here at least a quarter of the population is gathered in front of the Catholic Church for the 5 p.m. Mass. When I drive by, they stare and then vanish, in dread, no doubt, of an unfamiliar face.

Now I accelerate, always east on Route 200, lulled by Brother Juniper's misbegotten project in long-ago Lima. I've developed a routine: whenever I'm defeated by country, I try the radio for local happenings, and when, all too often, there's no reception, I listen to books on tape. I prefer tales set far away in time and geography. *Blue Highways, On the Road, Travels with Charlie* won't do. Far better: Dickens, Trollop, Dick Francis. The blue Suburban sets me free in more ways than one. It lets me rove where I wish; within, it's a yarn. And I'm never lonely.

To the south: glistening sinkholes, each claimed by a pair of buffleheads. Late afternoon, craving junk food, I turn off at Richey. Again, a town dominated by the three gods of eastern Montana—grain elevator, church, and school, dwarfed by its muscular gym. I pull up at the only illuminated sign, "The Stockman." Within, through smoke, I see one table occupied by a rancher wearing a grease-rimmed Stetson, his wife drinking Coors Lite, a young cowboy and his girlfriend. They are discussing grain prices and the disheartening weather. When I settle down at the bar, conversations cease to allow them to stare. I order popcorn and a Coors Lite. "You from out of town," the barmaid wonders.

"You bet," I say, having prepared my lie. "Shepherd." (a town near the Bull Mountain Ranch). "How's your team?" I enquire, turning the questions on her.

"Girls or boys?"

"Makes no difference." The bar's other patrons are weighing me with serious concern.

"Well, the girls are world class. The boys weanies."

"Not great," I respond, with a look as mournful as I can muster. "Sorry." This town must be jinxed and, what's worse, everyone in the bar knows it.

My "roadie" in hand, I'm now bound for Circle. Immediately, I lower Sam Waterston's volume to call Helen Waller. Will she and her husband join me, on my arrival, for drinks and dinner at the best restaurant in town—whatever that may be? Helen has been active as a spokesperson for the people of eastern Montana—kind of a celebrity in these parts. Over the static, she pauses uncertainly at my invitation, says she'll call back. More static. Waiting her reply, I resume Mach speed, drilling an amber tunnel through darkening prairie dusk. The ranging fields of wheat on either side appear mathematically perfect, each windrow aligned, it seems, by laser. But perfection doesn't extend to farmers' homes—bathed under unnatural yard lights, weathered toy front-end loaders, solitary lawn ornaments, all akimbo. When Helen calls back, just as I pass an entire field of John Deere implements, she says there's no *best* restaurant in town. There's only one—a diner that doesn't serve drinks.

The Travelers' Motel ("Best Little Snorehouse in Town") also enjoys a monopoly. "I've got six," says Paula, its owner.

"Six empties or six fulls?"

"No, six sheepshearers just moved in." Maybe because Paula appraises me as a sheepshearer, she asks no questions about the size, make, numbers, behavior of my dogs. For $29, she hands me the key to room 14 and then returns indolently to her cigarette and another sequel of "Touched by an Angel."

Tastee Freeze is nearby, across from the Assembly of God congregation. I go there on foot while the dogs, who've found solace in the flammable floral-print spread on one of the twin beds, watch me, accusing me with stares of betrayal.

All dinner long, Gordy Waller won't say a word. He examines his hands, knotted like old taproots, and tacitly agrees with his wife's every word, she spokesperson of Plains justice. Together they've raised five children on a "small" grain farm—all 40,000 acres of it. Yes, she answers, she knows everyone in the restaurant, everyone in town, everyone in the county, and, for what it's worth, most of their secrets. I'm the only one Helen doesn't know, and she's bent on battle. As soon as we order chicken strips and steaks, she wants me to realize that the people of the Northern Plains are misunderstood by America, especially, its government. She's in her 60s, hair proudly white, cheeks a complexion that in other parts of this world would be called sunny. Here they're tinted red from a lifetime exposure to prairie wind.

Farmers like the Wallers, she states, can no longer make a living. In a recent 11-year period their farm income rose 7.5 percent while their costs grew 23 percent. Today, to grow wheat in a good year ("which this won't be"), they must lose money. Experiments have been attempted in eastern Montana—"sunflowers, blueberries, Belgian endives, and other off-the-wall crops," but without success. Here, the growing season is short with wheat the only crop that will endure. "It's heartbreaking. In the last few years, the population of Circle has declined from 1,200 to 800. Every kid has to leave because the family farm can't keep them alive. There've been suicides."

"What's the solution?" I fire back. Gordy looks at me uncomfortably while the waitress produces our steaks, square and well-done, flanked by baked potatoes in tin foil and slices of tinned beets.

I can tell Gordy knows Helen's answer, drawn from the bones of one of her many prepared speeches: "We have to look at what we're paid to feed a hungry world and we haven't been paid adequately. Agriculture can't continue to grow food products less than the cost of production. If we don't take care of the land and you don't take care of the people who take of the land, we won't have the production to feed a hungry world."

"So what's to do?" I repeat.

The Wallers believe there's a conspiracy afoot. Agribusinesses—many of them privately held and thus unaccountable to the public—have colluded with the federal government to set artificially depressed grain prices. Government, according to Helen Waller, no longer provides for working people. It only looks after the rich. "Do you know," she adds, her features more florid than usual, "They're even putting toxic waste in the fertilizers they sell us. They may be trying to poison us.... That's how much they care."

"Please, what should we do to correct this mess?"

"The government and the farmers should decide on the farmers' needs each year. If we require $6 to cover our costs for a bushel of wheat we produce, then we should be paid $6 a bushel."

"Price fixing, in other words."

"Not really."

"If it's not price fixing, then what is it?"

"Support for the family farm." I pay the bill, more confused than ever.

Next morning at breakfast I'm again in Tastee Freeze, sitting beside a booth of six Mexicans, conspicuous because the waitress keeps calling them "boys," even though they're older than her. Around me, an assortment of geriatric ranchers and farmers who, when not smoking, work toothpicks across their bridges. I can hear snatches of their conversation while I bare down on my Raisin Bran: "He's the most ambitious man a fellow would ever meet,"

"He's got angioplasty,"

"Damn Chevy—I'll trade it in on a new one—me and Rockefeller."

The sheriff, at the next table, packs a pistol. When he gets an emergency call at the counter, he brushes it aside ("It can wait") so he can finish his breakfast.

The Mexicans, unlike everyone else, talk in whispers; I only catch a little of the melody of their Spanish. I'm curious because last night when I asked Gordy Waller about minorities in Circle, he said: " They just don't come here because the work's too hard." Across the partition I introduce myself. The Mexicans are sheepshearers—the ones sharing my motel. They've driven in one car from Greeley, Colorado, to earn $1.35 a sheep in Circle. On a good day they each sheer about 70 animals, to gross $100.

Driving west towards Jordan, center of Freemen country, the clouds that yesterday held promise of rain now hint they will part. I wonder if Circle will survive long into the second millenium.

With the dogs asleep at separate corners, I've slowed to 60 miles an hour and opened the windows. I ask myself: "How many ways are there of saying 'empty?'" Wickedly, I think of New Jersey, so far away. There's reputed to be almost 400 people a square mile, while in Montana we can boast of a biological monster: less than half a human per square mile. Today, driving "The Great Empty," I can inhale the vacuum.

Surrounding each ranch stead lie miles of winter-blown uniformity that shortly will become an astonishing carpet of grain, as it has for half a century. But the engine of plenty that powers eastern Montana, and turns an entire landscape the size of Belgium green, is now running rough. The moment eastern Montana farmers fire up their tractors, they watch all their prospects blow away. World economy now favors transportable wealth—the kind you can put on an integrated circuit or stash in your head. Land, lots of land, at least here on these angry flats, appears to be a commodity without a cause. Within these hardscrabble homes, once palaces to people who, on paper, were millionaires, live the scarred, the dazed, the alienated. And, as Helen Waller says, the rest of the world could give a damn.

Long before the granddaddies of these grain farmers reached these parts, eastern Montana was the hunting grounds of Northern Plains Indians—the Sioux, Crow, Assiniboine, Cheyenne. In the 1880s it was partitioned by cattle barons, for Texas longhorns to grow fat on its rich native grasses. Success was short-lived. Most cattlemen never survived the apocalyptic winter of 1886 and 1887, when 90 percent of the herds either froze or starved to death. Sheepherders and later homesteaders, attracted by the pipe dream of free land, took up the slack. By then the cattle barons had hived off to other parts, abandoning their brands, like the one that gives Circle its name.

A few miles east, to the left of the road, there appears an accumulation of planks. I turn off. The Brockway Bar, inspite of its "Welcome Stranger" sign, is abandoned. But the post office, which doubles as the town's church, is open. Its post master, Joui Mothershead, remarkably young and comely for this wasted place, seems proud Brockway's population now numbers 26. She explains that when the Chicago, Milwaukee, St. Paul & Pacific Railroad Company pulled up tracks in 1980, Brockway lost its way in the world. Just a few diehards, tilting against progress, stayed on. But Joui is a cockeyed optimist. She's certain that if someone could open a bed and breakfast, fix up the dry rot in the church, launch a cottage industry that will pay minimum wages to Brockway's educated 26, the town would boom. As we chat outside the post-office church, doors squeak in prairie winds, dogs bark at tumbleweeds.

I'm now cruising through the second tape of *Bridge of San Luis Rey* as well as Garfield County, famous for its 50-million-year-old *Tyrannosaurus rex* and for Freemen, who in the mid 1990s brought this lonely corner of Montana to America's attention on the evening news. These are badlands as dramatic as any in the Dakotas. Certainly no wheat farmer could plow these broken contours—earth that from space might resemble acne. "The dogs deserve a run," I think. We stop, they pee, I pee, and for once they choose not to leave the sanctuary of the open road. Front to back, the cracked, eroded, seared land is humbling. In spots that never could be plowed, there are tenacious stands of buffalo or bunchgrass, but the country seems little changed from the time before *T. rex*, when all eastern Montana lay at the bottom of the sea. Vacation country for Freemen.

Over the last eight years Jordan's population has declined from 575 to 470. Late in the 19th century, it was born on the bank of a lazy river called "Big Dry." Today all that remains of the town is one main street, one drugstore, one bank, no ATM machine, and five bars. What remains of the river is even less. Not far from saline seeps, I find Jordan's celebrated dinosaur museum, housed in a cinder block building, shut tight, with no trace of human life. I bang on its door, my only answer the cough of the wind. Discouraged, I find my way to the KD Café. Here I meet a cocksure kid and his sister, currently suffering from a case of the sulks, both sitting at the counter, while, behind it, their mother flips burgers and talks to a slow, middle-aged man. Grizzled Bud, ("I'm a newcomer to Jordan: been here only 50 years"), is another regular, and, from the end of the counter, he serves as spokesman for this exotic group. "I like it here because it's isolated and you don't have any kooks running 'round the country," he says of Jordan.

"But didn't you have a few kooks recently? The Freemen?" They challenged the American Constitution, refused to pay taxes and, through a complex check-kiting scheme, bilked banks out of millions.

"Well, yeah, but they didn't bother anyone.... The ones who drove us nuts were the journalists and federal agents."

I ask for a glass of water.

"I wouldn't tank up on Jordan water if I was you," urges Bud. "If you ain't used to it, you won't get ten miles down the road before you'll have to pull over. When geese fly over Jordan, they all loosen up."

The boy, Junior, his sister, Cynthia, are the first young people I've encountered on the road trip. Four years ago, they moved here from Billings, because Ruby, their mother had "taken up with a guy" from Jordan. Now, the guy is gone and their mother disillusioned. "I don't like the people here," the girl announces to our congregation.

The boy disagrees. Jordan is great "because of the parties."

"Ever heard of *the trees*?" asks the old-timer. "Everyone in Montana has heard of *the trees*."

The trees—in fact, cottonwoods—the only ones in Garfield County, serve as the site for most of Jordan's parties. "A little bit of everything goes on there. No limitations."

I turn to the boy. "Are you going bananas in Jordan with so little to do?"

His sister answers for him: "Yes," she barks. Then she returns to filing her nails. I ask her for a little explanation. Without lifting her head, she answers: "They're all alcoholics. All they think about is getting shit-faced or taking crank or having sex. They're all all cliquish. That's why I'm leaving."

"Where are you going?"

"Don't know."

The old-timer, unrepentant eavesdropper, explains. "The problem with this town is there's not a damn thing to do. In summer you can only go to the *trees*.... And then everyone in town is related four or five different ways. Last weekend there was a funeral. So many people came, they had to stage it at the VFW hall."

"You got to be careful who you chat with in Jordan. You may be talking to the whole town," says Ruby to the sizzling burgers.

"I know where I want to go," says the brooding sister. "A city that stays open all night long."

I had always hoped eastern Montana towns might resemble the MGM backlot—white frame houses, big porches, pies cooling on windowsills, and Robert Preston leading the town parade. Instead I've encountered people who, by their own admission, appear lost. I half-hoped I'd meet kids dedicated to dinosaurs, sandhill cranes, John Deere tractors. Instead, it's all about alienation, *the trees*, dropping out.

I need to leave. I pay the bill, impulsively deciding to abandon my friend, Route 200. I'll find a dirt road, head south, and then resume a westerly course on a stranger, Route 12. The map is a bit coy about the north-south connecting road, but Bud describes it as sound: all gravel through country that's "a whole lot of nothing."

The dirt road exceeds my wildest dream: explosive clouds dash eastward, dappling the Suburban with moments of chill. Dry creeks are celebrated by cottonwoods and, with them, the trill of meadowlarks, the busyness of killdeers. Hawks have settled onto fence posts—in most instances, the highest point in all the land. And a small lake, further diminished by drought, is awash in Canada geese, pintails, grebes, buffleheads, all exuberant with spring. Even when the dogs and I stop for a jog, antelope appear far too preoccupied by sex and grass to disperse. Over more than 50 miles of road, there's no voice to be heard from the radio. We're in misbegotten Montana and I become manic, singing a dirty ballad to the thump of static. And when I see hills to the west, antelope mingling with deer, I think to myself: "Yes, I think I'm falling in love, all over again."

At road's end: Ingomar. Nearly a century ago, this settlement claimed to be America's largest sheepshearing and wool-shipping point. Trains on the Milwaukee Road stopped each day at Ingomar; the town claimed many banks and an opera house. By World War II, fire, Depression and a lackluster wool economy had left Ingomar devastated. The only business still clinging to life would be a bar, formerly a bank, now call the Jersey Lilly, so-called after the apple of Judge Roy Bean's eye. Today, it's still renowned for beans, beer, and a hitchin' post that serves thirsty cowhands off adjacent ranches, some the size of an Eastern county. When I park at the Jersey Lil', there are no horses, only "the bouncer," a blue-heeler asleep on the wooden sidewalk in the shade of a new pickup. He sees Chui and Duma's inquisitive heads, growls, and returns to his coma. Inside, the well-lighted room is adrift in ranchers and ranch kids playing tag to either side of the bar. The barmaid offers me beans and she isn't miffed when I decline. I settle for Coors and popcorn and then I rove through the bank's office, now converted into a consignment shop, its old desks heavy with handwoven sweaters made from the wool of neighborhood sheep.

All of a sudden, I realize I've been overtaken by prosperity. The encircling ranches are efficient by virtue of size. Success comes with having over 1,000 head of cattle and a skeleton crew of ranch hands. And it now attracts outsiders. The new owner of the Jersey Lilly is a Midwesterner who made his fortune in burial vaults. First drawn to Ingomar on an autumn antelope hunt, he bought the bar and built a house. The barmaid explains that one day he intends to retire in Ingomar. When he does, he'll expand his enterprise by offering stagecoach rides, a bison petting zoo, even a hotel: "no bed and breakfast, more like a bunk and biscuit." On the walls of the Jersey Lil', pendulous with the heads of greater kudu, sable antelope, and warthog, the new owner proclaims he has been to Africa. Prosperity, I conclude, suits me just fine. I chug the beer, say my goodbyes, and through gathering dusk sometimes interrupted by the lights of a distant ranchstead, I speed toward Roundup.

Roundup is a hiccup in this landscape of coming affluence. On Main Street, built wide for teams of horses to turn, there are now boarded storefronts. If I hadn't stayed two nights, I might have guessed Roundup to be in decline, along with the Jordans and Circles of eastern Montana. Instead, I discover a renaissance of sorts, thanks in large part to outsiders who haven't given up on small-town dreams. To either side of the empty stores are banks and coffee shops, some serving cappuccino. On the outskirts of town, there's a nine-hole golf course, said to be one of Montana's best.

Roundup was settled in the 1880s by cowboys who met at the confluence of Halfbreed Creek and the Musselshell River. Here on a big platter of a valley they began gathering their range cattle each fall. In 1907 the Chicago, Milwaukee, St. Paul & Pacific Railroad also liked what it saw. At the edge of town it built a station and started developing high-grade coal in the Bull Mountains. The railroad also turned matchmaker, introducing prospective homesteader to shortgrass prairie. In Roundup, disembarking settlers set off into the dawn of new lives, and for not quite half a century, Roundup enjoyed prosperity. But then the Great Depression (which in Montana began long before the Wall Street crash), the "Dirty Thirties" and the Dust Bowl made mincemeat of the smallholder. In 1980, I can recall reading in the *Billings Gazette* a small insert about Roundup. The newspaper reported that railway tracks belonging to the Milwaukee line were being removed from embankments, hoisted onto flatbeds and shipped to Detroit, where they would be melted into car bodies. The town was witnessing its final roundup.

Today, rebirth is palpable. In the morning, after breakfast at the Pioneer Café, I drive Route 87 due north through a landscape worthy of IMAX, past sulfur-tinted hills and onto a plain rimmed by the frosted shoulders of the Little Snowy Mountains. Twenty-six miles out of town, at a cattle guard, I leave macadam to follow a country road along Flatwillow Creek. "Tom Elliott?" I ask a band of lean cowboys, stolidly weighing bulls. They study the Suburban, curious dogs, strange me, and silently point a finger down the road. Once I pull into the headquarters of the N-Bar Land & Cattle Company, a cluster of neat white frame buildings with green trim, I'm confident I'm about to meet someone who believes architecture to be more than a double-wide.

Tom Elliott is a deviant from Western mythology. He sits in his neat office, pensive and unassuming, commanding multiple computers. Bald, not a bristle of beard out of place, glasses wire-rimmed, he blatantly wears sensible shoes, not cowboy boots, even though he manages one of Montana's classic cattle ranches. He will later admit he seldom rides a horse, preferring instead to hike. And when he walks, this middle-aged man leans on an ornate walking stick that would look odd even in midtown New York City. Next to his office, in a conference room, where recently he conducted his weekly workshop, he has spelled out the ultimate mission for each of his ranch cowboys: "Have Fun!" Next to this, a smiley face.

Tom and his siblings inherited this historic 48,000 acre N-Bar Ranch from an enterprising grandfather. Tom assumed its management, and now he's increased the ranch's running capacity to 1,200 mother cows, 800 steers, 4,000 sheep. His stated aim is to keep the N-Bar Ranch profitable while making it eco-friendly. Everything produced here is done so with chemicals and, at the time of sale, is certified organic. On the N-Bar Ranch more trees are planted than cut, and all ranch decisions meet the highest standards of sustainability. Unlike any other rancher I know, Tom Elliott is vegetarian, practices Zen Buddhism, writes poetry, and meditates. "I got over the cowboy thing after a year. I leave cattle-branding to others. I'd rather spend my time walking, observing, studying the grasses, and thinking.... I want this ranch to be productive 100 years from now."

Roundup appears to attract others of Tom Elliott's ilk. He and Bill Milton, also a large landowner as well as Zen master, dedicate themselves to community projects, like building a trail park on the edge of Roundup, improving the hospital, and fighting to derail state bills not in the best interest of the community—like the one to build a maximum-security prison next to town. Thanks in no small way to inherited wealth, both are making sure Roundup doesn't go the way of Jordan.

Now Tom has a new neighbor—Theodore Roosevelt IV. He helped Tom thwart developers by buying a neighboring property, and on it Ted and his family have built a hill house, evocative of Maine. Here they spend a few long weeks a year. To the east of Roundup, there's another sort of rancher—the patrician, Henry Bedford, who controls two spreads totaling 77,000 acres. Bedford isn't as public in his support of high-minded causes. He began buying property in the early seventies, when Bull Mountain land was as cheap as anything in the state. A tall, sardonic man with a rueful smile, he sports a large hat and dark sunglasses as he studies his ranch hands roping and branding the winter crop of calves. "I'm just a supernumerary. My body's telling me I ought to do more thinking than riding." Henry's manager, he claims, is "the best around...and I've a son who's more competent than me. So I paint, play on the computer, think, and make the occasional decision. The thing about ranching is it makes you believe you're rich even when you're not. Of course, if it doesn't rain, we're all broke."

Henry Bedford urges me to meet journalist Wilbur Wood. "He's our local communist. You'll like him." So, on my last night in town, I take Wilbur and his wife, Elizabeth, to dinner at Stella's, "the best restaurant in town, but still marginal," according to the Woods. Wilbur is in his 50s, his hair disheveled, shirt misbuttoned, his smile decidedly mischievous. Unlike other members of the Roundup crowd, the Woods appear not to be people of great means. They live on a city lot, in the stone house Wilbur's grandfather built, now overrun by vines and cats. But Wilbur is universally admired by Tom Elliott, Bill Milton, and Henry Bedford because, with nothing to lose, he speaks his mind. Having lived in California and Paris, he's now returned to the Roundup of his youth simply because this slight Montana town is where he and his wife "want to be." Over well-done New York cuts and underdone baked potatoes, Wilbur becomes voluble. "You talk of Montana privacy. Hell, Elizabeth and I were far more private in San Francisco than we are here. There we were anonymous (unless, of course, we joined a protest march). Here, we're a public commodity. But that's OK. I'm in Roundup because of this river valley, these high plains, the Snowy Mountains. As member of the stressed human race, we can come to these towns and repair.

It's a place where the air gets to clean itself out, where I don't have to carry my identity card if I want to cash a check, where I can run out of money and not panic.... When our daughter goes out riding her bike through town, I don't worry—she'll be home by sundown. How many places in the world can you say the same? Hell, it's not perfect here in Roundup, but it's not as broken as it is elsewhere."

This morning the minute I open the door of the motel room for a jog, both dogs bolt, turn a corner, and vanish from sight. When I catch up them, they're savaging an arthritic mutt, walked by a lady who appears infirm as well. I call off Chui and Duma before there's any damage. I'm mortified—prepared, in fact, to pay reparations. But the dog's owner is not out for a buck. In fact she does the apologizing: "Please there's no bother. Max'll be fine. Spirited dogs you have."

Good folk, the woods, and all those Musselshell swells stay on my mind as I accelerate along Route 12, following the river. I'm now ready to presume prosperity is an essential to the Montana dream. Deny financial rationale to farming and ranching and this immense, endlessly beautiful land no longer makes sense. This road trip is becoming a journey from penury to prosperity. As I drive west I seem to track wealth and happiness. Now I'm entering country where the human spirit is downright boisterous. I have to assume money made elsewhere is Montana's yeast of optimism. It may always have been that way—locals, it appears, rarely get rich off of Montana. Outsiders do. They are the ones who have exploited all its treasures—beaver, copper, gold, beef, wheat, and now scenery. Today, in the East, the state has been abandoned by outsiders and repatriated by locals while the West continues to attract the outsider.

Driving west I encounter more cattle ranches, and while livestock is certainly no growth industry, its appeal is universal. For many outsiders cattle ranching is a lifestyle choice, not a business. On a spread of their own they may think of themselves as latter-day "Virginians," rugged individualists mounted on gallant horses, husbanding primordial beasts who, in turn, harvest the earth's bounty. Gallant stuff and it's exactly what I once fantasized, on my own. Now the affluent from Atlanta to San José play cowboy across Montana's open spaces. On good days, they may look across their very own miles of Montana and celebrate the luxury of possessing so much private space. But if rains fail, grasses wither, the earth starts to blow away—as it might this year—Montana may be no place for the faint of heart. Already, after bad years, I've seen so many outsiders vanish without a trace.

Before reaching Roundup I've noticed another change in the country. Trees. And with them, gobs of insects dying messy deaths on my windshield. Even without rain, there's been a series of big hatches on the Musselshell. Trout fishing and cattle ranching: a perfect set of twins. Today, I watch the river, meandering seductively. I've half a mind to pull over, let the dogs run and cast a Royal Wulff onto one of the Musselshell's many lazy pools, but I can't. I have a date. Kathryn, a new and wonderful friend, arrives in Bozeman the day after tomorrow. Together we'll finish the journey to Wisdom.

Lavina, Ryegate, Harlowtown: towns that once were invented by the Chicago, Milwaukee, St. Paul & Pacific Railroad Company to entice homesteaders. In each, the old railroad hotel looms bigger than the town—handsome, square, tall and now all boarded up. But these towns refuse to call it quits. In each, there seems another kind of outsider fueling the economy. In Lavina, master blacksmith George Ainsley was recently awarded a contract to reproduce historic hinges, lamps, kick plates for a new log lodge in Yellowstone National Park; in Harlowtown, Bill Schenk, leathersmith, has a two-year waiting list for his saddles. Why do such gifted artisans come to these small towns? Virginian George Ainsley explains: "Because I want my family and me to live in the only empty place left on the map of the United States."

Not altogether empty: I pass the site near Lavina where on September 17, 1877, Chief Joseph and a large band of Nez Perce crossed the Musselshell, bound for elusive sanctuary in Canada. Everywhere I drive, I'm mindful that the white man's history is of recent origin. Beneath it lies subtle artifacts of so many other Americans, shifted elsewhere. Hunger for land remains a constant. Just before Harlowtown, I spot a large gate leading to a small house and two acres of land. Above the gate a sign reads: "Need More Land and Cattle Company."

"Two Dot Bar" reads another sign as I approach the Castle Mountains, "Easy to Find, Hard to Leave." I'm thirsty, the dogs need a gallop, and here there's bound to be history. Indeed, the bar is the only sign of life in the town of Two Dot. Jean, owner and barmaid, brings me a beer and recounts how, seven years ago, she and her husband drove up from Vegas, saw a For Sale sign over the derelict bar, and, on a lark, bought it. Within a year, her husband met someone else and vanished for other parts. Now Jean has decided to sell because the work is too consuming for a single woman on her own. "I'm going to miss the hell out of Two Dot.... This joint is the heart and soul for all 30 inhabitants in this town. After seven years, I feel related to them all."

Soon, I'm joined by JoEllen who used to run an animal blood bank in Roundup. She wants to know where I'll be spending the night. I dodge the question by buying her and all the others a drink. I notice that between 5 and 5:45 in the afternoon, the bar has gone from empty to full, patronized by the entire population of Two Dot. I approach the shyest man at the bar. John Whelan, whose large ranch surrounds us, explains this community was named after George R. "Two Dot" Wilson, who, in the 1870s earned his nickname for his aptitude for branding irons. He was known to use any piece of metal that came to hand—often the kingpin of a wagon axle—to brand his cattle. When he wanted to disguise someone else's brand his "dot" could be made with a hot frying pan. John is shy no more. He buys me a beer and promptly invites me to fish his stretch of the Musselshell in the morning. I'm tempted to stay for a third beer, but there are many miles of road to drive before Bozeman and Kathryn.

I spend the night in the foothills of the Castle Mountains on a 100,000-acre cattle operation. It's called Bonanza Creek Ranch and has been in the same family for half a century. These days, cattle no longer can support a large family, and recently the Voldseth family built guest cabins as an additional source of income. The ranch is achingly beautiful, stretching between two mountain ranges, encompassing glacial ponds, native cutthroat streams, and miles of ponderosa pines. On a rutted road, when the dogs and I enjoy our long-awaited run, we attract the attention of black baldy cows and calves, as well as two ruffed grouse. Heavy clouds overhang the Crazy Mountains to the south.

At dinner I bemoan the weather with June and David Voldseth and their hired hand, Kerry, from Australia. Attractive, no nonsense, russet-haired Kerry would like to stay in Montana, but her green card is about to expire. "The only way I can break the Immigration Service is to marry an American."

"Any offers?" I ask.

"Just one, to date. Toothless Tim."

Toothless Tim is Martinsdale's barfly. Unkempt, rank, and devoted to weather statistics, he can be found most days cadging drinks at one of the town's two watering holes. "He even agreed not to sleep with me if we got married."

In the morning, I leave a $20 tip for Kerry. She studies the green bill: "You know, mate, this is the best offer I've received."

The prospect of seeing Kathryn tomorrow hurries me along, but outside of Martinsdale, I detour from the main road, unable to avoid a collection of opulent white frame buildings and a large Crow teepee. The sign reads, "the Charles M. Bair Family Museum." I learn it has recently been established to showcase the lives of Montana's most philanthropic family.

Until her death in 1993, Alberta Bair lived alone in this remote house. While she acted like a grandee, Alberta also loved shooting gophers from the front steps of the house and popping deer from the window of her Cadillac. The museum enshrines her serendipitous life: French antiques combined with Northern Plains beadwork, a pink Formica kitchen next to a hodgepodge of illustrated letters from her friend, Charlie Russell. Alberta's father made several fortunes, the most notable from sheep, which he ran in the hundreds of thousands on the Crow Reservation. Alberta who died childless, left her estate to the land and the people she and her family revered. Harlowltown's hospital is a gift from her. Every year, five high school graduates from there and from White Sulfur Springs receive full scholarships from the Bair Family Trust. The rest of the Bair fortune is earmarked to support Montana arts, education, and medicine.

Duma and Chui enjoy the Bair house as much as me. Across the lawn, Duma has turned her attention to the many gophers Alberta never shot, while Chui, always the lounge lizard, has pried open a screen door with her nose and is making her way to one of Alberta's most comfortable couches. This remote, seldom-visited museum. celebrates eccentricity and generosity, in equal shares. I've come a long way from Circle and Jordan.

Even the nearby Hutterite colony, population 110, appears rich. Here I stop to buy potatoes, said to be Montana's best, from a jovial man—in white shirt, black pants, black hat, black suspenders. The potatoes are an alibi—a way to inflict myself upon these remarkable Montanans, refugees from 19th-century Russia. Today they live in scattered farms across North America's Great Plains. Theirs is the ultimate communist life—no private property, all assets shared by the collective. Unlike the Amish they have no scruples about the use of modern technology. Their produce is organic, their yields said to be the envy of all the country. Girls, dressed in homespun skirts and bonnets; boys, sporting black caps, all blush when I say hello. They speak English haltingly, with accents, for they are taught twice—once by teachers from local public schools, then, in High German by teachers from the colony. Many Montanans, suspicious of all things foreign, treat these Mennonites with diffidence. Now they are as Montanan as any tobacco-stained cowboy. The jovial man heaving the bag of potatoes into the Suburban asks if I'm as worried as he about the drought.

There's no sign of Toothless Tim in picturesque Martinsdale, half-restored, half-boarded up. At the Crazy Mountain Inn, I settle for a chicken-fried steak (the best one I've ever tasted) and enquire of the energetic owner why this town looks so intact, why there are no double-wide trailers as there are almost everywhere in Montana.

"Alberta Bair wouldn't have it."

"But she didn't own the town."

"That didn't stop Alberta Bair. When a lot came up for sale, she bought it. Simple. She ended up owning the entire edge of town. She just hated the hell out of trailers."

Money—what an impact it can have on this beautiful land. I feel so crude to talk this way even to myself, but I'm ready to conclude there are only two uses for this state—leaving it in its original sinless state or repairing the damage of the last 50 years.

Now, fishing lunacy grips me. After hot coffee, I leave Route 294 to test an unexpected lake, awash in rafts of northbound duck. I begin wetting my feet on its west flank, experimenting with a Royal Coachman. My first cast, a long one, aided by the wind, stuns me with its precision. Damn, if I'm not good. The moment it lands there's a rise, 20 feet to the left. I correct and my fly lands within inches of the roiled water. I steady the rod and then draw the line home in quick erratic tugs. Nothing. Again and again I cast until the waters quiet and my casting goes to hell.

I press on—this time, the lake's north side, with a muddler minnow. There's not even a rise. After an hour, I look at my watch and leap back into the Suburban. I'm late and thunderheads are building in the west. On my way back to Route 294, a pickup, overloaded with large square bales of hay, stops me. "How ya doin'?" Asks the ranch hand, pressing Copenhagen under his gums. I shake my head in disgust. He studies my equipment bemused. "On Sunday in an hour, I got 11. Biggest ran four pounds."

"What did you use?"

"Nightcrawlers and oatmeal."

The roads I now travel, some paved, most dusty logging trails, are acknowledged on the map as broken lines. While I'm bound for Bozeman, my course is never a straight line. Random, even illusory, the first road runs beside the Milwaukee line, its trestle bridges and embankments now derelict. High on a hill, near a ghost town, I pause to admire three mountain ranges, visible with hardly a twist of the head. By chance, I spot an inconsistency on a rock and pry field glasses from the jockey box for a closer look. Sure enough, a peregrine falcon and, beyond, a pair of short-billed curlews, bound for breeding grounds in Canada. Their gurgling lullaby seems an invitation to a long journey. I study these heirloom birds, living Audubon prints, and feel a strange compassion for their mission. I cannot imagine how far they've traveled or the adventures that remains. Duma eyes them curiously, poised to spring. Just in time, I call her off.

Soon I swoop into the town of Ringling, once summer headquarters for the circus magnate John Ringling North. There were times, 70 years ago, when his private railcar brought him and his elephants here to summer. Today there's no sign of the bluster, only hints of a rebirth—a new steeple for the church, homes resided, children kicking balls on dusty roads. No one appears to know the road to Maudlaw until, at the town's sole bar, a grizzled patron leads me to the door to point south into the Bridgers. Armed now with popcorn and a roadie, I locate the Maudlaw road, a trail behind a wire gate. As soon as we climb, the road steadily deteriorates. At 6,200 feet the track becomes mud and melting snow. I can see no one has been this way since winter. I engage four-wheel drive. Game is scarce and, for an hour, ravens torment me, hovering beside melting snow in the lee of abandoned corrals.

At the top of the pass, I pull the car to the side and jog for a mile with the dogs. When I return to the car, gasping for breath in this thin air, I play with the radio dial and discover one station with perfect reception. It's Bozeman and the newscaster is chatting about El Niño and its effect on Montana. In southern California there are floods. In the Northern Plains drought. And because of the drought, fire—an oddity in spring—is spreading through the forests above Missoula. More firefighters are en route and there appears no relief in sight. "A disaster in the making," the anchorman intones, not once, but twice.

After topping the divide, the track follows Sixteen Mile Creek into a dark canyon, plunging vertically. Sometimes, brakes lock and the Suburban slips on old ice and congealed mud, snowboarding along the swale of the road. For the last three hours the dogs and I haven't seen any sign of human life. Finally, I engage the brakes as we enter Maudlaw, a town of boarded storefront, gray, splintered wood, barking dogs. But this is no ghost town. Prosperity's in the air since the town is surrounded by three monster ranches, one owned by a California bank executive, the other heir to the Sun Oil fortune, the last, Ted Turner. I turn on the tape player to hear the final installment of *Bridge of San Luis Rey* for guidance. Thornton Wilder writes of Uncle Pio: "He possessed the...attributes of the adventurer: a memory for names and faces with an aptitude for altering his own, the gift of tongues, inexhaustible invention, secrecy, the talent for falling into conversations with strangers." Not bad advice for a Montana traveler.

"Chui. Duma," I whistle. They stir, their heads, one blond, the other black, appear above the rear seat. "Company tonight. Kathryn. Remember?" Chui yawns.

She is sitting on her suitcase, waiting for me at the airport. Kathryn is quick to forgive my failure at punctuality. She says she has been enjoying the Montana air. Tall, almost equine, she hugs the dogs and defers to me with a kiss. I throw her bag in the back and I watch her move to the front effort-lessly, as if she is born to the West. For the first hour, on I-90, driving north, conversation is awkward. I haven't talked to a passenger in a week, and she doesn't seem inclined toward banalities. I ask a few questions about New York. I apologize for the interstate, telling her that the back roads beat every-thing. I describe the Bar 20 and how, on the threshold of spring, it will be waiting for her, after we reach Wisdom. She knows I'm struggling, and she lets me squirm even more; she looks away into a forest of hills. After Butte, we turn west onto Route 15 and, in time, Route 43.

The moment we leave the interstate, she starts to talk and I begin to babble. I tell her about the curlews, Maudlaw, the Bair Family Museum. She's "bummed" she missed it. All I want now is to spoil her with scenery. In the back, the dogs are attentive to the chatter, the first they've heard in a while. Chui places her muzzle on the back of Kathryn's seat to audition for a pat.

We follow the Big Hole River, slowing near a settlement called Wise River. Here I tell Kathryn about its colossal browns and rainbows. The river is low and they'll be stressed if rains fail. Too many thoughts of mine are running together: Lewis and Clark passed through here in 1805, I explain. She tells me she's read the Ambrose book. I describe how Chief Joseph and his band of Nez Perce fought the army near here in 1877. The river is deep, swirling, labored. With approaching dusk, I hear Kathryn whispering our destination. "Wisdom," she says to herself. "Wisdom," she repeats. She finds it funny.

As we cut through this broad valley, I let her know my thoughts. I tell her I've seen hardscrabble communities transformed by people of wealth, drawn to Montana by rivers and mountains. "But that's only in the west. To the east, it's a different tale—few outsiders and locals, consumed by inertia, discon-tent, anger. I'm beginning to realize space—Montana space—is so damn expensive these days. Only the rich can afford it. I'm damn glad I'm not a politician, because my remedy wouldn't be popular: more Mongol hordes, more outsiders. Montana will only survive if it's invaded."

The valley widens, clouds darken. Beneath a range of hills, just below the Continental Divide, we sight our destination, a blemish of lumber on the plain. We pause to enjoy the view, to breathe ionized air and let the dogs own this chilling landscape. The moment I open the door, they spot a rabbit and they're off, bound for a distant hay stack. The valley, filled with beaver slides, archaic wooden hay-stackers, is almost as broad as the heavens. "A cup in the sky," Kathryn says. I stare at her when I think she's not looking. Then we enter Wisdom—6,200 feet high, end of my 943-mile road, the beginning of Kathryn's Montana.

At dinner at the only restaurant in town, we meet a man dining alone. Kathryn invites him to join us. He explains he took early retirement from a software company in San Diego, and selected Wisdom to live the rest of his life. "Last year, I fished 150 days total. You can't do better—the Big Hole, Bitterroot, Beaverhead, Fiddler's Creek. This is ground zero for trout." Kathryn listens attentively and says not a word.

After dinner, we return to the Nez Perce Motel to fetch the dogs. We run them on the town's wooden sidewalks. Where the town ends—at the Anglers' Bar—they're invited inside by a dog-loving brunette sporting a handful of Slim Jims. Chui and Duma perform all their tricks—sitting down, looking innocent, rolling over—and earn themselves second Slim Jims while Kathryn and I are rewarded with Moose Drool. "Why Wisdom?" Kathryn asks the brunette.

"Honey, all you need of the world is here in this two-bit town."

At dawn the next morning, I notice something different outside the drawn curtains. With Kathryn still asleep, I open the motel door to release the impatient dogs. Clouds sit heavy above Wisdom's roofs. On the ground—standing water. Rain beats against my face.

I go inside. On the Bozeman TV station, the weatherman declares the drought broken. All Montana is overcast. Locales that haven't seen moisture in months may soon be drenched. And the rain will last for another two days. Good-bye El Niño. Welcome La Niña.

I return to gather the wet dogs. Rain, beating on my tousled hair, runs across my forehead, over my shoulder, down my chest. Half naked, I stand on the stoop, blinded by surprise. The owner of the motel sees me, gives me the high-sign and yells, "The million-dollar rain."

I return to the hushed room. "Kathryn," I whisper. She stirs. I'm thinking of eastern Montana and the happiness that must be written across the face of every grain farmer and cattle rancher from here to Williston. Kathryn stirs, rubbing sleep from her eyes, looking past me into the gloom of day. "The rains have come," I whisper. "It's a celebration. All Montana must be delirious. Go back to sleep. When you awake, I'll drive you to the Bar 20."

~

CHAPTER 6

Invaded by Memory

Today is August 18, 1996, a Sunday. I dash out of my small shed office to find out why Chui is barking. A low-slung car has left the West Boulder Road, crossed the bridge and is approaching. Since the sight of a luxury car is odd sight on the back roads of Montana, I study it as it scatters dust through the aspen. Someone asking permission to fish the river, I dread. When it approaches, I see it is an older Lincoln with Washington State plates. It's also pocked with dings. Through its tinted windows, I catch a glimpse of its driver: definitely no fisherman. Very deliberately, he uncoils his frame from the seat. Stoop-shouldered when he reaches his full height, he wears a finely creased straw cowboy hat, silver belt buckle, monogrammed boots that adds two inches to his impressive frame. I guess him to be in his mid-70s. He shields his eyes from bright sun, unabashedly scrutinizing me. My attire is decidedly exotic: hiking shorts, *chopli* sandals out of Nairobi, and a beat-up Lacoste shirt. From the way he politely averts his eyes, I know I've failed the first test.

He begins with an apology: "Don't normally intrude on strangers on Sunday, but I just wanted to come back to relive the events of my life 60 years ago. Ken Presley's the name."

For the last year I have been randomly trying to establish a Bar 20 history, thanks to the three pages of foolscap given me by Eugene Magat. But the trails were all overgrown. I knew Stanley Cox of press card fame had been central to this tale of house and ranch. On the Internet I had searched his name through an array of telephone books, in hopes Mr. Cox had produced a son and named him for himself. My search yielded a cavalry of Stanley Coxes. I sent them more than 50 form letters. When the responses started trickling back, most were of the "addressee unknown" variety. The few Stanley Coxes who replied did so with courteous "I never had any relative who ever lived in Montana" finality. In the end, I jammed the returned letters in a file and waited for something else to turn up.

Now here it is: the stranger's card, filling the palm of my hand. It reads: "Charles K. (Ken) Presley, B. Sc., P.E.M Consultant. Large Diameter & Specialty Drilling & Boring." This Sunday was not the best time to meet someone with a voluminous story. A friend and his young son have just arrived from New York. My then girlfriend is agitating for me to help her load a horse onto the trailer so she can ride with a neighbor. Would Mr. Presley like a refreshment after the dusty road? I ask, disregarding responsibilities. "I'd go for a whiskey," he replies. I invite them inside while I tell the girlfriend she'll have to wait.

Mr. Presley stays one hour. His tale will become a turning point.

As he wanders the Bar 20, nodding and whispering to his wife, his body suggests memories are gathering fast, like blue bottles. Finally he unlimbers himself in a wicker chair on the screened porch and speaks. He, Ken Presley, was last here, age 12. His father, the ranch foreman, had been a celebrated dude wrangler, known for horsemanship and roping skills.

He looks around. The place hasn't changed all that much, he concludes, casting his eyes toward the river. He explains that in 1935, the Bar 20 was a 2,000-acre ranch, owned by Naval Commander Stanley Cox. I had always hoped Stanley Cox was one hell of a guy—military in manner, patrician in outlook, fine horseman, upright neighbor, model rancher, dedicated photographer.

"Memory," Ken mutters, "it's like an artichoke. You pull off one leaf and uncover a whole lot more." For Ken, the Bar 20 saga revolves around its owner. "Old Stan Cox," I discover, was anything but hero. He was an Eastern cockscomb, married to an impenetrable woman, both of them dreamers of a cowboy fantasy, both incapable of playing the lead role in their own drama.

According to Ken, the Coxes had purchased the ranch through the sale of the family home, a royal Maryland land-grant estate, according to Ken. Why they sold a great house, in the same family for six generations, Ken didn't know. Stan had spent much of his life on the sea, having served as a naval commander in World War I. Stan, thought Ken, had been inspired by the works of Owen Wister, Clarence Mulford, and Will James. "Stan and Mrs. Cox were dudes," explained this gimped-up former cowboy. "No doubt about it. And for a year and a half—until my Dad couldn't take it any more—I watched and listened. I was a bottle-assed kid, ears all aflappin'. I'd never seen anything like it. Their life was all high hopes and outrageous misconceptions. And they were so different...."

The Bar 20 house had then consisted only of dining room, bedroom, and kitchen. Ken's eyes squinted as the memories tumble out, in no particular order: "In the dining room there was a wood stove. But soon after we arrived, Stan hired an old Norwegian—Jesus, I can even remember his name—Tosti Stenberg. He must have been nearly 100 years old at the time. He was hired to build a fireplace and chimney. Then Stan added a living room and an office [the room that had now been converted to my bedroom].

"The Coxes had a cook called Lucille Graham. That fall, Pinky Pearson of the Valley Ranch showed up to work as a hand, moving cattle and branding calves. He spun a few windies for Stan—old Pinky'd never let the facts get in the way of a good story—and then Pinky started sparking Lucille and eventually he married her.

"Mrs. Cox had wonderful goblets that were so thin they gave when you pinched them. Beautiful dining-room table. She had three Scottie dogs and one Sealyham. Each morning Mrs. Cox would line them up and feed them scrambled eggs and bacon with a mother-of-pearl handled fork. I'll never forget it. We'd never seen dogs treated that way. Heaven help you if you let a chicken bone drop to floor—the Coxes raised 200 chickens at any one time. The dogs, naturally, weren't allowed to have chicken bones, but what Bab didn't know is that they'd go out to the garbage pit to dig them up. They were always eating chicken bones behind her back. I thought that was funny as hell.

"Every spring Stan had the garden plowed up, just beyond the aspen trees, with his team of horses, Pete and Dolly. Mrs. Cox planted lots of carrots, lettuce, radishes, onions, asparagus, peas, and corn which was never too successful. Canadian thistles were rampant. My job was to chomp out the thistles. So if you ever think of having a garden now, make damn sure you've gotten rid of thistles. They grow faster than asparagus.

"No one ever came to Stan's house without going there on specific business. I'd say they were standoffish. You had the feeling the Coxes only dealt with enlisted men or servants. They gave Lucille directions. She was definitely the servant type. But Stan wouldn't dare try that stunt with Dad.

"One January, a good friend of Stan's from Philadelphia's main line came out to visit. Bayard something. They had been to prep school together. Nice guy. In those days, Stan had a single-cylinder engine with two flywheels. It ran a crosscut saw and cut several loads of firewood a day. So this Bayard came up to see us working the saw. He wore a top coat and fedora. It was well below zero. He was slapping his hands against his ears. 'Bayard,' Dad said, 'Goddamn it, why don't you put your hands over your ears?

"'No, I wouldn't do that,'" he replied. 'One time I was wearing earmuffs and a fellow offered me a drink and I didn't hear him.'

"Dad and I never forgot that remark. I was just a kid, but it sure tickled me. Bayard was deadly serious.

"In those days, Dad was making $75 a month as head foreman. Stan hadn't a clue what was going on on the ranch. He was nervous around horses.

"In February '36 Stan bought 50 head of poled Hereford shipped out of Texas. Anybody who bought cows in Texas to calve in February was not a cattleman. Stan did just that. It snowed all month; the temperature never got above zero. In the old dining room, you could melt steel in front of the fire and freeze a brass monkey's balls ten feet away. But Dad never lost one of Stan's calves. They were born in box stalls in the big barn, then put behind the stove in our house until they dried out and got onto their feet.

"Sometime in February, we were running short of grub. But what bothered Stan was that he and Mrs. Cox were out of whiskey.... I won't bother you just yet with the story but Dad wasn't a happy camper. We quit late in August of '36. Dad was damn glad to get out of Stan Cox's employ."

One hour has passed. The equestrian girlfriend, sitting on the fence, is tempestuous. My friend and his son, puttering in the grass, need entertainment. During this interlude the narrative pours from Ken Presley in a steady stream, clear, bubbling, freshly thawed—stories that needed telling for 60 years and only now have found their audience. One thousand questions about the Coxes remain, but today is not the day.

His whiskey polished off in a neat swallow, Ken rises, takes his wife's hand, and the two make their way out to the dusty Lincoln. The old man opens the door, removes his hat. "Thanks for the hospitality. As I say, I don't normally do this sort of thing." He repacks himself into the driver's seat, readjusts his hat, and fires the engine. The car purrs out of the driveway, his left arm gesticulating as he tells his young wife just what was what when he was 12.

So Stan Cox was not the all-conquering hero, the accomplished dude who launched a great enterprise from this spot. But who was he? Was this Cream-of-Kentucky yarn telling? Why did a childless couple leave a life of ease and privilege back East to entomb themselves in a remote and sometimes hostile Montana valley? What were they hiding?

The serendipitous appearance of Ken Presley has now fired me with renewed enthusiasm for putting flesh and blood to house and land. He has just pressed into my hands the clues I've been trying, halfheartedly, to find. With luck, they may tip me off to the Cox mystery, if indeed there is one. Who else lived on this site? Who preceded and who succeeded them? And did others eke from this place dreams of their own?

At the time I had something else on my mind. Several years after we bought the Bar 20, I happened upon an old acquaintance from New York. I first met "Mike" in New York where he worked as a broadcasting intern between between acting and bartending gigs. Pitching up at the Road Kill Café on one of Montana's lonelier road was a contextual jolt and we both spent a few minutes shaking our heads in disbelief. He explained he had come to Montana to realize his dream of writing "the great American novel." He thought this valley might furnish him with lots of rich material for a work, germinating, he claimed, in his mind. I wished him well and suggested that if times were ever hard I might be able to cook up some work. Mike's face, open and unguarded, lit with delight. We parted and for three months I heard not a word. Then one day Mike metamorphosed with his dog at the Bar 20. I duly showed him a few pesky items that needed attending while I was away on assignment—a fallen fence, fieldstones waiting to be laid for a path, dry log walls waiting to be oiled.

Mike was never cut out to work with his hands. The jobs I gave him took him far too long, his car was always breaking down, and there were a number of reasons why things never quite got done "to specs." Still, I wanted to help; I trusted in his cause. Mike had a winning personality and his dog, a coyote-cross, never left his side. Anyone so good with animals was, in the end, worthy.

Over the winter, thanks to my introduction, Mike worked as a fetcher for a contractor friend. Evenings, he freelanced for the *Billings Gazette*, reporting on town meetings and school-board functions. I was happy Mike had found a way of affording Montana. I just hoped he was making headway on the novel.

Then, in March, it happened. My sister received a phone call from the reserve caretaker, saying that one of our cabins had been burglarized. It wasn't just a case of the alarm clock walking away. Every stick of furniture—bed, tables, chairs—had vanished. I was out of the country, and when I heard the news, having never known of such a crime in our remote corner, I was mystified. New York City, yes. But never in Montana. After all, this is a state whose entire population could be housed in 20 blocks of Manhattan. Instead it's scattered across an area one and a half times the size of England, Wales, Scotland, and Northern Ireland. In Montana, cattle outnumber humans. Our local town, Big Timber, is so innocent, front doors are left unlatched, elderly women block traffic to share recipes on the main street, children on bicycles have the right of way, and most police phone calls are about stray dogs or love-sick bulls who've crashed a fence.

For a while, the police suspected our robbers were a group of high school seniors known to pry open lonely cabins, to party. But this crime didn't fit. The driver of the getaway car had skidded across the ice and crashed into our chain blocking the driveway. A chunk of headlight mount carelessly lay as evidence on the ice. And why steal a bed unless one is interested in refurnishing one's home or fencing furniture?

At about the same time my contractor friend had received a visit from Mike, inquiring whether he might be interested in purchasing a saddle that had been in his family for many years. It was an impressive object, covered in historic tool work. The contractor looked it over admiringly and said he would like to show it to his wife before committing to a price. Mike agreed.

My friend took the exquisite saddle to the police station, and after a few phone calls, the police chief traced it to the Lewistown Museum, the Central Montana Historical Society. It was revealed the museum had been robbed on three occasions during the winter, presumably by the same individual. Nine valuable Indian artifacts, including a beaded wooden saddle, ceremonial tomahawks, a warbonnet, two antique rifles, and mocassins had been removed. One item the museum described as "priceless" and valued at $20,000.

Mike's driveway and house were searched. The headlight mount fitted nicely into his damaged Cherokee grill. One quarter of all the purloined items from the museum lay under his bed. Most of the others were traced to the home of a Billings "antique collector." The contents of our cabin were never found.

Caught red-handed with stolen goods, Mike confessed to the museum thefts. He was taken into custody and bail was set at $50,000. After calling an aunt back East, Mike made bail on the spot. Sentencing was set for 30 days. Those, like I, who knew Mike suspected he would be sent to Deer Lodge, an infamous state prison, filled with hard-core criminals. Here someone as gentle as Mike would become easy prey, terrorized by every idle deviant. Poor Mike, I thought. I wished I could have helped him. The *Billings Gazette* which, until now, had buried the incident in small leads on page ten, now ceased reporting on it altogether. Presumably the newspaper's editorial board hesitated in covering this sorry affair since the criminal had been one of its own.

Mike had come to Montana with a secret. To a friend during the 30-day wait, he confided, by way of explanation, that his parents had abandoned him as a child, that later he had been abused by foster relatives. Throughout his life he had mitigated against the effects of mistreatment by appropriating the possessions of others. He had burgled purses at work in New York, the cash register at the Hard Rock Café, hardware stores, and supermarkets from Billings to Bozeman. The object had never been money. His compulsion lay in the process and thrill of the heist, the satisfaction of sweet revenge. Mike blamed the Lewiston Museum directors for securing their back door with a defective padlock. They had, he believed, given him an invitation to rob.

As to our cabin furniture: Mike never came clean on whether he had stolen it. According to my source, he found the subject tedious, waving his hand impatiently and saying it would be up to us to find out.

We never did. Mike skipped bail, fled Montana with his dog. Neither one has been seen since, and to this day the case remains open. I wonder where he'll turn up next.

While bruised, I was also intrigued. Mike had clearly duped me, but more provocatively, in Montana he had discovered something lacking elsewhere. Here was country that deified personal expression and freedom of movement like few other regions. In fact, Mike had settled on Montana for the same reasons as mine. He and I hadn't escaped New York for a California or Colorado or Wisconsin or Hawaii. It had to be Montana. But Mike had gone one better than me: only this state fulfilled his need for private vengeance. He probably thought a land which didn't secure their cabins or museums properly, and a citizenry so gullible to buy his line, wouldn't have the know-how to track him down. He was probably right. Simply, his luck turned.

My luck has now changed. On the first page of the yellow foolscap is the name "Kahle." On a whim, I check Montana telephone books and find a listing in nearby Livingston for a Dr. Robert Kahle, "chiropractor."

Dr. Kahle is retired, but, yes, he had once owned the Bar 20 although he is not certain he can tell me much."It was a long time ago." But he will see me on August 22. What I know of him is slim. He was the one who sold the place to the Magats at the onset of the hippie experiment, in the early 1970s. How long Kahle owned the Bar 20, from whom he bought it, why, how he used it, is uncertain.

I find Dr. Kahle's house in a small development behind a row of motels. Here there are a handful of modest ranch houses sprawled on a sweeping lane. His, sited at the cul de sac, is the largest, the kind developers describe as "deluxe." The glass on the front door is frosted and the bell sounds a long-winded chime through the house. For a moment, I'm not certain I've arrived at the right place. My dogs, confined to the car, study my nervous pacing on the stoop, hoping I'll relent and release them to terrorize the neighborhood. I look back at the door as Dr. Kahle opens it. He is bespectacled, wiry and tall, probably in his 80s. I can see from the pile of the carpet and the glow of the kitchen appliances, he has done well as a chiropractor. We sit at the kitchen table and he explains that his wife of 23 years is blind, hence the odd assortment of talking cuckoo clocks and door-bell chimes, her way of orienting herself.

He can't remember the year—might it have been in 1959?—when he bought the Bar 20 house and two and a half acres surrounding it, from Harry Brewer. Harry had been one of Dr. Kahle's patients and Harry was in a bind. His neighbor, Paul Payne, was about to be foreclosed on his property, amounting to many hundreds of acres of land. Harry wanted it but couldn't afford it, Harry explained, as he lay in Dr. Kahle's examining room, awaiting relief from his cowboy backache. Harry had to buy the damn thing—it made a lot of sense—but the only way he'd be able to afford it would be if he sold off all its "dude" cabins. Some of the smaller ones had already been spoken for, but the big one, the homestead, called the "Bar 20," was still available— a bargain at $7,500.

Dr. Kahle bought it, on the spot, and for the next 12 years, he used it as his family weekend escape. His sons were young, snowmobiling was in its infancy, and, during the height of winter, father and sons drove from town until their pickup bogged down in drifts, then offloaded the snowmobile to continue—across Wolfe Hill, down into Ellis Basin, along the West Boulder Road until they reached the old log bridge, negotiable only on foot, thus to arrive at the Bar 20...on snow shoes.

In summer, Dr. Kahle often dedicated weekends to improving the Bar 20's derelict buildings—reshingling the main roof, replacing an ineffective propane stove with an antique wood-burning one he had found in an old cabin in the Cinnabar Basin. But the Bar 20's first and foremost use during the Kahle tenure was hunting.

Dr. Kahle invites me into his cellar, as roomy as the house, carpeted and dark. On one wall are the heads of eight varieties of sheep. He lists them: "stone, Dahl, desert, rocky mountain bighorn," and when he is done, he breathes the words, in a sacred whisper: "Double Grand Slam."

I am impressed. But, Dr. Kahle insists, the Bar 20 was never a place for hunting mountain sheep. Just mountain lion. When Robert Kahle bought it, it was crawling with "lion and bobcat…Harry Brewer called one day in December. You see, ranchers were scared to death of lion and one had just gone through Harry's corrals. He'd seen its tracks.

"My hunting buddy had two black-and-tan hounds—great mountain lion dogs until one ate the other. We took 'em and got to Harry's place on the first of January that year. And soon—where Davis Creek hits the West Boulder—we picked up the tracks of the lion. All day we followed it, the dogs baying ahead of us, the country under snow as quiet as death. Then we saw blood all over the ground, where the lion had killed a deer. We continued…tracking it over the brow of the hill. We were tired as all get-out, but we kept climbing and tracking. Finally, just with night coming on, we treed the lion right on top of the brow overlooking Davis Creek and the West Boulder. The snarling lion was merely one dark shadow in a dark, gnarled tree. Shooting was the easy part.

"We carried the lion down to the West Boulder in the dark and got to the Bar 20 at 11 that night. The lion weighed 86 pounds and my hunting buddy was paid a bounty of $100. It covered the cost of dog food. So that was the first of our West Boulder lions…. In all, when I owned the Bar 20, I shot four bobcats and two lions. There they are."

Dr. Kahle steps aside, switches on lights to reveal two full mounts of his lions. They are grappling one wall of his rec room, frozen in the same snarling spring now for nearly 40 years. I wonder whether descendants of these same lions might prowl our valley today. I have seen only one, climbing the cliffs behind the Bar 20. Tawny, with a tail nearly as long as its body, it seemed to know how to skulk through matching limestone shadows. Soon it was consumed by shadows on the cliff.

Recently, neighbors in the valley have been reporting an increase of mountain-lion sightings. For the lion, recovery from the brink of extinction has been long and slow. Once, in the 1930s game departments declared it enemy number one. Strychnine poison and jaw traps, strategically placed by bounty hunters and wolfers, were effective weapons, killing unselectively. For the wolf, they meant virtual extinction, at least in the lower 48 states. Its comeback thereafter would only be possible by an act of Congress. The lion, on the other hand, is secretive. Canny as a leopard, it has recovered on its own.

"I would have liked to have kept the Bar 20," Dr. Kahle says as he flicks off the rec-room lights and trudges the stairs to the kitchen, "But in the early seventies my wife and I couldn't get along anymore. She had gotten a job in Livingston and I don't think she liked the Bar 20. If we had company she might enjoy it...but otherwise she wouldn't have much to do with it. She had been brought up out in the country, so it was no big thing for her to be in a remote place like the Bar 20." Dr. Kahle settles back at the kitchen table and repeats, "I would have liked to have kept the Bar 20, but it became our divorce settlement. She took it and sold it immediately [to the Magats]. I believe she made $25,000 on the deal."

I decide I've gotten what I came for—a mere sequence of life at the Bar 20, perhaps banal and uninspired, but strangely reassuring. Robert Kahle had been little more than a tenant, repairing its joints, enjoying its wildness, but hardly imbuing it with vigor. His story, in the end, is the story of so many: two people diverging because they didn't share a passion. Now it's time for me to leave. As I do so, the tall, lanky chiropractor, bent like a capital *S* over the table, begins chuckling. "Harry Brewer. Now he was quite the guy," he adds.

"One rainy evening…" Dr. Kahle recalls as I stand in the kitchen doorway, Kahle was at work, electrifying the Bar 20. Until then it had been powered only by a generator and its telephone, a primitive two-longs-one-short-ring-and-crank variety, had been installed by the Forest Service for fire control. Strung on small poles, zigzagging between neighbors, it found its way from Livingston to the end of the line, 40 miles distant, in the now abandoned mining town of Independence.

The downpour, Dr. Kahle remembers, was unremitting. "I heard a shout and went down to the river. The bridge had recently washed out, and during spring floods we could only cross by boat. It was Harry, yelling that his phone was out, and he believed a limb on my side had fallen on the line. With the river raging, I took the kayak across to collect him. Harry didn't know how to swim and had never been in a boat before, but I successfully got him to our side of the river [where] I climbed the tree and he spliced the break. Once it was complete, we set off for the return. I could see he was nervous. 'Now sit down Harry and I'll get you back. Don't stand up.' He stood up anyway and over we went, the two of us washing downriver. For a while, he was caught underneath the kayak, hanging on for dear life. Finally we both crawled out on the bank—unfortunately the wrong one for him. Harry had just quit smoking three months before. He needed a smoke real bad, so I gave him one. He sat in the rain looking at the bank where he wanted to be. 'How're we going to get back?' he asked.

"I said, 'Just sit down and I'll get you back.' He would have none of it. His wife, Mabel, was waiting for him on the far side. He yelled across the river to her to…get the horses. She rode five miles in the rain, around on the Forest Service bridge to collect him. And he never got in a boat ever again."

I leave Dr. Kahle's house, knowing it is the Harry Brewer connection I now need to fill Bar 20 gaps. Dr. Kahle has closed the door but I can see his shadow behind the frosted glass, watching. I'm also being studied by my dogs, marooned in the heat of the car. I let them out, refill their water bowl, and watch them tear across the impeccable Kahle lawn, irrigating it where they choose.

The Bar 20 is now no longer a collection of well-planed logs and a roof. It is a series of revolving symbols. For Robert Kahle, it had been retreat from the relative frenzy of Livingston, population 6,000. Then it became the great equalizer of an unpleasant divorce. For the Magats it had been access to a new world, the West, then it became their ticket to retirement. While I'm not yet sure about the Coxes, each in the end, it seems, had regretted the circumstances that led to its sale. But loss is accompanied by a sense of the inevitable. Somehow, however enduring, the Bar 20, it appears, can never be owned by anyone for long.

I gather the dogs into the pickup, turn the air-conditioning to full blast, and drive home fast to ride my favorite horse, Coop, before darkness.

It now is time for me to enjoy the Bar 20.

≈

CHAPTER 7

The Valley—From Horseback

The best way to appreciate the Bar 20 is by horse. From the start, I learned a good horse possesses an intuition for mountain travel, a nose for the historic trail. Without any coaching, my first Bar 20 horse, Dewey, had an unexpected desire, as soon as I climbed into the saddle, to lope past the house, across the wildflower meadow, up onto the bench that runs south, high above the river for two miles. On foot I had never noticed the overgrown trail he now followed, but from a high perch it resembled a highway. By following faint cuts in the brush, weaving in and out of drainages formed by intermittent springs, Dewey and I thus worked our way to the end of the plateau only to find ourselves in a maze of game trails leading into a dense stand of aspen and fir.

En route, 100 feet beneath the saddle, there were astonishing views of river—a shard of reflected sunlight, a gush of shadowed riffles. Just released from alpine glaciers, the river curls, trembles, shimmers in canyons below my horse's hoofs. On the trail, the river was chorus to Dewey's steady clomping, but in forest gloom its murmur was hushed, and now all I heard was just a breath of wind adjusting lodgepole pines. The faintest give in the brush was enough for Dewey to find his way to a bog beside a still spring, then, with a lunge, through knotted serviceberry into a clearing. When we emerged from forest that first time, Dewey led me straight to an old log house, as if he had always known about it. A catawampus affair, huddled on a steep slope, it came as a surprise. I hadn't clue this corner of the national forest had ever been inhabited. The cabin appeared to defy gravity, thanks to wooden braces hastily erected, I supposed, to stop it from snowboarding into the river. But on this crisp August day, I had no time to admire the old logs, for Dewey had started prancing, skittering, lunging away from the clearing as if the grass has caught fire.

My confusion was short-lived. Instantly I saw what was bugging him: two black bears peering above the cover, transfixed. It seemed we had interrupted a sow and her cub from a lunch of chokecherries and huckleberries. We laid on a spectacular rodeo for them as we rollercoastered about the clearing, me yelling, "Whoa, baby, goddamnit, Dewey, cut this shit, stop you sonuvabitchin' horse" and Dewey not listening, all the time pretending he was an astronaut. Finally the sow and cub turned and bolted into the forest, leaving behind a musky eau de bear, which further frazzled Dewey's mind.

These were probably Dewey's first bears, so he took no chances. Even when they had fled, he let loose with another booster launch, sending the two of us about level with the forest canopy. Perhaps he was thinking I'm bear as well, I couldn't be certain. I hung onto anything that came to hand—a clutch of mane, a hunk of neck. Even in my misery, I was grateful there were no witnesses. Fear of being seen is as serious an injury as bouncing along the ground. My heart hammered at my neck. I stopped breathing and I wondered whether my eyes were extended in the cartoon bug-eyed position.

Finally I managed to head Dewey down the hill, away from bears. Near the river, we stopped and, with my cupped hand, soothed him until he stopped twitching and began to graze. At last, breathing regularly, we crossed the Forest Service bridge, opened two gates, and jogged north to the Bar 20, both of us a bit more seasoned to West Boulder Valley ways.

Beginning in 1988, the horse, sometimes obstreperous and high main-tenance, was my passport to all the secrets and bonanzas of this valley. While I rode mostly alone, I didn't mind saddling them up for beginners. I enjoyed showing others the ropes, but as soon as we left the security of the homestead, I felt an awful responsibility. Nightmare accidents weighed on me, awake and asleep. What might happen when we come upon a bear, a snake, or even worse (and more common) old fence wire? Horses, I had learned, don't reflect or take stock. They go bananas first, think second.

The horse is central to the Bar 20. I've never doubted it complements the house, with its surrounding jackleg fencing built to equine scale; its logs organic, imperfect, alive. In this valley, house and horse, both willful, appear historic partners. From the screened porch, at dusk, I feel complete in the sight of a horse, whether slurping water from the fountain at the fence or head down in high grass or looking at himself in the rearview mirror of a car. I marvel how our horses always prefer grazing as close to us as they can get, if for no other reason than to monitor our comings and goings or, per-haps, to ensure we don't slip into the granary and distribute oats without their supervision.

Because of Dewey and a few others, in 1994 we acquired one more reserve lot, this one adjacent to the Bar 20. It comprised wooded riverfront, a wildflower meadow, a stand of colonizing aspen, sheer cliffs, and the life-less remains of an old horse barn. All that remained of this structure were weathered logs, fallen to the ground, like pick-up sticks—a salad of old doors, hinges, strips of roofing tin, and mouse nests.

By now, Chuck, our contractor, had returned to his roots in the East. Contractor Terry Baird, renowned for his work with old logs, took his place. When he first saw the rubble, he shook his head dolefully and explained that the cheapest course with such a derelict structure would be "to torch the logs and start anew." But Ken Presley's surprise visit had strengthened my resolve to restore, not reinvent the Bar 20. In the thirties, this building had been surrounded by corrals and served as winter shelter for Stan Cox's horses. The ranch then was just under 2,000 acres. We owned a pitiful 34. We didn't need a barn as large as the Coxes'. Our job wasn't to dazzle history but to give it a stay of execution. Terry Baird smiled enigmatically and said he would do his best with what he had.

Work began in early spring, and by July the barn was complete. Terry had achieved the impossible. Every log not rotten had been stacked upon a new sandstone foundation; and old barnwood, once stored in Terry's sheds, now formed the high peaks. The roof was salvaged corrugated tin, the rustier the better. Two doors leading to the attached tack room had also been recovered and restored; hefty horseshoes, found in the dirt, I nailed, superstitiously heel-side up, to flat surfaces above barn doors. As soon as the barn was complete, visitors to the Bar 20 stood transfixed by the structure and exclaimed it felt as old as time. Terry smiled another wan smile.

The logs yielded a surprise: a shard of paper. When Terry pried one old log from another, he found a corner of a Livingston newspaper, used as chinking. The date was December 21, 1899. One can only imagine that on Christmas day, when a weathered teamster, his hands dug deep into pockets, his head and neck bundled in a mackinaw, might have cursed the wind and then took last week's newspaper, crumpled it, and wedged it into a pesky crevice. The event must have occurred long before Stan Cox ever reached Montana, and it conjured in me legends of this place's busy past. I could even smell the sweet sweat of draft horses eating grain in this building whose life mission, I knew, was always to shelter horses.

"We always called it the old stagecoach barn," reported Loren Brewer in the shade of the patio adjoining his motor home, parked north of Big Timber. It is now midsummer and Loren, after some convincing, has agreed to talk about his father, Harry, and the Brewer years in the West Boulder Valley.

Loren explains the barn had been built long before he was born. "Way back in the 1890s," he guessed. "Just after the Indians had been run out of the country," a road was developed from Livingston in the West, east to the gold-mining town of Independence in the main Boulder Valley. As a boy, he'd been told that twice a week, a team of four horses and a stagecoach careened down the escarpment track, past a school and post office, named "Hawkwood," to halt at this barn. Here lathered teams were replaced by fresh ones, and the journey resumed. In the 1890s there wouldn't have been a bridge so, in continuing the journey to Independence, the team's first challenge would have been to ford the West Boulder River. For the two months of spring floods when the West Boulder turned into a torrent, the road was closed.

I estimate Loren Brewer to be in his young 70s: a big authoritative man with slabs of fingers that often describe a church spire when they're not tapping the table restively. Much of the time he sits under the awning by the mobile home, his wife and daughter, Linda Larsen, in attendance, while a newly acquired horse mills uncertainly at the edges of our gathering. It's a hot day and we drink lemonade. When Loren talks, his mellifluous voice reminds me of Gene Autrey's, and his stories unravel like ballads.

Loren's father, Harry Brewer, had come to the West Boulder Valley in 1937. He arrived shortly after Ken Presley's dad, Earl quit working for the "misguided" (Ken's word) Stan Cox. Harry signed on with the Bar 20 as Stan's replacement dude wrangler, but he, too, didn't last more than two years. He quit after "he got into a damn shooting match with Stan Cox over a horse, and I can't remember what it was all about." But when Harry Brewer walked out of the Bar 20, he couldn't leave the country. "We just loved that West Boulder Valley so much."

In those days, at the end of the road, three miles from the Bar 20, there was another ranch owned by twins, Aubry and Mabry McDowell. During summers they took in dudes. One was New Yorker Helen Fargo Arnold, granddaughter of the founder of the Wells Fargo Bank. Mrs. Arnold had married three times, been widowed once, divorced twice. Now alone, the heiress fell in love, like so many others, with the West Boulder Valley. She let it be known she was interested in purchasing land, and after a month at the Link Bar, she got word the adjacent ranch, the one separating Bar 20 from where she was staying, had come on the market. Within the year, hardly six months after discovering this corner of Montana, she became a Montana landowner. Her first projects were to upgrade the log house (now the reserve guest cabin, where the annual meeting had convened) and to hire a manager. Harry Brewer conveniently fell into the job.

Working for Helen Fargo Arnold was, for the Brewers, a family decision. "She was a wonderful lady," recalls Loren. "In fact, I'll tell you just how nice she was: for three years as a kid I had a sore throat. At the end of one season when I drove her in the big Buick out to Santa Barbara for the winter, she said, 'You're going to my doctor.'

"I did. He found I had some damn type of lump jaw, which he treated with radiation. It took a long time, but after two months, I was cured and Mrs. Arnold paid for the whole damn thing."

"To us, even my Dad, she was always 'Mrs. Arnold.' Very discreet, she wouldn't tell anyone how old she was, nor would she discuss her husbands. Years later, I found she had been widowed once when a husband suffered a heart attack. It had happened in a New York whorehouse.... Mrs. Arnold was a beautiful person but she would have had a heart attack of her own if she knew I knew."

Helen Arnold stayed in the West Boulder Valley for eight years. She decorated the master bedroom with a Russian sleigh bed, its footboard carved to resemble a swan. The living room was filled with Molesworth tables, bureaus, chairs, and couches. In time she added to her land holdings, with another ranch, this one, far away, on Sweetgrass Creek north of Big Timber. The combination of the two spreads was judicious. In winter, the one in the West Boulder Valley was always deep in snow, while the other was usually swept clear by chinook winds. Twice a year cowboys trailed Mrs. Arnold's cattle the 40 miles between each place. In spring, when calves were young, the journey took five days; in fall, with the calves grown, only three. Each night the buckaroos camped beside the herd, on the trail. "It was some of my happiest times," remembers Loren.

In 1947 Helen Arnold proved yet again she was a "very classy, lovely lady. She decided she had gotten too old for Montana weather, so she gave my Dad the ranch."

Harry Brewer was, in fact, given a choice of ranches—the winter ranch north of town or the summer place in the West Boulder Valley. "He didn't think twice," recalls Loren. "We loved the mountains. And when we got the ranch, Dad and I thought we had gone to heaven. It was the prettiest country you'd ever seen in all your life."

Giving away a ranch to one's foreman would, under any circumstance, be an astonishing gesture of good will. Even years later, members of the Brewer family have difficulty in describing the transaction. When Linda, Loren's daughter, wrote a loving profile of her grandfather in the June 16, 1976, *Big Timber Pioneer*, the most she could concede was: "Grampa became the owner of the ranch on the West Boulder." One elderly neighbor one drainage west of the West Boulder had previously confided to me: "Helen Arnold leaving her ranch to Harry Brewer was a cruel thing because she didn't endow him with enough money to pay the taxes."

Harry Brewer, seasoned horse and cattleman, had never before owned a place of his own. He was born in 1900 in Indian country near Camp Crook, South Dakota. His father was a ranch foreman. Years later, he would tell his son and granddaughter about the first time his father took him and his sister to a reservation. When several Indian women saw the two red-headed children, they scrambled onto the buckboard to run their fingers through their hair. Young Harry and his sister, Rowena, froze, frightened for their lives, their eyes beseeching their father to leave. It was a memory Harry coveted for over 70 years.

In his teens, Harry Brewer, trailing vast herds of cattle to railhead at Belle Fouche, developed a name for himself for his way with livestock. In 1936 his reputation as a horseman delivered him to Yellowstone Park as a dude wrangler. Pretty soon, horse and people skills began landing him one job after another at guest ranches, finally pitching him into the West Boulder Valley, in the employ of Helen Arnold.

Shortly after Harry Brewer became owner of the Arnold place, he discovered the capriciousness of ranching. Now, as sole proprietor of mountain acreage, he would receive only one paycheck a year, itself insufficient to cover costs. Beautiful as it was, this West Boulder place wasn't large enough to support a family. So the Brewers cut corners, neglected some improvements, overlooked nonessential fencing. Mabel Brewer, with one glass eye, didn't care for the remoteness of the valley, and during winter, she began to spend more and more time in town.

But during this period, standards of courtesy were never compromised. "The ranch," recalls Linda Larsen, Harry's granddaughter, "became known for hospitality. Everyone who stopped by was invited in for a cup of coffee. If it happened to be close to mealtime, Grampa asked them to stay and eat. If it was late in the evening, he always asked them to spend the night. It didn't matter if he'd just met them that day or years earlier."

These sentiments were echoed by another neighbor: "A lot of those old-timers had an innate sense of courtesy and decency that we lost. Harry Brewer certainly wasn't polished, but he was compulsively polite."

Rick Spellman, one of the reserve founders, also remembers Harry's charm, but, recalls another side of the elderly cowboy: "He always maintained a cordial relationship with us, but I later discovered he had a way of saying things about people he wouldn't say to their faces. He was a hard-bitten Montana rancher, not all sugar. If he sold you some cattle and you did well with those cattle, that would upset him.

"Of course, we mislead him," admits Rick. "He thought he was dealing with 7 buyers. Instead there were 20. I'm entirely sympathetic to his displeasure."

"Yup," reflects Loren Brewer. "Dad couldn't trust Rick Spellman and his group, especially Rick, who he felt wouldn't ever look him straight. He just didn't care for that sort of thing."

Harry Brewer is best remembered in the West Boulder Valley for another feud, this one with a neighbor whose presence is felt to this day. In 1939 the McDowell twins sold the Link Bar to Brad Wilmot (not his real name), a wealthy Chicagoan. "Brad," recalls Loren Brewer, "was an outsider who'd changed his name and made a lot of money from a company delivering bulk oil. He also owned a Chicago flea market and a string of truck stops called Montana Bud's. We got along wonderful for years and years, all the time helping put up their hay. Dad even went back to Chicago one time and stayed with Brad." Loren pauses, transforms his fingers into a church spire, and continues almost hoarsely. "Then we got in a bad jangle and never did get along with them after that."

Loren's scarred hands tighten. I can see I'm entering dangerous territory. Linda, his daughter, studies the grazing palomino. Loren's wife fidgets and then rises to fill our glasses with another round of lemonade. Just mention the name Wilmot even now in our valley, and neighbors report rumors of violence and bad blood. The Wilmot ranch, the "Rawhide," is now in the hands of his son, Matt (not his real name), a handsome, hardbitten cowboy who socializes with few people in this valley. He is seen infrequently, mostly driving a diesel pickup, his eyes fixed, blond mustache discolored by cigarettes, jaw clenched, just an index finger rising from the steering wheel, to say a wordless hello. To see him pass is an event; were he to stop and talk, neighbors claim that would be an occasion worth boasting about.

Mrs. Brewer fills our glasses and Linda looks to Loren for a cue. "You want to hear," he says impatiently." I nod.

"My Dad and I had a little sawmill on the West Boulder. So I called Brad back East and said, 'We can get some logs up Davis Creek but I'd need to cross a quarter mile of your land to bring em here.'

"He said, 'Sure. Go ahead.'" So we cut 100,000 board feet of timber and built a road through the Forest Service. Then we waited for Brad so we could site the track through his property. When he got here in spring, he said he'd changed his mind."

I jump in: "Brad simply revoked permission, for no particular reason? And you had gone to all that trouble with the logs?"

"Yup."

"So you never talked to him again?"

"Well, I did but not very nicely sometimes. He was an overbearing bastard. He liked to chew out his help in front of people. That was his style. Dad didn't care for that. And Brad himself wasn't much of a hand. Dad spotted that as well. If everything went Brad's way, then he was fine. But he always wanted it *his* way."

"Essentially," I interrupt, "he didn't measure up because he wouldn't play according to the rules. He wouldn't *neighbor* with all of you."

"That's about the size of things. It wasn't just us, he was that way with everyone. For years and years it was a common thing to let your neighbors go through your land if they were trailing cattle into the national forest. Well, he stopped that. Wouldn't let anyone cross his land anymore."

"One time Dad said to him, 'Brad, let's make a trade. I'll let you use my road if you let me use yours.'

"'No,' he said.

"Then Dad said, 'Then you stay the hell off of my road.' But Brad kept a-using our road.

"One time Dad and I was on horseback, up on top on the ridge, and there was Matt and Brad in their pickup. Dad rode right at them and, with a rope doubled up, started beating old Brad over the head.

"Brad yelled, 'Harry, Harry, you're going to kill me. I've got a bad heart.'

"And Dad yelled back, 'You sonuvabitch, you don't even have a heart. Get your ass off of this mountain and don't let me catch you up here with your vehicle.'

"That was a true story," Loren adds, scratching his chin. Telling it today has agitated him. An old feud, a father's honor, neighbors that don't measure up to preexisting codes—after all these years the issues haven't been laid to rest. I can see where, even now, Loren is resolved to understand no more of human behavior than is absolutely necessary. The story, he believes, speaks for itself. But then so much remains a puzzle—extravagant generosity counterpointed by vindictive pettiness.

Tired by the account, Loren Brewer tips his chair, squints his eyes, and studies an old photograph. He makes no attempt to conceal a yawn. He adopted his father's strict rule of conduct, in time only to find it failed. Its failure remains, to this day, unfathomable. In the 1960s, what had once appeared secure had become discomfiting.

Loren retreats into silence. Had his father been deposed merely by forces of change—one hippie, the other, arrogance and wealth? I wonder if there might have been more. Provincialism, for one.

Raising the subject of intolerance would be downright discourteous. Old Montanans, like Harry Brewer, never knew minorities other than Native Americans, most of them conveniently exiled into reservations. The old-time rancher may have been bigoted, but his prejudice was theoretical, targeted mostly toward totems. If Brad Wilmot was indeed a Jew, he was probably the first Harry had ever encountered. Rick Spellman remembers Harry once asking him, "What kind of name is Brad? Some kind of Jew name?" Little did he know Rick Spellman was himself Jewish.

"Harry," adds Rick, "probably hated Jews even though, up till then, he'd never met one." Even as late as the early nineties, Montana was a world of little diversity, a land where unexpected courtesies abounded but where human differences were feared. When Whoopi Goldberg bought a house near Livingston in the 1990s, one old-timer stared at her incredulously. He had never seen such a person before and had only heard the name of one black. He couldn't even "sex" her properly. He thus reported to a friend a "Negro" person had moved into the neighborhood. Must be that fellow Magic Johnson.

By the early 1960s, Harry realized that to survive the West Boulder he would need to expand. On one side lay Brad Wilmot. Here the lines had already been drawn. On the other, the Bar 20. Were he to acquire what remained part of the ranch Stan Cox had once cobbled together, the Brewer place might become profitable. With an additional 520 acres he'd be able to run more cattle without assuming corresponding overheads. Such a land acquisition made sense, and in 1960, two owners after Stanley Cox, the property became available. To tell this part of the tale, I now must backtrack.

A few months before meeting with Loren, I came upon a yellowing document in Denver. It had been put together nearly 40 years before by the Livingston Land and Abstract Company, whose principle was a certain Homer Terwilliger. The late Mr. Terwilliger helped me enormously by supplying me with Bar 20's chronology, through a litany of owners, some mentioned on the Magat foolscap, others new to me. Flipping through its many neatly typed pages, I began to worry that, once having penetrated the fifties, all that would remain would be a catalog of the Bar 20's dead. Firsthand knowledge of long-ago tenures would simply vanish, enthusiasms and disappointments, attending ownership, fading with them. Mr. Terwilliger's "Abstract of the Record Title" contained dry, legal descriptions of transfers back to the day when Bar 20 land was claimed as a homestead through a patent from the Federal Government. In between, only names of people, now either gone or too old to remember. Would there be no one to tell me of the Bar 20's whispered confidences?

I knew there was, at least, one living witness to the Harry Brewer transaction. Monica Payne, former owner of the Grouse House, had a Colorado address and, seven years almost to the day after we purchased what had once been her home, I found her telephone number and called. After a few minutes of meteorological chitchat, critical opening gambits in most western conversations, I asked her about her ownership of the Bar 20 and her life at Grouse House. At first, Mrs. Payne responded warily: "Isn't much to say about it really." But it wasn't long before her suspicions thawed. By my second call, memories—some brutal, others sad—gushed forth.

Monica Payne came to the West Boulder Valley a young bride, in 1958. She had been raised in Madison, Wisconsin, and, in her teens, she fell in love with square dancing. Thanks to this hobby, she met a man locally considered the best square dancer of all. Paul Payne, nearly 25 years her senior, was divorced with two children. He seemed "comfortably fixed," thanks to a shopping center his father had built and had left to him and his brother. Soon Paul and Monica were partnered each Saturday night. Monica square danced, he called the dances, and together they were such a sharp team they appeared on local television. The handsome, chain-smoking 45-year old then married his young admirer, age 21. The union appeared perfect. In addition to dancing, they shared another passion—hunting. In time, the prospect of shooting a trophy elk brought them to Montana. They loved "at first sight" Yellowstone country. Two years after their wedding, Paul Payne sold the family shopping center, the two packed up and relocated to the heart of elk country—Livingston, Montana. Now they could hunt and square dance to their heart's content.

Shortly after the Paynes alighted in Livingston, Monica gave birth to daughter Lynn. Unexpectedly, at about this time, Paul began complaining of a painful ankle. Soon he announced to his young bride, he wouldn't be able to dance anymore. It was a blow for Monica, but the news was leavened by some luck: the Paynes had discovered the Bar 20, just 22 miles outside of Livingston. This 600-acre ranch was now a shadow of its former self, but it still included over ten log buildings and embraced "the most breathtaking views I'd ever seen" on both sides of a river. The Bar 20 was a steal at $40,000.

Paul took out a mortgage for most of the land. His plan was to open it in summer to wealthy dudes, in fall and spring to hunters. Monica's parents, equally excited, sold their home in Madison, Wisconsin, preparing to join the team to help with cooking and maintenance. On November 14, 1957, Paul Payne closed on the property. The next day, Monica's father had a stroke.

Because of her father's illness and subsequent death, the move to the West Boulder Valley was stalled until spring. Monica's widowed mother's promise to work as cook still held, and as soon as snows melted, refitting began. Photographs Monica sent me show the Paynes favored sheer white curtains, white bedroom sets, knotty pine cabinetry in the kitchen, heavy oak side tables in the dining room, and a Naugahyde couch, where their spoiled Boston bulldog slept. In the first summer of their ownership, the Paynes hosted several dudes, some from as far as Texas.

Mysteriously, the moment the dude ranch business got under way, Paul seemed to lose heart in the enterprise. He decided to stop advertising, and then, without warning, he took a job as a roving salesman for H. Hicks Cadle, a Midwestern spice company. He left Monica in charge of the ranch while he hawked nutmeg and celery salt from one Montana grocery store to another, never explaining why he preferred a life of squalid small-town motels over home at the Bar 20, where he could steward the business of his dreams. "I put his behavior down to cautiousness. He didn't feel we could cook for dudes, and he believed mother and I weren't strong enough to handle the details while he was away."

But soon Paul began borrowing money from Monica's mother. "I was young and very happy and I didn't think too much about it all. I was crazy about ranching. We had five horses, a milk cow called Daisy, a lamb for

Lynn, a cat, and I just loved the West Boulder Valley. In winter, once I'd milked the cow at dawn, I'd go down and help Harry Brewer feed cattle. He used to say, 'You come out and drive the truck. I can't stand Mabel's driving—she's not too swift with the gears.' Evenings, Harry and Mabel would come over and join my Mom, Paul's daughter, Beverly, Lynn, and I, and we'd pop popcorn and play cards. Harry Brewer was a super good fellow."

On the second season of operation, because there was no more advertising, not one dude showed up. Now Paul was staying away most nights. The job with the spice distributor had terminated, and Paul had begun selling Exercycles door to door. "A smooth talker, Paul could make anyone believe him. To be frank, my husband didn't know how to handle money. He virtually ran away from home, and I never knew when he'd be back. He just blew the money he got from the sale of the shopping center.

"Soon there were bills—lots of them—and I didn't know how to cope with them—especially the bar bills. Paul was a drinker...I had no idea where he went when he was away. One time he abandoned his car. Another time, he lost his wallet. When finally he wasn't coming home at nights for long stretches, I knew we were having a problem."

Monica decided to file for divorce. She drove into Livingston to talk with a lawyer, and, when she explained her plight, "the lawyer laughed at me." He knew. In fact "everyone in town knew Paul had a girlfriend. I'd simply been ignoring the truth all this time."

Now there was an additional problem. Because Paul had missed a number of payments, the bank was about to foreclose on the Bar 20. "All we owed of the original $40,000 was a piddling $10,000, which, of course, we didn't have. Our banker never played straight. He'd been saying to all his cronies who longed for the Bar 20, 'Let's wait for it to be foreclosed and I'll sell it to you for nothing.'"

Among the first to hear of Monica's dilemma was Brad Wilmot, the Chicago tycoon who owned the ranch that had been renamed the Rawhide.

"He'd been bragging to his people when Paul left me that he was going to buy the place. And one day he walks into the house, lays down all his papers on the table, and starts telling me how much he wants this place and how much he's willing to pay for it. Frankly, I don't remember what offer he made me. I was never going to sell it to him. He wanted to buy the Bar 20, then keep people out of the valley. He wanted to squeeze Harry out, as well, and then he wanted to close the county road. 'I'll let you stay here,' he said, 'but I'm going to shut the whole place off at the gate to anyone else.'

"I made up my mind then and there I'd rather lose the Bar 20 than sell to Brad Wilmot."

Instead Monica Payne sold the Bar 20—at least most of it—to Harry Brewer. "On the last day the money was due, Harry called his banker in Bozeman. We drove there at ten at night. His banker opened the vault, made out a $10,000 draft to Harry. Then we returned to Livingston to meet my banker who held the mortgage—he was the one who had been undermining us. Harry knocked on the door of his house. The banker was having a celebratory party. Harry held out the check, but the banker wouldn't accept it because, he said, 'Banking hours have passed.'

"'Not for me they have,' said Harry—man, was he some Montana cowboy! 'You take it or I'll shove it down your throat.'

"And the banker took it.

"In all we had the Bar 20 for two years. I was devastated to lose it."

Through an agreement with the Brewers, the Paynes were able to retain Grouse House. The other cabins would be surveyed, then sold, with all assets split between Brewers and Paynes.

Now, Monica Payne had to face an even greater reversal. All the proceeds from the ranch were not hers but her estranged husband's. Uncharacteristically, he came to her and asked to be given a second chance.

"Paul bought us a house in Livingston—a little old shack across the railroad tracks. The payments were $75 a month. I laid down the law. I told him he couldn't go on the road anymore. He'd have to get a job in town, and he'd have to bring his paycheck home to me. I wouldn't live any other way. So we began. I put Lynn in school and I started a garden so we could eat. Paul got a job in a hardware store in town. For a while it worked.

"Then Paul had to go to Gardiner once a week for supplies. Soon he was staying overnight. In time I learned he was staying with the 'nice post-mistress.' Then I told him: 'enough is enough.' We were divorced in 1962. Five days later he remarried, and four years later he was dead of liver disease."

The Grouse House, left to Monica and Paul's daughter, Lynn, eventually reverted to Monica. She found a job in Livingston ("those people there were so wonderful"). In time, she moved to where there were better paying jobs—Denver. There she worked 30 years for one company until, finally in 1998, she retired. Throughout, she left the Grouse House "to its own devices," only vis-iting it once a year during summer vacations. In the early nineties Grouse House, having been abandoned for nearly three decades, began showing seri-ous signs of neglect. It needed a new roof, new windows, new porch. Why bother if she would never live in it? Time to sell, she thought. Out of the blue, she received my phone call. "And when I sold it to you and your family," she reported, "It was the greatest wrench of my life. I cried many a night."

Today, Monica Payne finds the sometimes harsh memories diverting. The once agile square dancer, is now in her late 60s, gray haired, and, as she says, "filled out." She does not regret her harsh Montana past and when-ever she hears "Bar 20," she says she impulsively smiles. On the telephone, I tell her she's always welcome to return to the valley and to stay at Grouse House. "Maybe this summer," she volunteers. She pauses and, before sign-ing off, notes, "You know we lived such a crazy life in that valley. At times it was a struggle, but I have no complaints."

Monica's photographs are today in my vest pocket. I want to see what nearly 40 years has done to Grouse House. Chui, the golden retriever, and Duma, black Lab, lead the way as I ride Coop, my powerful chestnut gelding, toward Grouse House. I drop off the dirt embankment, cut through high grass, and once we reach the river, Coop slows to test his footing on loose stones before plunging into the West Boulder.

My former girlfriend, a show jumper, introduced me to the deep, fast river on horseback. She taught me to fight its current, feel the horse lose purchase with the river bottom, swim, regain his footing, strike river rock, and then heave himself up the far bank. At first I didn't feel altogether at ease being captive of another irrational force, so I hesitated. But in time, I got over it and began to view our river as incredible fun, a set of wings. Even in spate, I still ride my dryland horses into the West Boulder River, overcoming their uncertainties. While the girlfriend caused much mischief in my life, she did teach me the lessons of a river. Now almost every outing on horseback begins and ends with a deep-water crossing.

When I met her, I had just floated free of another relationship. It was an old story: I was raw and exposed, not certain whether I was meant for togetherness at all. Sensing my uncertainty, she quickly adopted my way of life, and, at first, I could see no harm in helping her out. She arrived inconspicuously, her company hardly acknowledged, her intentions so innocent. I had a desire to protect her from her demons and soon we discovered shared interests—dogs, horses, and Montana. So it began—just a change in the weather.

Soon there were storms. In September of our second year together, she no longer could abide my aloofness. Soon her mood reached boiling point. One day, in a bitter rage, she and her hound dog drove away from the Bar 20, she shouting abuse while her dog quivered in the seat next to her. I watched, like a wooden Indian.

No doubt, in leaving the Bar 20, she acquitted herself. She gained the upper hand, and, for her, she was in command. Popping the clutch, spinning wheels, crashing against barriers, driving out of the Bar 20 forever—she had made her point.

The Bar 20 is now still. The dogs are no longer frightened. They stay close to my side, happy, it would seem, to see me resuming old ways. I ride Coop through the valley to look for golden eagles. Later, I sit on the screened porch to glimpse hummingbirds wage war over columbines, monkshoods, and delphiniums. My joy in quiet changes my face. In the mirror I can see the difference. When the sun sets, only the creeping cool tells me I've been reckless with time. The exhaustion of the last year is being nursed by the smell of fall in the air, the sight of grazing horses, overhead *agh-whits* of sandhill crane. As of today, I am no longer subject to the inquisition of thought. I can think what I will.

And by repossessing the Bar 20, I've regained its identity. No longer will it be coveted. Now it can be restored to those who truly need it. For the first time in two years, I'm looking forward, shamelessly, to sharing this valley with friends and relatives.

I realize during this quiet, the Bar 20 is mine only briefly. It's a fugitive place that no one can ever own. Brad Wilmot, the now estranged equestrian, and so many other inmates of this valley presumed to lock the gate and possess it. But it never could be so. Ownership to this place, to this valley, is fugitive. Title deeds in this region of Montana are not even 100 years old. Before then, the valley belonged to Indians and, before then, to river melt and the wind.

The dogs wait for Coop and me to set a course. When we do, they pitch into the river, lose their footing, and paddle to the far shore in a wide arc, bucked by the current. Once there, they scramble onto the bank and shake themselves, the rattle of their collars the happiest of sounds. Sleek like an otter, Duma reappears out of brush, followed closely by Chui, her gold coat lacquered to her ribs. Wet and well, they study me for a signal. "Grouse House," I yell to them. They wheel, but without the usual snap of exhilaration. They would have preferred "the meadows" or "the campground," but they'll settle for Grouse House, a mere 200 yards up the hill. Still every hike is, for them, the glory of the day.

By the log house I dismount and reach into my pocket to study the dog-eared photographs. Chui and Duma, soon losing interest in my wiles, ferret for ground squirrels. With the pictures, I compare today's look against the buildings, era 1960. Nearly four decades ago, the porch had been hurriedly encased in plywood, protection, no doubt, from winter. Now we've opened it, added windows and a wooden deck. During the intervening years, even when it languished, Grouse House was the picture of completeness, so different from the rambling Bar 20 house. On one side, built around a courtyard, on the other, trimmed by a screened porch, Grouse House has always possessed a resolved architectural principle, a sense of structural peace and self-fulfillment. Today, I identify with it. Isn't it remarkable. I think, how a home can inform its occupants of its dream, how this place, however serious the disrepair, whatever the turmoil, has always offered a generous welcome, endowed its inmates with calm.

I imagine Monica Payne wintering here, waiting for a husband who would never return. No doubt, the dependability of this place must have bucked her up. The log house, isolated at the edge of this high mountain meadow would have transmitted to that young, disillusioned mother the same serenity I feel right now.

Still, I've found something dark: while everyone worships this place, few can keep it. Each declares there is hardly a spot more beautiful in all the world, yet history proves over and over that here in this enchanted place, high hopes have been dashed, relationships dissolved, dreams violated.

Tonight might be a beginning. I look all around at the embracing valley. I scrutinize the aspen leaves gilt by fall, the embracing house, the neighboring Douglas firs and their limbed skirts rustling against the weathered logs. The West Boulder, beautiful and indifferent, has taught me we must all endure a cycle of love and loss, promise and failure, embrace and rebuff, before we will understand ourselves and our place.

~

CHAPTER 8

Talking with Horses

On one of my first visits to Montana in 1976, driving with a real estate agent from one spread to another, I stopped at a treeless ranch on the eastern front near Choteau. We opened the gate, drove around, and soon became hopelessly disoriented until we came upon a girl and her horse.

At first, she paid us no mind as she drove a recalcitrant bull away from bevies of cows, back to the meadow where he belonged. I squirmed out of the Suburban to lean against the hood. The bull's penis was unsheathed. Caught in *delecto flagrante*, he was in no mood to return to celibacy behind bars. He weaved and stomped attempting to shake his pursuer. But it was to no avail, for the girl and her horse were good hands. Looking no more than 18, she barely moved her fingers or reins. They hung over the horn of the saddle, limp as if they had nothing on their mind. Her tight, faded jeans had been swallowed by the saddle, and they moved to the same rhythm. Underneath her wide-brimmed hat, dark, sparkling hair, secured by only a blue ribbon, blew in the wind and, when she rode hard, her blouse annealed to her small, tight breasts.

The girl's mastery of the horse was subliminal—all knees, heel, and an ever changing gait. She may have whispered to the horse. I couldn't tell. All I saw were two beings, so closely linked they evoked a minotaur, arching and wheeling, careening right, sidestepping left until it danced into the abyss of mid-morning heat. This was, to me, a triumph of horsemanship. The bull must have felt so too. Soon, accepting he had been bested, he retracted his penis to mince his way through the gate and into the other field. I then spotted the girl was followed by her border collie, member of this same ballet troop. The dog took her commands from the girl's body, all three working together without a single audible command. I wondered if the border collie slept with her at night. And then I saw the coyote. He had been following the dog for much the same reason I had been watching the performance. Coyote, dog, horse, girl, bull: I had never seen anything so provocative.

Horses and horsemanship are at the heart of the Montana dream, probably for both sexes. Before we bought the ranch, whenever I imagined what I might become in the Northern Rockies, I saw myself on horseback, riding, mostly solo, lost in the incorruptible silence of great spaces. After we bought the ranch, I lamented I was still prone to attend public horse auctions and buy the one animal that, three days later, I would discover had been drugged and was incurably lame.

Late in the seventies, I heard of Ray Hunt, a horse magician. Unlike many other cowboys, he treated the horse with rare humanity. He broke them without drawing blood, he corrected them without brutality. Many years later his style and that of his student, Buck Brannaman, would be deified in a book and film, *The Horse Whisperer*, set near our West Boulder Valley, but in the early eighties when I came to know the remarkable Ray Hunt, there were not many Westerners who took him seriously.

Ray Hunt, I hoped, would initiate me. Being able to break horses, learning to think like them, working together with them were essentials in the cattle business, necessities on the Bull Mountain Ranch. What's more, if I were truly able to understand the horse, I might play a better role in that primal scene I once witnessed on the eastern front.

Those who saw the cowboy and the horse at that cold indoor arena in Tucson, Arizona, in 1980 weren't certain whether the performance had been voodoo or sleight of hand. Ray Hunt had taken us all by surprise. He began modestly: walking with one stiff leg to the center of the round corral, adjusting his wireless microphone and starting to talk conversationally. He explained he would be working with a horse, never before haltered, bridled, or saddled—a horse which, in fact, until this morning had never been touched by a human hand. When his short, sometimes impassioned monologue was concluded, he paused to grin, his hatchet face split in two by a row of tobacco-stained teeth. From the ingenuousness of that grin, I sensed this was no con artist. I knew in my bones Ray Hunt had to be the genuine article—a cowboy throwback, perhaps, to those companions of Charlie Russell, sitting by a campfire, listening to coyotes in the Judith Gap.

As Ray hunkered by the mike, an unbroken two-year-old pinto filly was released into the corral. She moved helter-skelter, her eyes bugged in alarm, her neck lathered in sweat. From my vantage point in the bleachers, she seemed trouble.

Exactly one hour and fifteen minutes later, she was saddled and as gentle as a kid's pony. Ray Hunt was sitting on her back, directing her from a walk to a jog to a lope by nearly imperceptible shifts of his body, moving her left, right, backyard through exacting figure eights, with only a jingle of his clenched lariat.

"If I hadn't been doing so much talking," said Hunt, almost apologetically, "I could have gotten the job done in 45 minutes."

Almost all the veteran stockmen present confessed to being bewildered. One admitted he had always believed the only way to break a horse was with a bag over its head, hobbles on its feet, a good stout whip, lots of cursing, some blood and about a month. Another said that if Ray Hunt had lived in Salem, Massachusetts, three centuries ago he would have been hanged as a witch. A solidly built woman wearing a silver belt and a large hat claimed that the last hour and a quarter had been "the high" of her life. An old-timer wryly observed that the value of the filly had jumped in an hour from $600 to $800. Only one horseman remained suspicious. "Kindness to the horse! It just don't work in the long run, no matter what this buckaroo says, or thinks."

I took down Hunt's address, a box number in Dillon, Montana ("I don't have any real estate," he explained, on the road 45 weeks a year. "So the post office there just helps me out"). Vowing to learn his witchcraft, I enrolled in a five-day clinic, scheduled for Bozeman, three and a half hours from the ranch.

After witnessing winter in the Bull Mountains, I had already accumulated a few opinions about the cowboy legend. Myth and reality didn't always conform. I had a small collection of coffee-table editions, showcasing the cowboy in bat-winged chaps, covered in the dust of a hundred cows, trailing across sere landscapes in northern Arizona, slouching on bunkhouse porches, tightening cinches of foaming cayuses, leaning against hitching posts at the Jersey Lil' Saloon in Ingomar, Montana. The cowboy's scarred face seemed forged by big skies and small-town rodeos. These romantic images suggested he was of independent spirit, incorruptible in attire, uncompromised by earthly comforts. The pictures would also hint he considers free enterprise—the sort found on a cattle ranch—his birthright. No, sir, this tough hombre wasn't to be tampered with by Easterners, governments, do-good environmentalists. And, what's more, he carried side arms. Watch out, stranger.

What the books didn't explain was that today's cowboys have to make a living. While their clones, suburban cowboys, hang out in Bozeman bars, lurching through replays of *Gunsmoke*, true cowboys are generally too busy, working for wages or standing in line at government agencies, waiting to sign up for cost-sharing programs, by planting—whisper the word—wheat. I'd also found the cowboy to be a stickler for current fashion, rarely departing from his confreres' taste in snap-button shirts, scuffed boots, down jacket, just-so broad-brimmed hat—white in summer, black after Thanksgiving. The verifiable cowboys I encountered were ill at ease with people who talk too much about things Eastern, can't live without a border collie or blue heeler, treat their wives ("her") as silent, unpaid partner, and would continue using branding irons long after the last rustler had been run out of the country. If anything, the cowboy was a stickler for habit and his own tumbleweed fashion.

Ray Hunt, I was sure, shared these limitations. In Tucson he had paid homage to the prototype, using metaphors with wild and colorful abandon. I spotted his horse trailer, backed up to the arena. It was modish and his tack, stamped with his brand, resembled every cowboy's.

But Ray Hunt, it seemed, was challenging cowboy religion—how he treated his horse. With what success, I wondered, could you penetrate this belief system? Would you be successful berating him for having misunderstood his alter ego? Would you go far telling him he had abused the creature on whom he most depended?

Maybe a future clinic would provide, answers. I called around Montana and located Whiskey, an unbroken two-year-old gelding, bred from a good line of stock horses, near Cameron, Montana. I was told I'd have to give $500 for Whiskey. Early one Monday morning, with autumn chill frosting the sides of his horse trailer, he and I drove into Bozeman.

Ray Hunt was just as I remembered—a few days past 50, an economical face axed with scars and split evenly by a contagious grin. His shotgun chaps and English spurs were stained with mud and he still walked with a limp— maybe his symbol of contempt for two-legged travel.

There were ten of us in the clinic, but watching from the bleachers in the indoor arena were 30 others—some just curious, a few Ray Hunt "groupies," the others, no doubt, skeptics. A decidedly Western audience: the women wore Wrangler jeans, thick leather belts stamped with names like Sharon or Barbi, and opened conversations with "Say, can I talk you out of a cup of coffee?" Before the session began, I heard one old boy say, "I wish I could do what he does. When I break a horse, I kind of spit in one hand and pour hope in the other, and wait to see which one fills up first." A border collie crouched next to the guardrail and quivered demonically whenever horses moved into his range.

Ray took up a position in the arena and faced us. As a hush crept over the bleachers, he cleared his throat. "The horse," he began, "he's no different from me and you. If you stick a knife in him and give it a twist, blood'll run out of him just as if someone did the same to you. But there's one difference: the horse is so good-natured that if you give him half a chance he'll make you look like a champion.

"I'm not going to teach you anything new. Everything I do has been known for thousands of years. It's just that few's bothering to give it a try, few's got the time to put all the pieces together."

Ray pointed to a poker-faced cowgirl. "It's like dancing," he said. "It's like me asking you to dance and you don't want to dance. Can you imagine what it would be if I took you and danced with you anyway? You'd be moving but you'd be hoping it would all come to an end pretty quick, because I'd just be dragging you. Pretty soon you'd slap me loose and call the law."

The girl guffawed, a few hearty cheers resounding in the bleachers.

"But let's say you wanted to dance with me," continued Ray. "When I reached for you you'd have a smile and a sparkle in your eye. You'd come with me and away we'd go. That's what I'm asking here. When I invite the horse to dance with me, she should turn loose. She'll want to go. So there it is, see. I can't teach you, but maybe you can learn to dance with your horse."

Our ten broncs skittered in the large corral. They looked feral—especially mine. Earlier that morning when I climbed a five-rail fence, Whiskey had reared and retreated. I called his name, but the little gelding only wheeled to mill with others. Now I dodged and darted and, at last, with Ray's urging, I extended my hand. This was key: soon I was able to urge him, prancing and retreating, into the smaller ring. Still spooked, at least Whiskey showed enough horse sense for me to hope we might, one day, bond.

Now it was Ray's turn. While I watched skeptically, he climbed into the small ring. Now, he explained, was a critical moment when these horses made their first material contact with a human. Consistency was key. The horse could count on him to respond with numbing regularity to repeated behavior. For four hours while he worked ten horses, Ray never once succumbed to a contrary impulse, even though things didn't always go his way. His overarching self-confidence had an instant effect: the horses' twitching, trembling, pawing, flittering uncertainty commuted to passive indolence. Throughout, Ray's heartbeat amplified by his chest mike, was steady as a metronome.

The first horse Ray cut into the other ring was a bay filly. Now alone, she circled warily. Ray's first job, he intoned, was to establish respect. To achieve it, he started edging toward the horse, making escape difficult but not impossible. It was vital, he explained, that the horse attempt wrong options only to discover them more tedious, less comfortable than correct ones. Here was the nub of Ray's horse philosophy. Were he to whip the horse for mistakes, he would only be "appealing to dumb instinct," not to the horse's native ability to make decisions, reason deductively.

"I'll just keep making it unhandy for her to turn away from me," illustrated Ray, meting out a gentle shove every time the filly attempted to flee. And when, finally, she stopped, turning her head to study Ray, he calmly announced the first of several victories. If only one of her eyes studied him, he said, it would be a half measure of success. The moment she yielded to watching him with her full head and both eyes, he nodded and explained: "You see, her mind is now working, both mind and body...one." He rode over to stroke her, said, "You never can stroke a horse too much." But no sooner was Ray within range than she bolted. Unfazed, he limped after her.

West Boulder: the river that continues to lure outsiders with temptations of freedom (LEFT). Chui and her kingdom—restored and loved again, the main Bar 20 house in 1992 (BELOW).

Photos (both) by John Heminway.

Photo by John Heminway.

Don Hindman in 1989 seeing the Bar 20 for the first time since he helped build it for Stan Cox during the winter of 1933 and 1934 (ABOVE). Chui and her acolyte, Duma, in pursuit of Richardson ground squirrels on the road trip east to west across Montana (OPPOSITE, ABOVE). Mentor, Larry Lahren, wilderness packer, archaeologist, champion of the Anzick Site and, according to some who frequent bars, the toughest man in Park County (OPPOSITE, BELOW).

Photo by John Heminway.

Photo by Kathryn Heminway.

Photo from the collection of Loren Brewer.

Photo courtesy of Eames Yates. From the collection of John Heminway.

Photo courtesy of Eames Yates. From the collection of John Heminway.

Harry Brewer and his son Loren gathering loose hay on the ranch Helen Fargo Arnold
would, in time, deed the Brewers in an act of uncommon generosity (OPPOSITE, ABOVE).
A smirking Stan Cox (far left), roughly 17, with friends at Pomfret School in about 1908,
shortly before he dropped out (OPPOSITE, BELOW). Stan Cox looked masterly in every
uniform he wore. Here, just returned from polo or riding to hounds, at the entrance to
Combesberry, in late 1920 (ABOVE).

The sporting, witty, Haydie Yates (third from left), abandoned by her husband, Stan Cox's brother, putting on a brave face to friends and dudes in Wyoming in early 1930 (OPPOSITE, ABOVE). Stan Cox's hired men in 1933 using his woodie as the power source for the temporary sawmill needed to build the Bar 20 (OPPOSITE, BELOW). Bound for summer pasture, in the years when the Coxes could afford to lose money on cattle (ABOVE).

Bab Cox socializing with a friend from the nearby Triangle 7 dude ranch in late 1930 (ABOVE). Bab Cox spoiling the children of her choice (BELOW).

In the face of such systematic pursuit, her fears at last thawed, until Ray scored victory number two by reaching across and stroking her with a firm, conclusive hand. Although tense, she didn't move, realizing that immobility had its reward.

Ray now had a further request. Standing still was no longer enough. The filly would have to approach him. Instead, she turned away. With a loose rope around her neck, he edged her back in his direction, easing her, albeit in a clumsy, involuntary gait, until she faced him. Again she tried bolting and again she was induced around, until eventually she chose the easiest of two courses—a coordinated walk in the direction of the cowboy. Once, twice, and by the tenth try the filly turned, of her own volition, toward Ray.

Apprehension, it seemed, had evaporated, her eyes rubbering after his, expectantly. "What I've done here," explained Ray, never allowing his gaze to break from the horse's, "was keep her interested in thinking what we both wanted to do."

Forever increasing the stakes, Ray began to play with his lariat. The horse, once again snorted, sensing, perhaps, she was now in for another unpleasantness. Ray tossed the rope over her back, coiled it around her fetlocks, draped it over her neck. "A horse has to learn about a rope," he justified. "Has to understand it ain't a mountain lion or a snake on her back." He was taking a liberty with this horse I would never have dared even with my best-broken saddle horse. The filly spooked.

But soon, right on target, she began to tolerate this snake. Soon Ray had all four of her legs tied in a granny knot. An invitation to a wreck, I thought. But no, the bronc waited calmly until Ray, moving dependably, untied the knot and eased her out of the predicament. Then he looped the rope around her neck and held her firm. She recoiled. But Ray's touch was consistent, not violent, and as long as she resisted, it continued more as nuisance than pain. Experimentally, she edged her weight in Ray's direction. At the very nanosecond she moved, he relaxed his grip to reward her. By the third gentle tug, she was coming to him with only the slightest encouragement. In one minute, Ray had successfully broken the bronc to the halter. Victory number three.

Saddling her was the easiest lesson of all. Reassured by Ray's gentle persuasiveness, she was now ready—so it appeared—to accept whatever he doled out. While he worked this one filly as model for us all, he had also applied his teachings to the other ten. None had balked. Now he whacked each horse with carefully measured back pats and then laid saddles on the spot. They had entrusted his hand. Ray had, it appeared, conjured a universe in which the horseman could be relied upon for soundness.

I was mistaken. When Ray tightened the back cinch, he pulled it sickeningly around the flank of her delicate girth. Sheer disaster. Indeed, the moment the filly felt hard leather over her groin, she recoiled with a hideous buck, pitching sideways, roller-coastering around the small corral, hell-bent to splinter metal.

"Her druthers are working against her," said nonchalant Ray. "She'd ruther be somewhere else. She'd ruther be doing something different. But pretty quick her druthers will be working for her, and then she'd ruther be here, with me."

As with his other prophecies, this one proved correct. As soon as the filly slowed, she moved toward Ray for him to readjust the cinch. "Might as well introduce the horse to everything that could go wrong," he explained. "That way she'll have nothing to worry about."

When the morning session ended, Ray had saddled all ten horses, releasing them into the large corral to habituate them to their new burdens. "The settling period," he called it. Two hours later, after I ate my sandwich and rambled around the corrals apprehensively, the horses were presumed ready to be ridden. Ray cautioned us always to check the all-telling eyes of our mounts before we made a move. He urged us to pat the area near the stirrups and along the rump to condition the horse to the inadvertent. It was dubious advice since I fully expected to be launched into space the moment I put one foot into Whiskey's stirrup.

To my amazement, nothing happened. There I was, seated on his back—his first passenger. So secure was he, his eyes half-closed as if from boredom.

Without the security of reins and halter we rode our horses into the larger of the two corrals. "Don't make no difference which way he wants to go," advised Ray. "Just let him move." I studied the others. Sure enough, they too were wearing big smiles.

Every morning that week, before we mounted our saddled horse, Ray rode among them to reinstill the first day's lessons. "I'm going to give them lots of respect and I'm going to expect the same from them," he explained. Not until each horse overcame its panic and voluntarily approached the cowboy was it ready to be mounted.

On the second day we rode the horses with halter and lead rope; on the third, with reins and a snaffle bit. On the fourth, Ray shifted us outside into a large pasture, and, on the fifth, we were loping the length of a fence. All ten riders and horses had, by now, been schooled to try several gaits, to reverse, to break from a run, to halt with precision.

Ray dedicated much of his time explaining the placement of the horse's feet. "How're you going to dance if you don't know where your partner's feet are at?" he asked each morning. "There ain't never a recess period or a lunch break on a horse's back. You got to know at every instant what's happening down there on the ground." I believed my horse was already seasoned in the placement of his feet. Why did I have to bother? "Look," he demonstrated, "You're turning his front end, but his hindquarters ain't yet broke loose." He was right. I was onboard a derailed train.

Ray pulled out a small red flag to catch my horse's attention. He rode alongside me, mounted on his compliant bay, and whenever one section of my mount parted company with another, Ray fluttered the device beside the horse's recalcitrant quarter. Soon front and rear were coordinating. By the third day merely the sight of Ray coming alongside was enough for Whiskey to turn like a swallow. On the fifth day Whiskey was performing slaloms on his own, merely from my gentle pressure on the reins. We had become partners.

Admittedly, our partnership had been forged from a few scrapes: I was never Ray's star pupil. In fact, about halfway through the course, he singled me out in a short speech, describing my mistakes of the previous day. "John was making the wrong thing easy... the right thing difficult," he announced. "His horse didn't want to move, so John started a-tapping his heels into his ribs until he did move. John should have stopped there, but because he wanted the colt to move faster than a crawl he kept a-hammering away until pretty soon that colt didn't know why he wanted to move at all. It was just as uncomfortable moving as it was standing still." Ray turned in my direction and flashed a generous grin that helped slightly to allay my embarrassment. "But don't you worry. We'll put it right today."

As Ray was "putting it right," I continued to demonstrate a bottomless well of inexperience. One day, after riding Whiskey for only two minutes, I noticed my cinch had loosened. I would have to dismount to tighten it, but before I could, he started skittering. The more he plunged, the more the saddle slid to one side. Now I was half on, half off and he wouldn't stop. He bucked, lunged, dodged, and with one resounding lurch, launched me head first into sawdust.

I was enraged at my own stupidity and embarrassed by the publicity. This wasn't the first time I'd been thrown. It was the first time in front of an audience.

One watcher, a broad-shouldered cowboy in his late 20s, picked up my hat and explained what had happened: "You were unprepared. Your horse got unprepared. And you couldn't help him out." Considerably humbled, I tightened Whiskey's cinch and tried again.

My benefactor's name, I discovered, was Kevin Stallings, a horse trainer and one of Ray Hunt's most dedicated admirers.

"Ray changed my life," he told me solemnly, later that day. Until four years before, Kevin admitted he had been tough on his horses, as tough as any cowboy could be tough. "If a horse bucked me off, I'd wallop him. Hard. I had the worst temper in the world." Then he met Ray Hunt and "kind of fell into" attending one of Ray's clinics. Since then Kevin has attended many more and now, as a professional trainer, he practices principles he learned from Ray. "I still get bucked off," he admits, "but now it only happens once or, at the most, twice, with each horse. When it happens I speak to the horse. I say, 'It's alright, I right, I understand.' Then I get back on the horse. Pretty soon, he stops bucking."

I asked Kevin whether a horse trained according to the Hunt technique would remain trained? Would lessons learned in a few mornings be remembered months later?—"No doubt about it," he cut me off. "An animal you start in his clinic will end up, after five days, better schooled than a horse worked over a month—so long as the person handling the horse keeps treating him right. The Ray Hunt horse will stay there."

Dave Young, a farrier, had also attended multiple clinics. Sitting in the bleachers, his hands knotted from concentration, he slowly revealed how the Ray Hunt approach helped him in his trade. "You can't get anything done with a horse by beating up on it, putting it under a lot of stress and pressure," he admitted. "In my business I refuse to use nose twitches. I don't believe in tying horses up—most shoers do when a horse gives 'em trouble. Now when I shoe a horse, I work with his head. I show him what I want him to do, and then I just let him do it. Like Ray, I never put any more pressure on the horse than's necessary."

Most of Ray's admirers, I discovered, knew virtually nothing of the man himself. And Ray Hunt wasn't at all forthcoming until the second-to-last afternoon. Ray then dropped a hint. "The horse," he said, "he's way more sensitive than any human I was ever around, well, with maybe one exception." I began speculating. Was he referring to Carolyn, the tall redhead who organized the clinics, managed his business, and who he recently married? My horse shoer friend, on the other hand, thought he might be paying respects to the old man who had taught him the technique. "Ray keeps his past to himself," another noted.

When I cross-examined Ray, he dodged my questions by saying that the message, not the person, was what counted. Finally, on the last day, he relented and agreed to get better acquainted over supper.

At the appointed hour, I left my motel and drove to the edge of the fairgrounds. Here I found Ray and all his earthly possessions: a large Arco mobile home, a canary-yellow Cadillac, two horse trailers, five horses. With Carolyn, Ray travels in convoy between clinics, some separated by over 1,500 miles. The Arco is the Ray Hunt family home.

Inside, at 6 in the evening, Ray was surrounded by four admirers, among them a local rancher's six-year-old daughter, who wouldn't let Ray and Carolyn out of her sight. After introductions, all seven of us drove to a Bozeman steakhouse, dark, manly, buzzing, its waiters and waitresses moving in rhythm to the beat of Waylon Jennings. We filled two tables—one by us, the other for hats. Once seated, these horse people went mute, so absorbed were they by the menu. After an ecclesiastical silence, Ray got the attention of the waiter and addressing him, a third his age, as "sir," he went for Scotch on the rocks followed by the "Cowboy special"—New York cut with all the trimmings.

Once the clerical work was complete, Ray listened gravely to my questions. At first, I thought he might have decided to remain silent, but soon, as others talked among themselves, the details of his life poured forth. Without formal chronology, they were propelled by astonishing passion—words alternately gushing and trickling, timed to musical laments as they breathlessly headed for resolution in the now of life. Highlights were weighted equally—triumphs, injuries, acquisitions, marriages, deaths, all brushed aside in no particular order, footnotes perhaps, because Ray saw narrative as mere hiccup, compared to the leitmotiv of his all-consuming mission. And throughout the soliloquy, Ray Hunt insisted, he was "just an everyday fellow."

Ray was not, as I assumed, from a ranching family. His father raised grain, alfalfa, and sugar beets on a small farm in Idaho when he was born in the Great Depression, one of eight children. Ray didn't want to burden me with tales of poverty's woes. He'd rather tell me of its pleasures. Each Hunt child had a specific chore. Ray's was the team of horses used to pull plows and clean irrigation ditches.

The Hunts owned a stud, which they bred to others' mares to guarantee replenishment of horse blood on the farm. As a result, there was a never-ending need to break colts for use as plow horses. When Ray turned 15, this task fell to him. His technique was to get an old horse to help a young one.

"You'd get your wagon out to a gatepost," he explained, "then swing the tongue off to one side. Your old horse was harnessed, let's say, on the right side, and the bronc on the left. You'd tie your bronc to the gatepost until you was ready, and then away you'd go, the old horse kind of acting like a guide to the young one. After three or four days of this work, I'd put the colt in front of a drill or a harrow—not heavy work—and I'd only use him for half a day so his shoulders didn't get sore. Then in the afternoon we'd replace that horse with another young colt, and pretty soon we'd have several young plow horses pretty well broke."

Ray very nearly succeeded in avoiding mention of his disability. He was born with a club foot, the only member of the Hunt family who "couldn't get around too well." But his deformity didn't compromise horse work. In fact, the more he stayed on horseback, the better. "Whenever I got to running around too much I sure would know about it. It felt like someone put a knife into my ankle joint and gave it a twist. I'm not complaining. Some people, after all, don't even have a foot."

With only two years of high school behind him, the senior Hunt was forced to sell the farm—not an uncommon story of the era. Now Ray had no base, no support, and would never return home. But, as it turned out, the sale of the farm was a heaven-sent opportunity. "All my life I'd wanted to be a buckaroo, so when I got the chance at...age of 20...I went to work in Nevada for a big cow outfit called the T Lazy S. It was 360,000 acres of ranch—big enough for 6,000 head of mother cows, 9 permanent buckaroos, and a cavvy of at least 80 Morgan saddle horses.

"Well, it was a dream come true. Up till then I had always thought work was pitching hay and digging ditches. Now all I had to do was ride a horse. I couldn't believe a person could do this kind of work and get paid for it."

At the T Lazy S, Ray staked a reputation for "starting" horses, particularly problem horses. Five years later the ranch owner sold out and this time Ray moved on to California. But the ranch life there was, he found, too confining. "A big California outfit," he explained, "would only be 30,000 acres, kind of like your own backyard."

So Ray went "freelance," hiring himself out to ranchers to break horses, irrigate meadows, harvest hay. He recalled those days somberly. "As a horse trainer I was below average. My attitude toward horses was forceful. They were my slaves—'the horse better do it or else' kind of thing." The result, he admitted, was, at best, "a fairly good horse."

"You see, I'm ashamed for what I done. I was tough. That's what a cowboy was supposed to be. He wore a high hat and high-heeled boots and made a lot of racket, and he was some hombre, see."

In 1963, a horse called Hondo changed Ray's outlook. He was, simply, more horse than he'd ever seen before. "I simply couldn't get tough enough with him. I could knock on him and hammer on him but I just couldn't get him to quit bucking. Things were so hopeless, he might have ended up being sent to the canners."

In exasperation Ray asked a friend if he knew anyone who could help. The friend had a brother and he was a "good hand."

"Good hand" indeed. The man was 20 years Ray's senior, an ex-ranch worker by the name of Tom Dorrance. Almost from the start, the older man had a startling impact on Ray. "He's the greatest horseman I've ever met. He's also the greatest person I've run across. He's an inventor. He thinks things out. He takes nothing for granted. He can just look over a fence and notice only the head of a man on horseback. Without even seeing the horse, he'll tell you not only what gait that horse is on, but what lead and whether or not the horse is upset."

With Tom Dorrance's spare advice, delivered as the old man perched on the rails of a corral, Ray Hunt began to communicate with Hondo. Soon, the once uncontrollable horse, was broken. Tom was "the horse's lawyer," and Ray, by his own description, "the buckaroo who knew no fear." It was a lucky alliance, for by the end of a week, Hondo had advanced beyond Ray's mastery of horse training. Hondo would prove to be the greatest horse of Ray's life. Ray went on to show him in hackamore and bridle-class events, at fairs and rodeos from the Cow Palace in San Francisco to Reno, Nevada. They won first place in every single event. "I don't take an ounce of credit," Ray insists. "I just got out of the horse's way. He was a smart horse and an outstanding athlete. As a horseman I would only classify myself as average."

Average or not, Ray had become, thanks to Dorrance and Hondo, an altogether different horseman. He no longer viewed the horse with cowboy biases. What once he deemed a "servant," now could feel, think, reason. Any sensitive horseman, he came to believe, could influence those decisions by appealing to the animal's native logic. Ray began to experiment with this, then-revolutionary, concept.

In 1970, a horse Ray had started slipped on wet hay and fell on top of him, smashing his crippled leg in seven places and forcing him to wear a cast for months. Painful opportunity, it allowed him to accept an invitation to teach a one-semester course in horsemanship at a college in Alberta, Canada. The response to it was such that Ray decided his theories might have a wider impact. A year later, eight after Hondo and Tom Dorrance had entered his life, Ray Hunt launched the clinics that continue to this day. "What was the good of starting a few hundred horses each year," he said, "When, if I could get others to catch on—just think of the effect it might have on the horse in general."

At first, cowboys looked upon Ray Hunt as a crank. His clinics were under-subscribed and Ray struggled to cover the costs of gas and feed. Today, a decade later, his workshops are fully booked weeks in advance. But it's not fame or money that motivates Ray. "I have no interest whatsoever in found-ing an empire. Maybe someday I'll buy a small piece of land to call home, but in the meantime making a lot of money don't mean nothing."

During the course of the year, Ray will travel more than 50,000 miles through the West from California to North Dakota, occasionally south to Texas. Once he conducted a class in Australia, and last year Ray made his first trip to, "a strange place"—the East.

"I wouldn't want it wrote down," he said. "No brag. But I've probably started more horses than any person living today. Just figure it out. In my clinics I help start 750 horses a year, and for the 20 years before that I'd say I handled no less than a hundred a year. There's no one I've heard about who can match that."

Dinner had ended and we were sipping our second cup of black coffee. I asked Ray whether he could say, one decade after the clinics were initiated, if he considers his life work successful.

"Not really," he said, "Very seldom do I ever see a horse today doing some-thing he enjoys doing. He's still, as far as I'm concerned, abused." Ray settled himself into his seat to nurse the cup. "It's not just the cowboy. It's often the youngsters. When you see those 4-H kids a-hammering on the horse, you got to stop and think. What gives them the right to instruct the horse in the first place? Do they know any more than he does? No. Absolutely not. A ten-year-old has as much right teaching that horse as he has teaching school.

"It aggravates me. It burns me no end. If this child is having problems with a horse, a dumb horse, then tell me. Who gets blamed? The dumb horse, of course. It's never the human who's dumb, is it? He's supposed to be the smart one. So if you ask me if the horse has been abused in the West I got to say yes. The cowboy didn't mean to. That's just the way it was."

We stood up, stretched our legs, and collected our hats. "Have you a dream?" I asked Ray.

"Yes," he replied without a second to consider. "I dream that one day some little girl or boy will be working a horse next to a road and somebody, stopping to admire that it's being done with good sense, with humanity, will ask: 'Where in the world did you ever learn that?'

"And the kid will reply: 'Is there any other way?'

"I don't suppose it'll ever happen, but I can dream, can't I?"

CHAPTER 9

Loner

Yesterday I called Matt Wilmot. His recorded message was belligerent: "Rawhide Ranch. I may or may not be able to return your call. Leave a message if you want." Already cowed, I left my message—an invitation to the Bar 20 for a meal or a drink. On Matt's machine, I explain I'm interested in the valley's history and I have a few archival photographs that may be of interest.

I've made up my mind I must meet this enigmatic neighbor. My neighbors tend to go into alert mode whenever I mention his name. Most say he keeps to himself, all they know of his movements being hearsay. One tough West Boulder horse outfitter found Matt Wilmot so "hardheaded" when he grazed his cattle in the national forest that the outfitter was left with only one course of action: "Negotiation—that is after I deprived him of oxygen for two minutes."

Loren Brewer, in the shade of his mobile home, explained Matt's problem this way: "he was a spoiled kid and had a terrible temper." Another source, a woman living in another valley to the west, grimaced when our conversation turned to Matt Wilmot. She noted his father, Brad, was married twice. His first wife died young of a lingering malady, and his second wife was the first wife's nurse—a woman so meek, compliant, and submissive she endured physical and mental abuse from everyone, especially her sole child, Matt. Still, when she died the considerable fortune she had inherited from her husband, reverted to her son and now, while Matt should be "filthy rich," he looks like "an old rodeo hand." No one disputes Matt has now become a fine rancher or that he knows lots about cattle, horses, and mules. But, as neighbors in this valley, both he and his father, she explained, "were utter failures.... Matt," she summarized. "should have been drowned at birth."

I am more than ever convinced I must meet this fellow. The legends of his cold-bloodedness I dismiss as tall tales. Whether true or false, this valley is, for me, reflection of all people living here. Who are we to say which are the admirable ones?

Real estate brochures call this valley "untouched," but realtors must only be looking at the wildflower meadows, stands of Douglas fir, Engelman spruce and gin-clear river. Look close and you will never be able to deny the West Boulder encompasses a complex human history. I make this claim not just from what I've heard but, in large part, thanks to a cheap metal detector I bought in Livingston.

Late summer afternoons, when I walk the old byways of the long-ago ranch, I've developed the habit of carrying the detector. One road in particular, terminates at our barn. These days it's covered in wild rose and burdock. Still, the horses treat it as a bridle path, and, on it, they've trampled a track. They've even managed to skirt some proud ground—remnants of a landslide, I'm told, from the 1920s. On the far side of the high ground, they've relocated where the track begins as accurately as if they were land surveyors. All day long the track is all but invisible, but in evening shadows, even from a great distance, it comes to life as a furrow, straight as a laser, diagonally cleaving the escarpment. Most visitors don't see it, but old-timers nod wisely: "the old stagecoach road," they say. This was the highway that more than a hundred years ago connected our valley with Livingston and the world. Down its rough surface rattled and plunged stagecoaches bound for Independence.

Today, in the chill of evening, I can conjure the sounds of metal brakes, creaking shafts, foam-flecked teams, jolted passengers, all talking of El Dorado.

The metal detector helps. It becomes an extension of my arm, a wand to invoke history. With it, I effect a movement much like raking leaves. From the barn to the base of the landslide, the machine goes ballistic. And with each erratic move of the needle, I stop, switch off electronics and shovel the dirt until I find what drives the detector to its high whine. Sometimes it's an old bolt, a hinge, a horseshoe nail, or, one memorable evening, a portion of a wagon axle, a century old (scrape away a little rust, it might even be put back into service). So I'm reminded this wild, sometimes inhuman, valley, is filled with ghosts. They've certainly left their mark across this valley, but here nature is so powerful it has conveniently buried the debris and moved on.

No matter their claims to the contrary, people are always driven to leave a mark—not just with hardware, but through the trappings of their lives and the little disguised echoes of their comings and goings. Everywhere I look, even though there might not be a house in sight, I see human evidence. One doesn't really travel the West Boulder Valley. One passes through the "Ellisson," "Johnson," "Brokaw," "Delandorf," "Hoiland" places—names that become inviolate, prefiguring nature, outliving death. Warmth, hospitality, exuberance, rapaciousness, hostility lie heavy across this consecrated terrain in a crazy quilt of passion. And the road threads through them all to become, in time, a narrative—mine, yours, no matter. I wait to see leaves changing, clouds building, bears emerging, and all the time, across the sulky landscape, I hear voices.

The mute, perhaps foreboding, Matt Wilmot might be verification. He's stamped himself upon this valley, just like the rest of us. He makes fences to last a lifetime. Like a twister, he cuts down wide swathes of trees to either side of his barbed wire. His gates are built so tight only professional wrestlers can open them. And across his land there's an aroma that smells: "Don't mess with me."

I'd like to understand the Wilmots, father and son. I can, with a little work, relate to their ambition of possessing an entire valley and most of a fine trout river. Such a mission is as seductive as having an island to oneself. Strategic power is erotic, one graceful finger of land a start but no match for the bust, hips, thighs of an entire geographic feature. Owning land is, let's be honest, mostly a male thing.

Today Matt Wilmot must feel a tad thwarted for his landholdings are boldly divided by the West Boulder Reserve. He owns the Steen Place to the north. Seventy years ago it belonged to the Bar 20. There, in sight of the road, next to an old cabin that prefigures any one alive today, he has erected a metal shed and a house for his manager.

But Matt Wilmot lives elsewhere—in absolute seclusion on his 490-acre parcel, devastatingly beautiful, with a stretch of river that is legendary—and all his. Here with assistance from a steeplechase course of "no trespassing" signs, he has withdrawn to his own reflections. But Matt Wilmot has a problem: to travel from one section of his land to the other, he must negotiate nearly three miles of reserve, owned by outsiders, most outsiders like me.

In 1962 Brad Wilmot believed he could obtain some of the intervening land from plague-torn Monica Payne. But his charm failed him. And as recently as 1988 Matt Wilmot approached the reserve with an offer to purchase all its undeveloped land. The association minutes would suggest Matt Wilmot had relied solely on numbers to make his case. He had directed his ranch foreman to notify the reserve caretaker of the offer—its tone: "take it or leave it." It implied Matt Wilmot knew best what to do with undeveloped grazing land. As a bona fide rancher, he had the wherewithal to put such wasted property to good use. That, in sum, was the nature of the offer presented to the reserve. Wilmot hadn't even bothered being artful with words, nor did his proposal pay lip service to the conservation biases of reserve members. He must have believed money spoke for itself, for he chose not to make the case in person.

The offer was made in absentia at my first West Boulder meeting. During that hot July day, I was slouched deep in a chair, aimlessly trying to fathom the minds of my fellow members, assembled in the guesthouse, formerly the home of Helen Fargo Arnold and, later, Harry Brewer. Suddenly a pickup drove by and slowed. I stared at it through the window. I didn't realize it at the time, but Brad Wilmot was at the wheel. When he slowed the pickup, he never looked our way nor even acknowledged us with the signature finger wave. While I didn't know who he was or what the deliberate drive-by was all about, I can recall the brooding character of his slow crawl. Without looking at us, he seemed to infiltrate the room. I'm not certain if others noticed, but, if they had, they might have sensed some sort of brute will, maybe a presentiment. But the portentous moment came and went in the blink of an eye.

With dizzying speed, Matt's offer was then unanimously rejected by everyone in attendance. The reserve's reaction was similar to Monica Payne's response, 26 years before, to Matt's father: "No. Never. Absolutely not to you."

With post-hole diggers, barbed wire, and no-trespassing signs, Matt Wilmot has successfully guarded his land against encroachment and from envious fishermen like me. In doing so, he's proven to be a fine conservationist, most of his property remaining as inviolate as it has for decades. But why does he remain so aloof?

Three days after I leave a message on his machine, Wilmot returns my call, much to my surprise. Yes, he'd be interested in my pictures of the Bar 20 in the 1930s. I suggest a date two days hence. In abbreviated phrases, he agrees, but a day later he bows out with another message: "Tomorrow night. It ain't going to work for me." After another round of calls, we settle on an evening one month hence. "OK if I bring a friend?" he asks.

I'm exhilarated to meet the West Boulder Valley's very own Prince of Darkness. Neighbors have noted the occasion's novelty. Matt Wilmot rarely visits other people's houses. "Hope he doesn't lose his temper," Kathryn warns over the phone.

Late one July evening, I hear the pinging of Matt Wilmot's diesel pickup crossing the bridge. When he steps out and reaches his full height, I see he's rake thin, wiry, and not as tall as he appeared at the wheel. His hair, now more gray than blond, has recently been barbered, one millimeter shy of a Marine cut. A cowboy hat rides his head at a just-so angle, and his full blond mustache is inflamed from tobacco. To this Easterner, he appears a studied rendition of the Marlboro Man, with legs bowed in the fashion of Western horsemen. His manners courtly, but guarded, he greets me and heads toward the house stiff and slow as if walking is not his preferred form of locomotion. At first, he appears too preoccupied by the sight of the Bar 20 to talk. He steps into the living room and looks around. No, he won't have a drink.

"How 'bout coffee?" he asks. I tell him there'll be a few minutes delay while I brew it. "Don't bother," he interrupts. "I've got some two-day old stuff in the pickup." Not responding to my protests, he returns with a thermos.

Matt Wilmot's friend, Steve, is originally from Iowa, a newcomer to Montana. He and Matt met in Arizona. He apologizes for his disposition, but he recently lost his wife and he's "working his way through the grief." Horses, cattle, Montana—they're all new to him. He is by profession, he explains, a counselor, his speciality the cycle of abuse from parent to child.

"Hope you don't mind," I say to the two men, "Steak, baked potato, and salad."

Wilmot is quick to respond: "I'll do without the salad. I don't want anything green touching my lips. The only salad I ever have is Jell-O salad."

I wonder whether he is pulling a fast one on me—expansive landowner posing as a hayseed. But Wilmot isn't inclined towards parody; the lines around his mustache, I suspect, cleaved mostly for commands, rebuttals, action. We dine on the screened porch in near darkness. I serve the steak, tell him and Steve of my life, my intrigue with the history of the West Boulder Valley, Bar 20, and Stanley Cox. For long minutes Wilmot concentrates on the steak, saying little, his face indecipherable. My words now feel like patter. Between sentences, I listen to the bats flighting between branches, just beyond the screens. Wilmot yawns and then watches me stealthily, as if trying to place me—animal, mineral, or vegetable. He notices the tape recorder on the table in front of his plate and tells me to turn it off. Maybe he'll now say something important.

"That Mrs. Cox: I kind of remember her being a looker," he volunteers. That's the sum total of his recollections: he was young and can't remember a whole lot. He says he knows little of the valley's history, nothing of neighbors, and he doesn't pay much attention to what's going on these days. Outside, the wind in the firs is warm.

"I don't know much about the homesteaders, but my understanding is they stayed only about seven to ten years." He turns to look at the fireplace. "Are them andirons old?" I tell him they aren't. Matt stands up to explore another Bar 20 room. "It really feels right. John, you've done real well here."

High praise. I thank him. He stretches. "John, I got the best part of that meal. That was good. I enjoyed that. You did good."

I think to myself, he speaks good cowboy. "Are you doing your own cooking up there?" I ask him, pointing up the valley.

"Yup. And I ain't doing very well."

Steve interjects for the first time: "He makes good pancakes."

Matt has nothing further to say. He goes onto the lawn to smoke, and while he is gone I ask Steve, defeated and remote, about his work.

He comes alive. "My specialty," he says, "is adult dysfunction due to early childhood trauma. Post-traumatic stress disorder.... Origins are very important to this condition. Childhood is where you learn to be dysfunctional."

"Were you abused?" I ask him.

"Yes," he replies hastily. My next question is cut short by Matt who returns to say it's time to leave.

"One last question," I ask, rising to meet Matt. "In 1939, your father when he bought his place up the valley after he made his fortune—did he intend the ranch to be a money-making operation or a hobby place?" I had seen a copy of the Rawhide brochure, printed soon after Brad Wilmot's purchase. Its purple prose was dizzying in its enthusiasm:

> Fully twenty trails of positively unusual beauty, wind their way to hidden lakes of unfathomable depths, and to waterfalls of primeval beauty upon which few white men's eyes have been privileged to feast. There is ever present the languid murmur of stately pines protected by the watchful eyes of Uncle Sam's Rangers. For those who prefer easier riding there are trails in the valley along the ever chattering mountain streams, rushing, as for centuries to their destiny.

Neither Matt Wilmot nor his father, I suspect, would have written those lines. They must have been penned by a hack in Minneapolis. He draws his finger across his mustache—a thoughtful gesture—then replies in his own way: "No, he did all right. He ran this ranch as a dude ranch for only three years."

"Why did he get out of dude ranching?"

"Kind of wanted to get into cattle a little more."

He cuts me off: "You want to hear about Arizona?" I don't, but Matt doesn't pause for my answer. He tells me he has a desert ranch near Yuma, Arizona, where he runs Braford cattle. There he goes in winter when the West Boulder gets snowed in.

"That Braford's a good combination," Wilmot explains. "The Brahman produce small birth-weight calves and the Hereford puts some hair on them." I study his face to see whether this is all a show to dodge my questions or whether he really isn't interested in the history of this valley. He resumes his own counsel for a moment, then adds: "I like cattle because I need something to preoccupy my mules." He rubs his mustache once again and says, "And I like to build corrals."

I have half a mind to give him the andirons if he likes them so much, but he cuts me short by moving toward the door. A presentiment of hopelessness and the gloom of dark have together fallen upon the Bar 20. Most days night is welcome but tonight will be darker than most. When I light lights through the Bar 20, Wilmot takes his cue to leave. He rouses the anguished Steve, and together they move to the door. We've both been evasive, Wilmot in concealing his remote self, me because I failed to ask tough questions, settling instead on Pablum. I'm intrigued Wilmot has allowed himself to be seen in the company of a counselor. Perhaps he has chosen for me to do all the work. He will thus deny me every hard fact and only let slip hints of dark forces and wily contradictions.

I go for broke. "Do you ever suffer from depression?" I ask.

"You know depression is no more than anger directed at yourself."

It's not the answer I wanted. It sounds, in fact, like a canned sentence lifted from a self-help book, but it seems to work for Wilmot. Now, he springs the screen door and walks into shadows. Duma pads along beside him, auditioning for a pat. Instead, Wilmot delivers a sharp rap to her muzzle.

At the gate I watch the mismatched Steve and Matt make their way to the pickup. In ten minutes they'll be back at the Rawhide. I can imagine what it might have once been like, filled with dudes and laughter. Now with the Wilmots, especially Matt, it must be a different place. Wives and children, each in their own way, have come and gone, mostly forever. Today, except for Steve, the special bend in the river will be empty. I watch as the pickup slowly crosses the bridge and gets swallowed by dusk. Matt Wilmot, I think, has adopted an end-of-road personality. That's it: he's as jagged as the landscape.

Two months later, Matt returned to show me the promised photograph albums. Tonight, he is accompanied by a girlfriend, blond, tight-fitting in slacks, her pretty face no longer able to disguise, I think, her eventful life. No, she won't have a drink, thank you. Like Steve, she met Matt in Arizona and had never before been to Montana. She explains she fell in love with the place at first sight when she discovered she could drink water straight from the river.

"How do you keep your house so clean?" Wilmot interrupts. "Who's your cleaner?

I shrug. "We have a wonderful house cleaner." He seems relieved as if I'd just inducted him into a family secret. I go to the kitchen to make coffee. For some reason, I open the cabinet beneath the sink. Something is odd with the bacon dripping can. I look closely and note a mouse has climbed in and died. Now it's embalmed in fat. The mouse's awful end—a death of plenty— makes me uneasy. I turn on as many lights as I can find. I wonder if I should show the mouse to Matt to demonstrate that the house isn't perfect. Instead, I return to the living room, where Matt and his friend are solemnly studying the andirons. I give them the coffee and then turn to Wilmot's albums. These old books recall pre-Rawhide days, when the ranch was alive with summer dudes. Even during the Depression and the Dust Bowl, the 1930s appear to have been a lighthearted time. I ask whether I can photocopy a few pictures.

"Sure. Just be quick. Gotta go."

The woman sits in quickening shadows, saying not a word, visibly cowed by the sight and footsteps of her friend, prowling like a zoo animal from room to room. When he's out of sight, her eyes glaze. I have the feeling she has done so much in her short life, she finds delight in uneventfulness. Matt and she probably met at some self-help gathering and discovered common ground of pain and abuse.

Wilmot repeats his former compliment: "You done good, John." Impatiently, he smokes outside my office as I photocopy.

Now the cigarette is ended: "Gotta go," he says, taking the albums, my work still incomplete.

I cannot be certain why I like the farouche Matt Wilmot. Might it be because he is exactly as he appears? While his manners are courtly, what he says is painfully direct.

But I have an urge to test him one final time. I ask: "Would you ever let me fish your property?"

His answer is swift, as if he had been waiting all this time to respond. "No." He collects his albums and as he leaves, walking stiff and straight, his bearing inviolate, he repeats himself: "I'm just not interested in saying yes." Matt Wilmot couldn't make himself clearer.

I always knew his answer would be no, and now I am relieved. He owns his swatch of valley, his ribbon of river, and he has every right to do as he pleases. While courteous to a fault, he cares not one dot what I think. These days his entire life is an exercise in suppression and pacing. Feline, dangerous, primal, he lives the model West Boulder life, healing himself.

Tonight when he departs the Bar 20, I have begun to penetrate the astonishing bond between landscape and people, and to understand how nothing, in the end, is perfect.

CHAPTER 10

Up the Valley

I am on horseback once again. We have left roadhead, three miles beyond the Bar 20 and have been climbing steadily into the narrowing valley, past Matt Wilmot's no trespassing signs, onto national forest, finally into the Absoroka Beartooth Wilderness Area. Mount Rae, a solemn hulk to the east, is still covered in a monk's fringe of snow. Shell Mountain to the west, is now obscured by stands of lodgepole pine, uniform like dozing soldiers. Below us, to the right, the river is an invisible escort, the sound of its breath rising and falling with the stirring of forest canopy.

I am not in the lead. That honor is Larry Lahren's—friend, outfitter, and archaeologist. Actually, the true trailbreakers are Chui (Swahili for "leopard"), my golden retriever, every few minutes running the gantlet between horse legs to check on me, and Duma ("cheetah"), black Lab, delirious with the smells of the forest. From my position Larry seems indomitable, a forest linebacker, a Paul Bunyan on his horse Blue, a Johnny Appleseed with an iron glove. He's all shoulders and beard, a sheepskin vest shrouding the huge engine of his chest. While built to massive scale and mounted on the brawniest of horses, Larry, like all of us, seems a tad dwarfish in this landscape. His horse plunges into muddy creeks, rebounding with the groan of harness leather, and, all the while, this massive woodsman leans to whisper in his horse's ear, careful his words not insult the forest hush.

Wilderness is what powers the Bar 20. It is our ocean, we its beach-combers. Like a sea, our wilderness has depths that may never be plunged, mysteries on the scale of sea serpents, massiveness to rival infinity. Wilderness gives us pure water, grizzly bears, mountain lions, and weather so fluky, predictions are comic. By law, Wilderness will never hear the snarl of a combustion engine, the rustle of roads, the buzz of society. Its only human intruders are those precious few content to travel on foot or by horse. Even on the Fourth of July, trails appear derelict.

This wilderness has become a Bar 20 ritual. Hardly a summer week will pass when I don't escape to its meadows for a picnic or into higher reaches of the river to be provoked by cutthroat trout. I try to remember rain gear, spare food, a sweater, in case of a surprise, like July snow. But all too often I forget, only to return in the dark, chilled, a T-shirt plastered to shivering shoulders, boots encased in gooey weights of mud. In autumn I climb into the forest at some peril. Larry once emerged from it with a broken shoulder, after his horse slipped on ice. In a nearby wilderness, Larry's only son slipped, slid, and plunged to his death. Some inexperienced elk hunters have been found very stiff six months later, in spring. The Wilderness is what this land once was—a place where humans are dwarfed by nature. It is an expanse that evokes the miraculous landscapes of Albert Bierstadt, Thomas Cole, Thomas Moran. Traveling through it by horse, one reverts to the language of the art historian: "Pure Nineteenth Century exuberance... the dewy dawn of Creation."

Today the sky, between the canopy, is uniformly blue. In the hopscotched light on the trail, moths settle for molecules of water and salt. My horse likes to travel inches from Larry's—a nose-to-butt routine, which may be a bonding experience for him but, to me, seems hazardous—an invitation to a good swift kick. After one hour of travel, the trail emerges from the forest.

We top a ridge to let our horses chomp on new grass. I've crested the rise many times before, but, invariably, the moment the meadow is revealed below me, I suck in lungfulls of air from surprise. In its midst, the river squirms, a changed soul from its rambunctious self beside the Bar 20. Serpentine, it slithers across the treeless meadow, its water clear like bottled air. On the elbows of meanders, knotted vegetation thickens into stands of brush, deep enough to bury a moose and her calf. To the right: vaulting limestone cliffs festooned with black caves and away down the valley, hills traded for mountains, all of them quilted in snow. Even here, a few hundred yards from the river, I sense the itch of life, the languorous swirl of very smart brown trout, shifting across mottled stones, all senses a-jangle, as they await the perfect mayfly.

Even though he's been visiting these meadows since childhood, I've heard Larry say the valley is a magnet, that he lives for this view. Today, in the saddle, he studies it in silence, then neck-reins his horse into high grass, his deliberation a signal for me to follow. Is this hulk of a man ruminating about history, about shadow figures who once ghosted through these highlands? From the way he moves, hard to say.

Soon Larry picks up a trail, fainter by far than the one we've been following. It climbs, without foreplay, up an incline and again we're covered in the chilled soup of forest. Thirty minutes later, we break out onto another meadow, this one altogether different. With Mount Rae crowding the sky, the water is not predictable cerulean, but the black peat of age.

Lost Lakes weren't formed by the West Boulder but by an impoundment of glacial melt and a creek that is today mostly shadow. Lost Creek rises on the edge of Mount Rae and has been filling this glacial cirque for eons. The ground is pulpy beneath my horse's hoofs. He's uncertain whether to advance for a drink, but I don't let him think too much. I dismount and lead him to it. So, too, Larry, who then turns his mount and the two packhorses into a stand of lodgepoles and ties them to trees. I do the same, and liberated, we walk the banks of a shallow lake, the dogs quartering to our right as we advance.

Larry hasn't been here in a decade, but on his last visit he stumbled upon something that surprised him. He's returned today because he wants me to see it, although he's not certain we'll find it. After so much time and weather, he thinks it may be lost forever.

Larry has been wandering the West Boulder Valley much of his life. He believes it has been playing host to human beings for many millennia. The site he found is not associated with hunter-gatherers but with latter-day trespassers.

For an hour, we explore, kicking through high grass with cowboy boots, communication no more than murmurs and nods. There's a small rise between two lakes, and when we scale it and pause, panning the basin from north to south, Larry remembers being here when the lakes were one, joined together as a large sleeping body. Today the water table has fallen and the lake is now a skeleton, one bony finger no more than a secretion. "You can see why once, you'd want to hang out here. Fresh water, good protection from weather, and you're right on the edge of the Stillwater Complex, one of the richest ore bodies in all the world." Indeed these lakes are still remote, visited at most by a handful of backpackers who discover them by studying topo maps.

When we enter a stand of timber, Larry again despairs the site has been consumed by the elements. As I mutter a banality about fate, Larry clears his throat and rumbles, "Here it is."

Only a few feet of two walls of the cabin remain. Their punky logs lie scattered across the ground, but at one corner they're still stitched together. We pace the cabin's original dimensions: 12- by 6- feet. "Hardly room enough to swing a cat." The entire structure was assembled without nails, and the logs, their butt ends rough-hewn, were felled with an axe. There is no hint of windows and only a suspicion of a door. Deer have lain against the logs for shelter and their droppings have turned hard on what once was a floor of bare earth. Nearby, a moose has shed his rack, now darkened, it too having assumed this enterprise of history.

"Skookum Joe is still pretty much will o' wisp," Larry explains as we ride down the trail to the meadows. He would be Larry's odds-on candidate for the builder of this cabin. In drib and drabs, Larry tells me Skookum's real name was Joseph Richard Anderson. He was born in either Canada or Norway sometime between 1835 and 1843, ran away from home at age 16, reached Montana by way of Cape Horn and the Pacific Northwest. In what is today Washington State, he lived with Chinook Indians, earning the sobriquet "Skookum," meaning "good" or "big." With them he learned how to survive in the wilderness. The rest of his shadowy life was bent on the search for gold. "Going it alone," in Larry's words. "The sound of his hammer and shovel must have been heard in virtually every drainage of these mountains.

"At the time, this was still Indian country," Larry explains as we return to the horses. "The Bozeman Trail, hardly 20 miles from here, had a short-lived history as highway for settlers heading out for Western farmlands. In these hills, help for a white man was far away and undependable. This country was still part of the Crow Reservation, and any pale face who messed around on tribal lands probably did so at his peril."

But solitary Skookum Joe was able to deal with the only other inhabitants of these valley—seasonal hunters—the Mountain Crow, by keeping to himself. "The Indians viewed Skookum, always alone, highly paranoid, eccentric in every way, as a kind of shaman. They just left him alone."

The cabin we saw today must have been his base, Larry ventures, during the course of one summer when he prospected the Lost Creek drainage for gold. There is a record he was camped by the Natural Bridge on the Main Boulder in 1870, on the East Boulder in 1872, the Clark's Fork in 1879. Today these crumbling logs remain the oldest known visible European structure in this part of the country—probably well over 120 years.

"I'd expect other outsiders to have been in this country before," says Larry as my horse steps gingerly into the West Boulder River, "But their shelters—whatever they were—are all rotted."

Our intention is to camp about six miles from here, to spend a few days in the back country, trade yarns, catch a few fish. My horse crabs against the current until he climbs onto a sandbar, then lunges up a mud bank, once again into high grass. "I'm pretty confident," continues Larry, "There were Frenchmen in this country before the Lewis and Clark Expedition. In the journals, when Captain Clark floated the Yellowstone in 1806, he wrote about passing the mouth of a creek near here. It must have been either Mission Creek or the Main Boulder. He dubbed it 'Stinking Cabin Creek.' He'd have to be referring to a fur trapper's cabin. They always stunk." We leave one meadow for another, this one studded with massive glacial debris. "The fur trappers had come out of Quebec. Most were illiterate. No records, no diaries, no honor. Anything near 200 years old would have completely disintegrated by now."

Lack of records is the hobgoblin of research in this valley. So many early pioneers were either illiterate or unaware they lived lives of consequence. The West Boulder's past can only be reconstructed through inference. What did Skookum Joe meditate about in his cabin? Did he ever find gold here? Grizzlies? Indians? Artifacts? How did he survive? What happened to him here?

The timber now elbows the trail on the right. To the left is a steep embankment that plunges into the West Boulder, now narrow and swift. I pause to study one enchanted bend of the trail. It overlooks a perfect waterfall—unsullied, pure, and explosive. Once, in a moment of insanity, I tied a nymph to my line, straddled a downed log at its base, and flicked the fly into the center of this deep pool. Here, in this minute space at the foot of the falls, viscous roiling water, stormy at one end, gushing at the other, seemed just "right," even though standing on slippery bark in hiking boots was a high-wire act. On my third cast, I felt a tug. My line straightened, whipsawed, and sang like piano wire. The pool couldn't be more than ten feet deep, yet I had more than twice that amount of line in play. The fish quickened, then darted beneath my perch. Now I would have to fight it, drunkenly, the butt of the rod in one hand, its tip sprung between my legs as the fish fled downstream with the current. Soon rapids swallowed the fish whole. Lurching awkwardly on my slippery log, I fought the trout for ten minutes. Three times I knew it was lost, then after maybe 15 minutes, I reeled it toward me. Between my legs, out of the river, I pulled an astonishing 20-inch brown trout—inconceivably large to have come from this bantam pool. I choked with private delight and thought smugly I was now the only person in the world privy to this secret, teased from beneath the falls. A minute after I released the fish back to the pool, I slipped and fell.

Today the log is gone, swept away, perhaps, by last spring's high water. I look into the pine-dark river. Had there really been a 20-inch brown trout? How stupid did I look when I fell? Might it all have been a dream?

Four miles upstream in a glade by the river, Larry and I drop from our saddles, remove packs from the other horses and spread our camp onto the ground. Within an hour, a scene of classic serenity is born beneath the trees: two small sleeping tents and a tarp-roofed kitchen. Now I head upstream with dogs. Within an hour, I've collected a batch of small cutthroats for breakfast. While I always maintain Duma and Chui are faultless, if they possess one sin it is their approach to fishing. Nothing gives Duma, especially, greater joy than the sight of me with a fly rod. It is her invitation to water sports. And no sooner do I flick my fly into water than she becomes airborne, overcome by an uncontained belief my bobbing fly is prey. I should have learned by now these dogs should never be invited fishing, but I always forget, so mistakenly committed am I to a conviction my dogs are capable of reform.

Today is no exception. Once I wrestle Duma and Chui from the water, tether them to nearby aspen, they follow my every move, bug-eyed, staring me down as if I have just performed an act of unspeakable sadism. Whenever my rod bends, Duma quivers uncontrollably, her whimpering audible above the rush of the river. The sight of these gullible trout leaping above the burble of current, airborne at the end of my line, drives her into a frenzy. The notion of a subtle, silent stalk for trout is as foreign to her as a day without a Milk Bone. After I take as many fish as we need for breakfast, I unleash the two trembling dogs and watch them leap into the quiet pool in case there are still unsuspecting fish.

"Skookum Joe," Larry says, over a whiskey beside the hissing fire. "He probably got into this country in May each year. Good place to start after the snows melted. The problem is he was so damn secretive. They say that every fall when he came out of the mountains he'd carry a lard bucket of nuggets. We know he hit it big in 1880 in the Judith Mountains, and later he and a few partners found the Spotted Horse Mine, but each time he lost out for one reason or another—"too many partners," he used to say. "But in these mountains he must have done as well, although he never let on. He was so protective of his claims he'd remove claim stakes, unload specimens, bury workings, destroy assay reports. Strange, wonderful dude. It was clear he discovered the Stillwater Complex [now arguably the richest deposit of platinum and palladium in the world], but he never benefited from it." Larry pulls a paper from his back pocket and reads from it. "When he lay dying in a Billings hospital in 1897, he wrote one of his investors, "'We've got it at last, Bud, the richest thing in Montana. I'll draw a map so you can locate it easy. But not tonight. I'm too tired. They keep trailing me, Bud, but nobody'll ever find it without me. Tomorrow I'll draw a map.... I believe I've located the main lode. You'll find it just three miles above....'"

Larry laughs hard, loving every minute of the drama. "You see his penciled scrawl came to an end just then. And no one to this day knows the location of the mother lode. I'm convinced Skookum Joe found it, no doubt about it, but, like all those guys, he cashed in his chips before he could make a penny." Larry is hunched over the fire. "Life, isn't it? It's all in the timing." He lifts himself to his feet to shift coals. With my foot, I nudge Chui to stop her from rolling any closer to the flames. The two dogs have crashed within range of sparks. We've given them fat from the steak, and now they're as good as dead, the sweet aroma of their farts jamming the air between clouds of pine smoke. The night has chilled. An owl cries. Mosquitoes hum out of range. Bats vector above the river, and, in the sweet contemplation of a day well spent, our conversation meanders between silence and nonsequitur.

I'm thinking of Skookum Jim, wandering this trail not because the mountains were beautiful but because they'd make him rich. He lived the best tale of all, and now its secrets are buried with him amid the logs of his cabin.

"We always think we're alone up here, but we're not," I say. "All these ghosts...."

"These days, everyone who gets to Montana, buys a place, believes they're the first. You might want to call it: 'the lie of the land' syndrome. They don't like to be told that in Montana they're trespassers.

"While I was born here, my right to this land is just as flimsy as yours." Larry disappears into the dark for another log, his tread as light as an Indian's. "My problem is I'm of German-Norwegian blood. That's a tough background: I can't sit still and I don't quit. I have to be self-employed because we don't like to kiss anyone's ass, and, worst, we don't get along with anyone. Add to that my obsession with this land. I'll never be able to leave it.

"I guess women have been my downfall. The last one was a psycho. 'Asshole,' I keep telling myself. 'Don't do it.' But I do it just the same. Dammit if just the other day I'm in a bar and I run into this redhead. I can't get her out of my head. I dream about her all the time.

"So what do you think about this pickup line next time I see her in that bar?" Larry chuckles to himself, preparing his voice. "'You're the reason I went through puberty.' Well, what do you think?"

In the dark, I can't tell if he's serious or not. Once known as "the toughest man in Park County," Larry doesn't seem to be the kind who'd ever need to scramble to find a woman. "Man," I whistle between my teeth. "I don't know, Larry," I reply perplexed. "If I used that line, everything'd go to hell. She'd either laugh at me or pull a punch. Why not say something more subtle, like 'You want to see my stone tools'?"

Larry grunts and continues to stare down the flames. "Honest, Larry," I continue, "I'm not the one to ask. I couldn't pick up a babe in a bar if my life depended on it. I've just as many problems with women as you do. As your counselor at this moment in time, I stink. Look at all my mistakes. Count them. Imagine, if I had fallen into marriage with one of them. No, I've just about given up on the whole damn thing."

Again we resort to silence, sipping whiskey, listening to the purr of river, the piping of bats.

"Did you ever know Huggins?" I ask changing the subject once again.

He looks over at me, trying to see where I'm headed. "Well, what about him?"

Two days before, I had been struggling, yet again, to reconstruct the ghosts of the Bar 20. Beginning with the title abstract, I had found that on November 14, 1957, Paul and Monica Payne had bought the property from a Robert and Dorothy Huggins, who had themselves purchased it on August 14, 1951, from the most mysterious owners of all, Stanley and Lucille Cox.

Six years of ownership seems so fleeting—hardly time to leave a mark.

"Yeah, I knew Huggins," rumbles Larry. "He owned an implement dealership in Livingston. I was just a school kid and he gave me a job the summer I was 15. I was shy and the whole family seemed so charming, all of them good-looking. I worked three months for him, installing sprinkler systems on farms across the county. When it came time to get paid, he let it slide and I was just a kid and too shy to ask for my paycheck. So he got my summer labor for free. Quite a deal, wasn't it? Shyness. I guess I was an asshole then as well. What do you know of him?"

The picture he paints of Huggins, I answer, matches the one I'd uncovered: a rich man uneasy with money in anyone else's hands.

I had begun my hunt for Huggins with an Internet search. A Californian named Ferguson was referred to me. His secretary gave me the phone number of Huggins's son, Bobbie, living near Laguna Beach, California. Bobbie's wife, Paula, answered and, over the course of three years, we came to know each other by telephone. Paula described herself as "tall with dark brown curly hair, 122 pounds. 5′ 6″. 'All legs,' my father-in-law used to say. I've been a tearoom and ramp model ever since I was 16. My cheekbone is where the cut-off button on the phone is."

Beside the fire, I explain to Larry, Paula had never been at a loss with me for words and memories. Without ever meeting her, she became visible from these telephone talks, a smiling woman delighting in self-analysis, unabashed with strangers, readily joshing about the chaos of her life. Some days her mood was carefree and fun-loving, other times she seemed in despair with a life run riot. In every way she appeared the ingenuous caricature of what we call "Californian." "I'm a doll-collector," she said once. "Fibber McGhee and Molly's closet—that's me. Boxes and boxes everywhere in this house."

"One August she lamented to me about her own mother who had 'lived nine years too long.' Now she weighed 60 pounds, had shriveled from 4′ 10″ to 4′ 8″ , was 'riddled with Alzheimer's' and 'when she goes, it'll be a blessing.' Another time she reported she had found and then lost her Bar 20 pictures. 'We're in chaos here. I've got a bridge luncheon and my husband decided to redo our deck around the pool. Redwood got bleached out. Planters have dry rot. Give me a few more days. Everything's in upheaval.' "

"Are you sure you're interested?" I ask Larry.

"Yeah, of course I am."

"When, finally, I found Paula with a moment to herself, I asked her to settle on one subject, the Bar 20. 'Aah,' she sighed."

I had a copy of the entire manuscript of our conversation. I pulled a flashlight out and began to read to Larry beside the fire.

"'Bobby and I were high school sweethearts. He fought in Korea, and as soon as he returned we were married. I was 18. He was 20. He played football, and, while a good athlete, he's small and was always being carried off the field. We were both only children, really. My parents had no money, but they treated me like a little princess. Bobby's parents were wealthy and didn't understand teenagers. We had a beautiful wedding, but everyone said it wouldn't last. Now we've been married nearly 40 years and we've got five kids....'

"'My father-in-law looked a lot like...Oh, my God, Paula, how can you forget? You know that actor with the blue eyes...Paul Newman, yes, that's it. People stopped my father-in-law in the street and thought he was Paul Newman. My mother-in-law was the one who came from money. Bob was a builder in Glendora, California. He kept building one house after another up a hill, then he ran out of houses to build. He thought California was going dry. So he started looking for ranches everywhere else—all the way from New Mexico to Montana.'"

And in Montana, Bob Huggins settled on Livingston, Montana. Here he bought an implement dealership as well as the American Motors franchise. The Huggins also acquired the then 1,640-acre Bar 20 Ranch, as their summer place, and for six years, every June, they settled into Grouse House at the top of the hill. While they owned all the cabins, they chose never to live in Bar 20, the Coxes' residence which they called "the river house." Soon it suffered from neglect. "'I can remember it well,'" says Paula. "'It was fully furnished and had a very dark living room, as big as a barn, filled with old NATIONAL GEOGRAPHICS, oriental carpets, oriental lamps, and wormwood furniture, all custom made with leather cushions. I didn't like any of it so I threw out all the NATIONAL GEOGRAPHICS and traded the rest to my aunt for a fur coat.'"

Chui rolls toward the fire and I retrieve her just in time. It's a cue for Larry to poke the coals and gather them toward the flames. "They just don't get it, do they? History's icky. You gotta unload it. I tell you, that Paula's not a whole lot different from everyone these days. Keep going. I'm getting into it."

I think back to the picture Paula sent me—the supersaturated color photograph, dated 1957, of Grouse House with green-striped awnings over each window and the crowd of guests sitting on the stoop. "We had a vegetable garden down there by the Bar 20," Paula explained. "My job was to pick bib lettuce. No easy task with all the snakes in the garden, and having to wash the lettuce in the stream, then carry it up the hill. We never kept horses on the ranch. All we did was provide summer pasture for longhorned cows from Texas. My in-laws thought they were pretty. They ran the place like a dude ranch, but only for friends, all of them nonpaying. Their friends' kids all had summer jobs on the ranch. In addition, my mother-in-law had full-time help. Towels and soap and everything had to match. Once a week all the linens went to a laundress in Livingston. It was lavish. I remember getting up from the breakfast table and planning for lunch and then, after deciding upon a menu for dinner, getting up from lunch and going down to pick lettuce. This was day in day out. My mother and her help made wonderful meals. I was expected to be a hostess like my mother-in-law, but she always yelled at me, my father-in-law always teased me and I never knew what to do. My mother-in-law reveled in the ranch. She was raised with a lot of money.

"'My husband worked for my father-in-law in Livingston and he had a terrible problem with him. He never got paid. One time in the living room of the river house there were words. I got scared and went into labor and nearly lost the baby. It was hard for my father-in-law to part with money.

"'My father-in-law was always puttering, and he wasn't good with young people. He'd tease a lot. Bobby's cousin was overweight, and he was teased mercilessly. I had long legs and they teased me about them. They used to say

I was like a moose going across a field. I cried all the time, in our cabin down by the river. I'm a Pasadena girl and you have to realize this was all very traumatic. We had bears all around the cabins. I got chased by a nearsighted moose. There was no dryer. There were miller moths. Our water was heated by a wood stove. Mosquitoes were horrible. And it was so cold I got dressed under covers. It was, believe me, traumatic.

"'But then there was so much fun. We were barely out of our teens. Everything was so new and awe-inspiring. We walked up to Nurses Lake. I used to hike that cliff behind the Bar 20. My husband was a fine fisherman. When his mother would ask him to catch fish for dinner, he would say how many and what size? All I caught were tree limbs. We were terrible southern Californians. Tans and fast cars: that's what people assumed we thought about. They were right. At meals, we'd play footsie and we were perfect fools. My father-in-law was looked up to as one of the rich people from southern California. He was a great character and talker, and everyone was enchanted by him. All of us stood out.

"'In those days, Livingston was a funny place—you got paid when the ranchers got paid. You'd carry notes from all these people—that was a killer. I remember making the rounds with my father-in-law. I especially recall one ranch we visited. It was over 100,000 acres and had thousands of sheep, but the owners lived in a log-and-mud house. All the girls ran around pregnant. That family was rich beyond belief. They paid in cash, but they lived without anything.'"

"Yeah," interrupts Larry, "I know exactly who she's talking about. Some of the best people Montana ever produced. Go on."

"What amazed me about Paula is she really never knew any of the neighbors. There seemed to be a social divide up in this valley.

"These were the words she used: 'In the West Boulder Valley, most of our neighbors scrounged out a living. Harry Brewer and his wife were very countrified and real laid-back Montanans. Lot of these people were very educated, but you wouldn't know it. None of them wanted to have any-thing to do with us—so-called high society.

"'When my father-in-law sold the ranch, I think he did well with it, but I don't really know why he sold out. He was not one to tell us anything. In those days, he was comfortably rich. Later he made some booboos in the stock market but that's another story.'"

"That's about all there is to say about the Hugginses' tenure. Paula explained that ever since leaving the Bar 20 some 33 years ago, they've lived in California. Never been back to Montana. Her husband had a sequence of professions—liquor store in Laguna Beach for nine years, then an Instatune business—whatever—then a Surf Store franchise, which they set up for one of their sons. Now Bobby Huggins is retired, and apparently he hates it. Bad shoulder, can't golf. That sort of thing. She called him 'Mr. Overdo.' But it seems to me he was a Mr. Overhave. Rich, handsome, have-everything guy who was indulged by parents. When he became a grown-up the only pressure left was sport. Like so many of us, he couldn't quite work out his mission. Now he's into bridge.

"'The only one who really cared about this place was the father. 'Leaving Montana,' Paula told me, 'Broke my father-in-law's heart. Ever since that time he kept talking about going back to Montana to chop wood. Then he died and that was that. Now,' she added, 'I miss Montana as well: I think about chopping wood there, as well, but there's no way. Here at home I can hardly keep my plants watered.'"

The moon has risen and the forest shadows have turned blue. Now all that remains of the fire is warm ash. "I don't get it," I admit. "I think I can fathom the others, but the Hugginses—they were damn scattered. In this valley it's almost impossible not to become besotted. *Le Mal de La Vallée.* Heartbreak Valley. But passion passed them by. They could admit it was 'awesome' and all that, but it was just another place. For them it was more memorable that they were judged different—the rich folk from California. A badge of honor.

They liked being known for their class and wealth even though they could stiff a kid like you out of his summer salary. Noblesse oblige. And then the old man moves on to his next diversion, and, after a year or two, he realizes he's made a big mistake. He didn't understand his own heart and, when he did, it was too late."

Larry and I stay in camp two more days. We would have remained a third, but late on the second day heavy clouds spill over the rim of the West Boulder Plateau, drowning Mount Rae, Shell Mountain, and our camp in wet, evening gloom. When I fish all morning of that second day, I discover that the farther up the valley I hike, the smaller and more voracious the cutthroat. Early in the afternoon I leave the trail at a spot where passage is narrow and the only approach to the river is a ledge of scree. The more inhospitable the access, I reason, the less chance of human visitation. When I finally reach the river, my shorts ripped, I find the water has narrowed into three pools, each separated by large glacial debris. Duma discovers the pools first, and by the time I work my way around a massive boulder and overtake her, she has plunged into one and is merrily swimming in circles on the trail of anything foolish enough to present itself to an overweight Lab. Chui follows her example, swimming against Duma's clockwise course. I wrest them both onto the bank, leash them to fallen trees, and choose another pool as well as a fly—a shop-worn Royal Coachman, the first I spot in my convulsion of dries, distributed between four pockets of my vest. My hand is unsteady from anticipation.

The effect of my first cast is electric. I cannonball the fly into the spillway without even semblance of artistry. Immediately, the reel hums and, within a few minutes, I've landed my first cutthroat. Hardly ten inches long, he gamely leaps and lunges like the fantasy fish I once held below the falls. The others, succeeding him—all 31 of them in an hour and a half—share his ardor. I catch each without guile, skill, or discrimination. And for each caught, there is another lost. My barbless hook might as well be a finger that sometimes stays rigid, otherwise tires. This is fishing influenza—a state of disorientation where the flow of water makes me feel airborne. Floating in this pool might be as mystifying as spearfishing for birds or hand gliding for butterflies. Aficionados of the sport would drum me from their midst if they had seen me catching, releasing, catching, releasing, so many, so fast, without even pretense at style. I don't care. I'm in a water-altered state of consciousness. Nothing but flow and fish matter. For a nanosecond I think I might be lost forever, spotted not until spring, a jumble of bones and rod, dogs and smiles. I don't care. And then the sensation passes. Clouds cover the sun. The dogs begin to shiver.

On the trail back to camp, I ponder whether I've been catching the same uneducated fish time after time. I think not. These wiry cutthroat, each with a red slash at the corner of the mouth, range from fingerlings to whales topping 12 inches. The pools are alive with them, all innocent of predators, ravenous for anything that floats. I think of those puddles as history—a rapacious community of fish, all innocent of modern man, living in as dense as the ones known to exist back in the 1930s.

Breaking camp the next morning in rain, verging on snow, is painful. Larry says not a word, so intent is he in assembling the perfect dry load for each pack animal. I help but with little expertise, less enthusiasm. I stand propped against an aspen, hands plunged into the pockets of jeans, I watching this mountain man leave the valley in which he says all humans are but birds of passage. On the trail we lose sight of each other as clouds and drizzle envelop the trail. Chui stays a religious three feet to the rear of my horse. Duma is lost from view until we emerge, after four hours, at the end of the wilderness trail. Wet as an otter, she slumps on the ground next to Larry's horse trailer and falls asleep, in brilliant sun.

I have been thinking about all the ghosts, the hauntings that preceded our own. Spotting snow-fringed Mount Rae once again, I think: "You find a valley as beautiful as this and you stay. You dedicate your life to it. It consumes you. How can I inoculate myself against my passion for this place? If I left, I may as well lose an arm.

I wonder how others can be so different. Skookum Joe and Robert Huggins, unwittingly. For them, a place could be left as easily as it could be loved. They each saw the valley as purpose.

Larry, unsaddling his horse, doesn't need to look at me to guess what's on my mind. "I'll tell you what," he says, adjusting his big hat for shade. "We always think we're the first. But we never are. We keep returning and repeating. We always believe we're inventing something, the first time, but it's all reinvention. Throughout the world, there's only a handful of stories and we keep repeating them."

"Yeah. Me especially. I should know better, but I never do. I just keep repeating one mistake after another. Stupid dumb romantic: that's me."

"Hell, I'm the same. But I tell you what I've learned," Larry continues, wiping sweat from his chin. "It's a warning I heard it a long time ago, true then as it is today: 'Never fall in love with something that can't love you back.'"

We load the horses and the dogs and drive up the valley, home.

CHAPTER 11

Fathoming Cox

My trail now led to Stanley Cox, the pivotal name of Bar 20 history. He and his wife were the third recorded owners of this ranch, once it succeeded to private ownership following the federal government removal of the Crow Nation, its original owners. In spite of occasional refinancing, the Coxes held the deed to the Bar 20 from December 19, 1933, until they signed it over to Robert and Dorothy Huggins on August 14, 1951.

In our house, on our land, the Coxes weathered the Great Depression, a World War and, I suspect, a goodly share of personal tragedy—all of which they stoically endured without a murmur of public complaint, such was their way. The Coxes were not easy people. From my chats with Loren Brewer and Ken Presley, I learned both these men's fathers had been discomfited working for Stan and both had left his employ after an exchange of words. Few came to know the arch Mrs. Cox, although Chuck Reed remembered her as "a looker." What else could I fathom from the sparse oral history of the valley? One sunny afternoon, my eyes fell on an imperfection on the frame of my office door. I leaned over and saw minute, elegantly wrought initials, "SC." More than 50 years before, Stan Cox had stood exactly where I stood, studiously whittling his monogram. Perhaps he had believed these letters would serve as further claim to the land he expected to own forever. Or perhaps they were carved the day he lost the Bar 20—a letter in a bottle addressed to future inmates to explain that the hand carving these letters had once carved out this land. What had been on Stan Cox's mind when he stood here? How had he and his wife built this place? Why the Bar 20? And when finally they left, did they hold back tears or were they relieved?

Questions about the Cox's tenure at the Bar 20 haunted me to the exclusion of others. They were the fountainhead dreamers, risking, it seemed, everything to be here. They had sold their Eastern holdings to buy one of the most beautiful stock ranches in Montana, even though they had no practical experience running cattle or horses. They had persevered at this enterprise for 18 years, spinning setback as success and glorying in narrowly perceived triumphs. For me, their endeavor had been honorable, their failures memorable. In recalling their 18 years in the West, I kept returning to a popular Teddy Roosevelt quote:

> It is not the critic who counts; not the man who points out how the strong man stumbled or where the doer of deeds could have done them better. The credit belongs to the man who is actually in the arena, whose face is marred by dust and sweat and blood; who strives valiantly; who errs and comes short again and again; who knows the great enthusiasms, the great devotions; who spends himself in a worthy cause; who at the best, knows in the end the triumph of high achievement, and who at the worst, at least fails while daring greatly, so that his place shall never be with those timid souls who know neither victory nor defeat.

"There are a lot of unanswered questions I have about Stan Cox," Ken Presley said, on that sun-bleached Sunday when we first met at the Bar 20. A few days later on the phone he repeated the lament: "One question in particular: I'm baffled about the Grouse House. You see, not a year after the Coxes bought the Bar 20 they had some dealings with a Larz Anderson from

Cincinnati. As a result, he and his family were *given* a plot of land and on it he built Grouse Creek House or 'Grouse House,' as you call it. The Andersons lived there for a few years. They arrived in a big Auburn with their three kids, a black chauffeur, and his wife, the cook. Larz was very friendly, not nearly as standoffish as Stan. I remember him saying he should have bought Chrysler because it had taken an upturn. At the time I didn't know how a fellow could buy Chrysler.

"Then the Andersons packed up, never to return and Stan didn't talk about them ever again. I'm only curious now how those two fellows got together in the first place. I can't imagine Stan just gave Larz the land to build the house on. I can't work it out. Larz Anderson and Stan Cox were very different sorts. A damn strange deal from the start, and it evidently ended in failure."

In Livingston, John Fryer, owner of the bookstore, Sax and Fryer, also had a question. John's family have been selling literature to the scattered settlers of Park County for much of the 20th century. One day in the summer of 1995, I stopped by to see whether Stan Cox had been one of his clients. Always radiant with the pleasure of living in this generous community, Fryer fetched an album and then leaned over the well-rubbed oak counter to ponder my question. "The Coxes. Hard to forget. Very military bearing he had, and she always so well turned-out." John Fryer pointed out a photograph of Cox. Taken during the era when subjects rarely smiled, one suspects Stan had a flair for looking his best in the company of photographers. Hair meticulously parted, shadows emphasizing his cheekbones, commanding nose, showing fine breeding, he appears a matinee idol cowboy.

"Whew," I whistle, startled by his good looks.

"Mrs. Cox rarely came to town she was so terrified of travel on that muddy road. There was a story going around that once when she simply had to get to town, Stan had to throw a bag over her head so she couldn't see the precipices to either side of the road. Otherwise, she seemed to stay permanently at the Bar 20.

"I must have visited the Bar 20 a few times when I was kid. Once for sure." Fryer smiles. "I couldn't have been more than 12 and the house was dark and grand and pretty awesome. Never seen such a place in all my life. It made you want to lower your voice, out of respect. No sooner had I sat down on a couch, Mrs. Cox started in on me. You see, we country kids always wore jeans, which had brass studs in the rear. She was worried my studs would pop the buttons on her upholstered couch, so she ordered me to stay standing. That was a pretty terrifying moment for a kid like me.

"What I can't work out about Stan is the change. Before the War he was sort of a bantam. When he came back, all the stuffing had gone out of him. It was if he had had a nervous breakdown. Something snapped and I wish I knew more."

Late one September, I invited Sandra Cahill, her cousin, Alberta Francis, and Sandra's mother, Ginny Christenson for dinner beside a spitting fire. The Christensens have owned the 63 Ranch for over 70 years and they would know the Coxes. Mrs. Christensen arrived, leaning on both Sandra and a cane. Her hair had been frizzed for the evening, and she walked curled up like a leaf. She was quick to tell me she, like me, was an Easterner. In 1931, her parents gave her a trip out West when she graduated from Rosemary Hall boarding school. There, at a rodeo, she met Montana dude-rancher Paul Christensen. "It wasn't love at first sight, but it grew," she whispers to me over her tall glass of water. For two years she and Paul conducted their romance from a great distance. Once he rode 12 miles in the snow to place a telephone call to her at college, only to be told she was still asleep and couldn't come to the phone. In 1933 to the dismay of her family, the two were married. The marriage lasted for much of the 20th century. Now widowed and having ceded daily control of the dude ranch to her daughter, Sandra, Mrs. Christensen is retired from the daily chores of the ranch. When I helped the frail matriarch into a dining-room chair, I could feel her arm muscles, as hard as branding irons. Crumpled at the end of the table, sitting next to poker-straight Sandra, she said little, her eyes rubbering from one speaker to the next, watching the conversation as if it were a tennis match.

Even though the Coxes had been a generation Mrs. Christensen's senior, she had known them as virtual equals. I hoped for insights. At first it appeared no one understood the evening's rules of engagement, but when I began explaining how little I knew of the Coxes, how much I wanted to relive the life of this valley in the thirties and forties, the old woman began to nod, the cousins, first to laugh, then to spar.

It wasn't until after dinner, Mrs. Christensen cleared her voice and spoke. Her words seemed to be chosen with precision. "Stan's wife had a reputation of no matter what time you arrived at Bar 20 you would never be fed. The Coxes were different. She just wasn't very hospitable. Once when I arrived on horseback she said, "Oh, would you like a glass of water?" Nobody just offered you water. Mrs. Cox just didn't want you in her house. In fact, I don't remember anyone being invited into the Cox house. You had to be formally introduced. Western hospitality wasn't known to them."

Alberta added: "Mrs. Cox gardened with gloves. She was a Spring Byington-type—all fluttering hands and chiffon dresses."

Sandra interrupts: "Spring Byington? Was she out of the silent movies?"

"That's pretty low.... No, I think of Mrs. Cox with gloves and hat. And as for Stan, I thought he was pretty old. Everyone talked about him going to war and said he was too aged and shouldn't. But he did anyway and came back worst for wear.

"Wounded, was he? I just don't think he could have been that old. I thought he was about the most handsome man I'd ever met."

"You always liked older men."

"Now that's enough," interjects Alberta.

Soon the subject turns to a Canadian bull rider called Whirligig, who lived with a lonely widow in a nearby valley and "was a beautiful drunk." My Cox interview has been concluded.

Here in this valley, memories of this couple seem to be leaves blown by winds of chance, scattered across the ground randomly. I want the leaves back on the tree. So far, haphazard recollections would suggest the Coxes were Eastern patricians, uncomfortable even with the prospect of striking up a friendship with someone of their own milieu. The more the Coxes removed themselves from scrutiny, the more I became convinced they either disdained others or there was something to hide—perhaps a dirty little secret from their past. A childless, reasonably affluent couple who left their roots in the East to live like remittance people in a remote and hostile valley—it didn't hold together.

Just before leaving, the three ladies make a final point: "Don't forget that between the wars, this place in summer wasn't all that remote for Easterners." Mrs. Christensen had been tallying names: "In a 50-mile radius, I count at least 16 dude ranches." Alberta begins to list them: "the Link Bar, X Bar A, Aller's, Clydehurst, Hell's Canyon, Snowy Range, Bow and Arrow, Dot's Dot, OTO..." Her voice trails off. "Most of them are gone. The war killed them off. You see, dude-ranching isn't all that easy. That's what the Coxes found out the hard way."

"You're saying the Bar 20 became a dude ranch?" I ask, surprised.

Mrs. Christensen's eyes meet mine and she nods. "You bet."

So Stan and Mrs. (at that time I still didn't know her first name) Cox had had to make a life-style accommodation in order to hold on to this place. It must have been a comedown for the diffident Mrs. Cox to serve as innkeeper to strangers.

Helping Mrs. Christensen into the car, I begin to see these buildings in a new light. Strange that I discovered so late in the game the Bar 20 was once a dude ranch. What credentials did Stan have as a hotelier? How had they marketed this place? Did they stay here throughout winter?

A few weeks after meeting Mrs. Christensen, I received a large manila envelope from Connecticut. The lettering, round and clear, resembled the calligraphy in fashion during my grandmother's time. It began:

> A friend recently gave me the June 1992 House & Garden and I
> devoured your article that brought back memories of a month spent at
> the Bar 20 Ranch in October 1941. Now fifty-four years later I want to
> tell you about the couple who owned it & loved it then—Stanley and
> Lucille (Bab) Cox. He was a classmate & best friend of my stepfather,
> Francis Thorne (at Annapolis) & served in WWII as a Navy Com-
> mander...He died after being wounded which left him very frail, in the
> early sixties & they never went back to Montana after the War & moved
> to Virginia.
>
> We stayed in the Grouse Creek Cabin, which was wonderful then &
> spent the days riding, fishing & exploring, with one trip to Yellowstone
> where we stayed in Gardiner & drove through the Park after a snow-
> storm, the only 'people' & fresh animal tracks on the snow. Utter Joy!!
>
> I am sending all the memorabilia & you can keep it or not as I am 82
> & my heirs are really not interested, but I can remember when I was
> 28 (reverse?) & fell in love with Bar 20 & Montana. It is wonderful to
> know that it is loved again.
>
> Very sincerely, Hildegarde Hard

I was ecstatic with this windfall. My article, written and forgotten three
years before, had described my family's discovery of the West and my sister's
magpie approach to decorating. Fine—I had undertaken this assignment
with some equivocation, not certain I wanted my Montana life subject to
others' scrutiny. Now there wasn't any doubt I had done the correct thing,
the article having uncovered Mrs. Hard. She would be the first Cox "equal,"
to come my way.

Today, Mrs. Hildegarde Hard and I talk and correspond regularly. Always
high-spirited, perceptive, and candid, she continues to supply me with leads
in my search to fathom the Coxes. In unearthing her many memories of the

remarkable couple who once owned the Bar 20, she sees herself belonging more to the memories than to the present ("Had a bad case of the dizzies this morning.... It's embarrassing: I still have a rotary phone and no cable TV"). Once when I volunteered to drive over to see her, she called back to say: "I'm sorry, John. I really don't want to meet you. I'm a crotchety, rickety, old woman and I want you to think of me when I was out at the Bar 20. You're a kind of hero for me, and I don't want to spoil it.... I just wish I could see Montana now. I'll be 87 a week from yesterday and I don't know how long I'll be for the world.... Give my love to Montana."

I owe Hildegarde Hard so much. In her generous letter, written on pale blue stationery, this remarkable lady unwittingly allowed me to consider the congruity of lives. She led me to believe that Stan and Lucille Cox, for all their foibles, had a worthy dream that, who knows, might match my own. I answered: "I wish I had the means to repay you for your wonderfully munificent gesture. It is a rare and thrilling occurrence these days to witness truly spontaneous generosity...." Because of Mrs. Hard's inspiration in 1994, my research of the Cox Family began in earnest. It has led me to courthouses in Massachusetts, Montana, and Virginia. It has located Cox relatives in Texas, Colorado, Louisiana, Hawaii, France, and Georgia. I've even communicated with the Secretary of the Navy. The Cox search has been a notable journey for it has revealed candor and generosity of a high order, as well as bureaucratic reticence dazzling by its hardheadedness. The Cox name has taught me much about the laws governing the proprietorship of memory. A few times, I was chided for trespassing into other family's confidences. Mostly, I've been welcomed. When people are long dead, the laws of privacy often are waived and everyone joins in the search for truths common to every generation.

While Stanley Mirick Cox would fabricate another date of birth when he attempted to enlist in the U.S. Navy at the onset of World War II, it is undeniable he was born March 22, 1891, in Brooklyn, New York. Stanley belonged to a well-to-do family—his mother, Lauretta Mirick, the daughter of a prominent Brooklyn doctor; his father, having graduated with the class of 1885 from the Columbia School of Mines, the son of the general manager of the Spanish American Iron Company, based in Cuba. The Coxes would later have another son, Arthur (known to his three wives as "Bub"). In all letters written by Stan's father, there's little mention of work. It would seem from the slight record that Arthur Cox was consumed by friendships with the likes of artist Frederic Remington, family get-togethers, sports, and good times. It is possible family wealth, first accumulated by Stanley Cox's grandfather had begun to erode as early as the 1890s. But at the turn of the century in a time of plenty, there seemed little cause for concern. Jennings Cox, Stan's grandfather, proudly boasted that while in Cuba, he had invented the daiquiri (named after the town where he was based). Even as an elderly man, Stan's father, Arthur, continued singing with the Columbia College Glee Club and remained proud of his deep and resonant voice. As a young girl, Mrs. Hard recalls being brought to a New York concert, where she was enchanted by the sight of this old gentleman, the volume of his fine tenor voice. Arthur Cox's love for music passed to Stanley. So too his love for the sea.

Cox summers were almost a religious ritual. From June to September, the Coxes escaped the heat of New York for Bass Rock, a summer colony near Gloucester, Massachusetts. In photograph albums there appear a succession of rented houses on the water—one shingled with a large, lazy sun porch, another a mock-Tudor with a porte cochere and one decidedly distinct all-stone redoubt, crenelated in the style of a Scottish fortress. The interiors of these houses were wainscotted and paneled, the living rooms filled with portraits and photographs, bedrooms dominated by bright floral wallpaper.

In these photographs, Cox women, wearing long white dresses, stand apart while their men, in homburgs, dress shirts, and bow ties, mount and ride polo ponies into the surf. Cox boats at the turn of the century are mostly sailing vessels. Onboard the women, hooded by large hats, half stern, half coquette, sit in wicker chairs, soberly enjoying the salt air. In these albums there are occasional children—blurred streaks diving off docks into the cold North Atlantic.

Stanley makes his first appearance in one album, perhaps at age six, solemnly staring into the camera, dressed in tweed plus fours, tweed cap, and hugging a dog. Later he can be spotted playing in the surf, a frowning child, arms around other boys, all of them devoted to sport. Sometimes young Stan is seen included in shooting parties with cronies of his father's—an earnest boy, wedded to his gun, seemingly mute in the presence of so many grown-ups.

Central to Stan's boyhood was an act of uncommon heroism. He was never to forget the incident and, in fact, at the Bar 20, 39 years later, he would use it as evidence of his good character when applying to the U.S. Navy, begging their indulgence to overlook the statutory rule of age. The story is reported in the *New York Press* on October 31, 1903. Later the account would be picked up by the *Boston Record*, the *Brooklyn Eagle* and the *New York Sun*. Each told how young Stan Cox

was in the Bass River when he heard a scream for help, and saw a child struggling in the water. With the coolness of an old sailor he threw his boat up into the wind, leaped overboard and swam towards the sinking boy, and then dived after him. The river's current at that point was swift and running in eddies. When Stanley came to the surface with the limp figure he exerted all his strength to keep afloat, instead of breasting the current and reach the nearest point of land. The watch in the Life Saving Station saw the leap, set out in a boat and brought both boys ashore.

The boy who was saved from death was Frank Deveau, 8 years old. He was dead apparently, but prompt application of the 'rules to restore the apparently drowned,' brought him to. Cox was unconscious himself, but was revived first.

For his "courage and coolness," Stanley Cox was awarded a bronze medal by the Massachusetts Humane Society. Probably the most cherished accolade of all was a letter from his father, still revealing after all these years. It speaks to the Cox code of behavior and to the family talent for secrecy:

> My dear Son, You have done well and as I told you this morning I am proud of you. It's a grand thing to do a brave act and to do it quick and the stuff that a chap has in him that makes him go overboard to save another is the stuff that real men are made of. Live up to it always old fellow and don't talk much about it. Pop isn't saying very much about it either but you know he feels mighty glad you did it and you can bet he won't forget it. You're all right Stan. Affectionately Your Father Arthur M. Cox

Stan intended to preserve the newspaper cuttings and the letter of commendation from the Massachusetts Humane Society the rest of his life. Instead, they fell into someone else's hands, as a family touchstone.

Athletic, handsome, and already driven to keep his own counsel: these are the first impressions we gain of young Stanley Cox. His father's employment is unsteady at best—the perpetual shifting of jobs as a salesman, sometimes in manufacturing, otherwise in the textile industry. We already might be tempted to suspect Stan had established his personal code wherein honor and duty come before wage-earning. What appears to sustain the family style at the turn of the century—houses in both New York and New Rochelle, as well as the summer "cottage"—is the one-time hard work of Arthur Jennings Bryan, Stanley's grandfather. Otherwise, Arthur, now portly and balding, but with a finely trimmed mustache, is only an indifferent provider, happiest singing, playing cricket, and seeing friends. In a packet of Cox memorabilia was concealed a telling 1904 correspondence between the anglophile Arthur Cox and the Marquis of Dufferin and Ava, then British Foreign Minister. Apparently the Coxes had met his Lordship during an

American tour. To honor the occasion, Cox had commissioned a miniature portrait of the Marquis of Dufferin and Ava's wife. It's clear from correspondence, the Coxes were entertaining the notion of a grand tour of the continent and, indeed, in his response, his Lordship extended Cox an invitation to stay either in London or at Glandeboye, the ancestral Irish estate.

Arthur Cox had also met Dufferin and Ava's daughter, Flora, who, no doubt, had been impressed by the vision of Cox plenty. A few weeks after her return to London, she cabled him: "In great difficulties turn to you. Written today could you lend me 1200 pounds… Beg you keep matter Private, and no account, tell Papa dreadfully worried count on you help me will be forever grateful cable answer, Flora." There is no record of his response, but two weeks later came Flora's thank you: "Thanks letter you are a dear if you could manage 300 pounds would be sufficient, Flora."

Stanley, slight, athletic and dutiful, was sent to a private school in 1906. Pomfret had been founded 12 years before for the sons of wealthy Easterners. Here Stan excelled, and for the rest of his life, he would cherish his leather-bound album of days spent in redbrick Connecticut. Within, one sees him at his best rowing, playing baseball and football, shooting a rifle, posing solemnly with friends. Occasionally, there are aberrations of horseplay, but mostly one's impressed by Stan's soberness on the fields of play. Included is a photograph of Stan's room, with carefully rolled comforter overhung by a Yale pennant. While records do not exist to support this guess, it's fair to assume he also took an interest in the glee club and in art. Like his father, he, too, fancied the sound of his voice, not quite the classic tenor of his father's, but with more range. Stan also must have developed an interest in art, for during rough patches of his life he would attempt to sell his drawings, all maritime in nature—faithful and meticulous, if not inspired, renderings of tall ships—salt barks from Sicily, "toothpickers," schooners, and trawlers cluttering the Gloucester waterfront each summer.

Academically, however, Stanley Cox was no great shakes. In 1910, one year before graduation, he left Pomfret under a cloud, never to merit even a mention in his class yearbook. Was he kicked out on account of an incident or had his grades been deemed unacceptable? What had been his father's response? No records remain. We don't even know if Stan Cox earned a high school diploma.

All was not lost: from his Pomfret days, Stan salvaged a lifelong friendship with Francis Thorne. Thorne, another dropout, was Hildegarde Hard's stepfather and, without doubt, he remained close to Stan Cox, even when geography intervened. The two stayed in touch until the end, their friendship evolving from Pomfret to embrace adventures on the waters of Long Island Sound, autumns dedicated to waterfowling, careers in the Navy, evenings harmonizing, and, most memorable of all, evenings knocking back "tappies—" their term for cocktails.

Stan Cox would always claim he went to Amherst College, but as with other milestones of his life this, too, would be slightly misrepresented. Gerald M. Mager, Amherst's registrar reports: "Since Mr. Cox attended Amherst College for only the fall semester 1911, we have virtually no information about him. He was dropped from the college for poor scholarship." So ended Stanley Cox's academic career. From now onwards, he would quietly go his own way, rarely attempting to be first, camouflaging his past when necessary, studiously seeking financial security without the nuisance of a paying job.

At the age of 19, Stan was thrust on the labor market. Family friends secured him a position with Bonbright & Company of 25 Nassau Street in New York, and while he would variously describe himself as a cotton-yarn broker and stockbroker, he undoubtedly began in the lowest ranks of the firm. Photographs of him during this period would suggest him to be a bit of a dandy—with three-piece suit, gold watch fob, white panama hat, Malacca walking stick festooned with a gold handle. Work never interrupted Stan's summers idylls on the Massachusetts coast, and it was here, in Gloucester probably in 1912, he met Isabel Dean Hyde. The Hydes, from Philadelphia, were among the wealthiest members of this summer community. Isabel's hair was dark, and, in the few photographs remaining of her, she stands out as the most stylish of the women present. Her figure was trim, her hair raven black and very full. Occasionally she wears a large bonnet to disguise the still innocent features of her face. When she smiles she does so modestly. On a cold day in February 1913, the two were married quietly in her parent's house on Drexel Road in Overbrook, Philadelphia. He was 22, she 21, and, for the Coxes, at least, there's would be a very good match. Exactly one year and one month after the wedding, Isabel gave birth to a son, Edward Hyde Cox, in her family home in Pennsylvania. Of all photographs of Isabel, there is but one—taken before they were married—with her arms around Stan, while there are many of Stan embracing his other friends, all male—such was the time. Whenever Stan and Isabel are together, husband and wife are invariably separated by centerboards, horses, cars, and sandy beaches. Even more remarkable, among Stan's albums and personal effects, carried through two World Wars and from one home to another, until his death in Virginia, there is not one photograph of his son.

Soon Stan's position in New York evaporated and the young family moved into the Hydes' mansion outside of Philadelphia and, in summer, their cottage at Bass Rocks. In 1917, during the days of the American buildup to participation in the War, Stan Cox joined the Navy. He enrolled as a Lieutenant Junior Grade in the Naval Reserve Force, agreeing to serve for four years. In late June 1917 he took a ten-week crash course at the Naval Academy in Annapolis, Maryland. Even though he failed his navigation examination, he graduated and was later appointed ensign. Before the year was out, he had executed his oath of office, and at the beginning of 1918, was assigned duty onboard the U.S.S. *Sigourney* cruising the French coast. From Norway to the

Bay of Biscay, the 800,000-man U.S. Navy was mostly dedicated to convoy and antisubmarine activities.

Stan's active role was short-lived, and in July he was admitted to the U.S. Navy base hospital in Brest for an undisclosed condition. More than likely he suffered from severe seasickness. When, two weeks later, he was released for shore duty, there was yet another undisclosed lapse in his record. The commandant of the Third Naval District "ominously chastises him for non-performance of duty." In 1919, after the Peace Conference at Versailles had been convened, Stan returned home for a 15-day leave. By now he had seen his wife and child a total of seven days during the year and a half of his voluntary service in the Navy. Strangely, he spent the first seven days of this leave in New York with his mother and only the final eight days with his wife, son, and her family. On February 24, after less than two years of his four-year contract, he tendered his resignation, citing personal reasons: "I have a wife and child dependent upon me and it is extremely necessary that I get into business again...in order to avoid greater financial loss.... I have been been unable to give my business any attention since (being ordered to active duty). While he awaited a reply, he was assigned temporary duty on board the *Louisiana* in American waters. On the Fourth of July, his resignation was accepted by the Navy, and, immediately, he lit out for his in-laws' house at Bass Rocks, with no indication he had made any effort to find gainful employment. Two weeks later he wrote the Navy requesting information about the Naval Reserve Force and asking "what provision is there for promotion and confirmation of rank?" Such requests for acknowledgment of rank and service would become a fixation of the young naval officer.

When the Hydes returned to Philadelphia in October of that year, Stan, Isabel, and young Edward went with them, and for the next six months Stan continued to be casually employed by his father-in-law out of the house on Drexel Road. That year, 1919, was not a wholesome time to live in any large city. During the third week of October alone, 4,600 Philadelphians died of Spanish Influenza. The pandemic would account for the death of 500,000 Americans and, worldwide, some 22 million people. On February 14, 1920, after a short illness, Isabel Dean Hyde Cox, age 27, added her name to these statistics.

Stan remained with his in-laws and his son for about a month. During this period, there is no reference in all his correspondence of loss, nor the changed relationship with in-laws or even plans for the future of his son. Three weeks after Isabel's death, he was writing the Navy once again: "It is respectfully requested that I be sent a campaign medal as issued for the late war with Germany." One month later, now living at his mother's home in New York, he was turned down for duty in the Naval Reserve on grounds of debilitating seasickness and for his dereliction of duty while based in France. He prevailed and by the following year he was reinstated, his peccadilloes seemingly forgotten. Now he was Lieutenant Junior Grade in the Naval Reserve, a position that enabled him to collect a small stipend. The money would help even though he was again intermittently employed by Bonbright & Company in New York.

Two months after Isabel's death, Stan Cox had effectively relinquished his son to the care of the Hydes. While grounds for abandoning a six-year-old child seem inconceivable, we can speculate he justified his decision because, perhaps, he felt rejected by the Hydes, who clearly had never warmed to a man they regarded as a diffident provider, husband, and father. But formalized contempt would not have been enough to exile Stan permanently from the Hyde family. Something else was about to happen.

In the summer of 1920, Stan, without a comfortable place to stay at Bass Rocks, decided he would set out for the American West. He and his young brother Arthur took the Northern Pacific Railway as far as the town of Big Timber, Montana. Here he was met by a team of horses and was brought north into the Crazy Mountains to the K Bar L Dude Ranch, owned by Paul Van Cleve and his family. For nearly a month Stan rode horses through mountain meadows, fished glacier-fed creeks, and, in the evenings, sang popular songs for the entertainment of fellow dudes—one in particular. Her name was Lucille Reierson, traveling with her mother. Lucille, or "Bab" to her friends, was 24, petite enough to wear a size 6 dress, wealthy, and very unhappy. Two years before, she had terminated her education at Smith College to marry Bill Fay, a charming roguish man, a few years her senior and a Catholic. Fay's wandering ways had led to irreconcilable differences—enough to justify a divorce. While legal proceedings were under way, her mother decided to remove her from the family home in Bronxville, New York, to enjoy a change of scenery in the West.

The change was enormously successful and during the fall, on their return, Stan and Bab had begun to see each other on a regular basis. Lucille's father was Charles Reierson, managing director of the Remington Arms Company, which had enjoyed much prosperity during the Great War. Lucille had grown up in Texas, where her father was born, but, along with her mother, had moved East for his work. His roots proliferated through the South, especially in Louisiana and Mississippi. Lucille's mother, on the other hand, was the daughter of a Presbyterian minister from New York. From one, Lucille had inherited fine Southern manners and a sense of fun, from the other a severe code of conduct, reflected in the perfection of her attire and poise whenever she went out in public. Subsequent actions would thus suggest she might have been consumed less by propriety than by the semblance of propriety.

In 1923, dressed in a white gown shipped from France, Bab married Stan in Bronxville, New York. Shortly afterward they acquired land in Darien, Connecticut, so Stan could continue his work as a cotton-yarn broker, with Bonbright & Company in the city. The job didn't last, and, for reasons soon to be revealed, they decided a new landscape would help their lifestyle. They moved to Talbot County on the Eastern Shore of Maryland. Here Bab's father bought them Combesberry, a Georgian manor house. Built in 1730, it was surrounded by magnolias and willows and overlooked Island Creek. Here was the ultimate squire's home, and Stan accommodated himself to this role by supervising its restoration and the construction of a new wing, to include a library as well as sun porch, well situated for evening sundowners. Bab came into the marriage not only with support from a wealthy, doting father but, as an only child, with family antiques, all of them perfect for the genteel Maryland setting. Once again, Stan was near the sea, and now he owned his own sailing boat, perfect for excursions into Chesapeake Bay and for duck and goose shooting in the fall. It appeared that this naval veteran had finally found his niche.

For Bab, Stan was the ideal husband. Throughout her life it would be said, she always needed a man for protection. While she was capable of managing a house and a staff, she required a manly presence for support. That he be dependent on her for financial support, all the better. So dedicated was she to Stan that she forcefully exiled from their lives anyone even with even a remote claim to his affections. Whether he abdicated to her possessiveness willingly or not, we can't be sure. What is clear, Stan severed himself from all further relations with his mother and father, he destroyed photographs of Isabel, and he conclusively abandoned his son, Edward. Many years later a remote relative, attempting to understand the Cox family tree, telephoned Edward, the son, to ask about his father, now deceased. Edward had little to say. All he was willing to reveal were the circumstances of his only weekend at Combesberry where he, age 12, had been sent by his grandparents. While there, "he discovered Bab was ashamed of him. She and his father never took him to visit their friends. When they went out for cocktails, they left him at the house. They didn't want anyone to know he was Stan's son."

Stan never explained his behavior to anyone. In his will written in February 1931, shortly before he and Bab left for the West, he wrote: "I have made no provision for my son, Edward H. Cox, for the reasons that my said son is already well-provided for." Instead he directed: "I give, devise and bequeath (everything) to my wife, Lucille R. Cox, absolutely." His claims to the contrary, Stan's will was never revised between 1931 and his death in 1960. So final was Stan's abandonment of his son that in 1953 Edward directed his attorneys write the following letter to the Chief of Naval personnel: "A client of mine, Mr. Hyde Cox, of Manchester, Massachusetts, is the only son of Stanley Myrick Cox, who served in the United States Navy both in World War I and World War II. If the latter is living he would be the legal heir at law of his son if his son died now. However, the father and son have been estranged for many years because the mother died when Hyde Cox was an infant, and the father left this part of the country and went to live in the West...and has never shown any interest in his son by his first marriage, who was brought up and educated by his mother's parents.... It would be of interest to my client to know whether or not his father is still alive...."

The rejection must certainly have had a devastating effect on the young man. All his life, Edward Hyde Cox remained devoted to the memory of his grandmother, the woman who raised him. When her husband died, she moved in with Edward; together they lived on the Massachusetts coast where he looked after her until her death. Now, with a comfortable fortune, he spent the remainder of his life, a scholar of American literature and local history, a devotee of Mozart, a philanthropist, and, according to all "a very private person." Alone, unmarried, he lived all his days at his home, Crow Island, an imposing stone house on the edge of the Atlantic, not far from Bass Rocks, where his parents had first met. Around his home he built a wall and a gate. He was waited on by a butler and strangers were never welcome.

Throughout his life, which ended at age 84 in 1998, Edward Hyde Cox studiously avoided any public mention of his father. In 1999, his former caretaker, Scott Patterson, recalled only one conversation in which his boss revealed, when he was young, that he had had a few girlfriends. Generally, he explained, he was scared of women probably because of his "'stepmother's manipulation, control, and rejection.' As for his father he had nothing positive to say about him."

Edward Hyde Cox appointed his great friend, Edward Lathem, as executor of his estate. When interviewed, the courtly but chilly Lathem, emeritus Dean of Libraries at Dartmouth College, made it clear he would reveal nothing of Edward Hyde Cox's relationship with his father: "There was in Hyde a lack of association and concern for his father and, even dead, Hyde would not want to be drawn into a story about him."

The Coxes remained in Maryland for only eight years. Photographs from these days show Combesberry in every season—washed brick with sun porches to either side. Stan must have played polo for there are shots of him, handsomely attired in jodhpurs and polished boots, reclining on the front steps next to the fig tree. Most pictures are of Bab with her beloved Scotties. Even at the helm of a sailboat, she has her arm around a dog; and when she is photographed feeding them treats, she wears a white collar, a stick pin, and a string of pearls. Her cool eyes rarely look at the camera, and when she watches the dogs she appears all business.

The Coxes might well have owned Combesberry longer had it not been for the collapse of the financial markets at the end of the decade. By 1931, the unlimited resources of Mr. Reierson had now been tested and it seemed prudent, if the Coxes wished to maintain standards, for Stan to find a more substantial job other than raising backyard turkeys. Unfortunately, in neighboring towns there was no appropriate situation for someone of Stan's stature. Probably, the Coxes may also have felt their lives under the scrutiny of neighbors. Bab's natural reserve was now being tried on a daily basis, and soon members of the community began to feel the sting of her rejection. Those who came calling informally were turned away at the door. They might well have wondered whether this woman with the consciously genteel air was looking down on them. What right did she have to think she was from better stock?

There's another set of circumstances that might shed damning light on this period of the Coxes' life. During 1925, at the time of the Coxes' move to Maryland, the record of their lives is interrupted by a puzzling lapse. For about four months the Coxes removed themselves from their home in Connecticut and left no forwarding address. They might well have been engaged in house-hunting along the Eastern shore of Maryland. Or was there something else?

The hiatus could be explained by the testimony of a lady, now living in Georgia. For reasons that will become clear, I must change her real name and lend her the nom de plume of Alice. She is in her mid-70s, has enjoyed a wonderful married life, is proud of her children, now grown, and has recently retired from a long and successful career with the state of Georgia. She is admired for her organizational skills and, according to friends, is gracious and generous to a fault. Alice is also very curious about her birth.

Alice grew up near Gulfport, Mississippi, the daughter of a wine keg maker. When Alice was in the sixth grade, she learned from her mother, she had been adopted. Later when she became engaged, Alice's very secretive parents confided in her that her birth mother, a distant relative of her adoptive father's, had been from Texas, had gone to school in the East and wanted, above all, Alice not be brought up a Catholic. Alice assumed she had been born out of wedlock. She learned that a few days after birth, she was left with the King's Daughters and Sons Protestant Baby Boys Nursery in New Orleans, the first girl ever admitted. She stayed only a few days before being whisked away by her adoptive parents. The year was 1925 and the baby's Christian name was Lucille, while her biological parents' surname was obliterated from the records.

Many years later Alice's adoptive father told her he would never have adopted a child that wasn't kin. For Alice, these words were a hint. Indeed, when she conducted her research, she learned Lucille "Bab" Cox was a distant cousin of her adoptive father. Her adoptive mother later revealed, that her biological mother's husband had had a son from a previous marriage. Not long after giving Alice up for adoption, the couple then went to live in the West. They never attempted to visit the girl, but every few years the father of the biological mother, a prosperous man out of New York, would come calling. He rarely stayed long. He would sit in the corner of the parlor, she recalls, studying her. While she was never told the gentleman's name, she now believes him to fit the description of Charles Reierson.

"I am convinced beyond a shadow of a doubt," says Alice today, "Lucille Cox was my mother." Alice is petite like Bab, and, from photographs she has seen, she believes she shares her bone structure.

Throughout all her life Alice has accepted the circumstances of her birth, so grateful was she for the generous, kindly, and supportive couple who raised her. During this time, she condoned the necessity of her adoption—that she had been born out of wedlock to a woman who probably was in no position to give her the love and care of settled parents. "In those days, I'm sure illegitimacy was common, but raising an out-of-wedlock child would have brought great scandal upon the family. Everyone covered up such occurrences."

When I pointed out to Alice that in fact she must have been born at least a year after Stan and Lucille were married and that the two were hardly living from hand to mouth, she wrote me the following note: "It was a shock to me [when] you said Lucille and Stan Cox were married in 1923. We had supposed that their marriage occurred after my birth…. I wonder if even you know what that news did to me. Considering the times, I could understand that an unwed mother had to give up her baby and I could feel sympathy for her. I was happy with the parents I knew; never resented the circumstances. But married and financially stable, to give up, want no part of the child you bring into the world—that goes beyond my understanding."

Later I received a call from Alice's best friend who gave me her evaluation of the adoption: "I have a feeling there was an agreement that if Stanley gave up a child, Lucille was prepared to give one up too." For the Coxes, children would have been an interruption of the equanimity of their marriage. Bab had found in Stan a willing co-conspirator to her possessiveness, and Stan, indifferent at best to any relationship threatening to jeopardize his way of life, was willing to abdicate to her will. Without children, Stan could live the life of a retired naval officer–country squire, and she would command Stan's unequivocal attention.

The news of the adoption floored me as well. I had been conducting my research for one reason—to come to grips with the personalities and motivations of those who had proceeded me as owners of a stunning Montana property. Now I had uncovered a very private secret that, without me, might have been swallowed whole by the limbo of history. All of a sudden, I felt I knew more than I deserved. I was now a Peeping Tom, a voyeur, an eavesdropper, witnessing the calamities of long ago folly. Weakness and selfishness were items not on my agenda and yet, now, strangely and with some shame, I felt relief. I had always imagined Stan as a crack naval officer, a man of high moral fiber, someone who did the right thing. While he certainly possessed many commendable attributes, there were others that, at best, could only be described as murky. Because of these blemishes, I realized, to my surprise, I may have cracked the code—that I could begin to fathom the man who one day—maybe 50 years before—had carved those perfect but perilous initials—SC—on the frame of my office door.

For Stanley and Lucille "Bab" Cox, the exquisite Bar 20 was not providence, as it was for my family, but escape—a place where they could barricade themselves against the discomfiture of truth.

CHAPTER 12

The Middle Years

I
t may only be a coincidence, but at Combesberry there is a trapdoor beneath the staircase where the 18th-century pirate who built the house is said to have stashed his loot. When the Coxes designed the Bar 20, they installed a false bookshelf that serves as a concealed door, leading from the drawing room into the dining room. Later, when in the early 1950s the Coxes moved to Virginia, they copied this architectural device, fitting their final home with another trompe l'oeil, a mysteriously hinged bookshelf that becomes the entrance to their bedroom. The Coxes, it seems, judged subterfuge and disguise as their privilege. Keeping a secret—and they clearly had several—was for them next to godliness. Thus in Montana, with so negligible a population, they believed they would be in a promised land suited to their needs.

In 1932, the West Boulder Valley must have seemed perfect for concealment. There the Coxes were not the only ones with such a mission. When Mrs. Christensen visited me for dinner, she recalled: "In those days, these hills were full of old bachelors, just like Ted Koscinski, the Unabomber. There was one: Bill Smith he called himself. We called him 'Greasy Bill.' He was on the lam. They said he had murdered someone in a brawl in Buffalo, New York. After that, he moved to the loneliest cabin in this valley, changed his name, and tried to disappear from view. He was none too clean. Smelled like a wild animal, and folks said he dined on coyote. When he walked by, every dog in the country barked."

Both the Coxes had had a taste of the West at the K Bar L Ranch, where they met. Arthur or "Bub," Stan's younger brother who accompanied him on that trip, found it so captivating, he quit his job in New York. As soon as Bub returned to New York, he drove straight back, this time to Cody, Wyoming. Bud's 1924 photograph album, entitled "Danglin' In Wyoming," shows he spent most of the autumn and winter in the backcountry, hunting with buddies and one woman. Within a year he had bought a dude ranch near Cody, planning to dedicate himself to the outdoor life. No doubt, Stan and possibly Bab had accepted one of his invitations to visit. Over time they, too, fell for the romance of the West. The Rockies were far more compatible with their secretive ways in 1933, than a life being country swells on the socially active Eastern Shore of Maryland.

Stan prepared himself for life in Montana by reading every novel by Clarence Mulford, the creator of Hopalong Cassidy. So besotted was he by these yarns he decided to name the ranch Bab bought him after Hoppy's— the Bar 20. Later, Jess Gile, one of Stan's many managers at the Bar 20 grumpily recalled that everything Stan knew about cattle ranching, he'd learned "from a Will James novel and from the life of Hoppy."

While Stan was different from the garrulous and swaggering Bub, they did share at least one genetic instinct in common. In 1928 Bub married a witty New Yorker writer who he'd met at the Valley Ranch. In his wife, Haydie Yate's wonderful memoir of her years in Wyoming and Montana, *70 Miles from a Lemon*, written a decade later, she brought flair, dash and humor to what must have been a heart-wrenching time of her life:

> The stranger I had married was both a hunter and a dude-rancher. But the dude-ranch part of his activities fell to me. He concentrated, with

practically no breaks for refreshments, on hunting. From crag to crag among the mountains, he pursued wild animals throughout the autumn and early winter. Just what he was still hunting in spring and summer, I was never able to discover. Whatever the species of wild animal, nevertheless it kept him at the vanishing point almost perpetually.

After the first year or so, when I'd caught on to the rudiments of ranching, I didn't note the Nimrod's absence; for I was the mother of a most engaging and companionable baby son whose name and age, even his very existence, his remarkable father never seemed to remember.

'Who's that baby?' my elusive spouse would ask as he rode into the corral on a sweat-soaked horse and dashed into the saddle shop for more ammunition.

'That's Eames, our son,' I'd say.

'Oh, I thought his name was David—or Christopher—or Bunkie, or something. Well, so long, Kid.'

Not unexpectedly, the marriage didn't last. When a handsome man showed up in the corrals one day, Haydie married him. And when Bub discovered he possessed neither wife nor source of income to support the ranch, he sold it, found another wealthy woman called Belle, and bought yet another ranch, this one in Montana on the East Boulder River. Photographs of this period show him as a heftier version of Stan. Today neighbors still remember him as a heavy drinker whose problem became so serious that in the mid-thirties Stan would commit him to an institution. Naturally, not one word of these happenings is breathed in all of Stan's correspondence. In fact, visitors to the Bar 20 were never told Stan had a brother or that he lived but 14 miles away.

Bub and Belle (they called their place, *sigh*, the 2 B Ranch) could take credit for having introduced Stan and Bab to the West Boulder River and the place they would call home for next 18 years.

In September, 1932 her Texan grandmother wrote Bab. The elderly lady was clearly concerned:

Have just heard of your plan to leave sometime soon for the far west.... I feel I must get something off to you before you start. I'm truly sorry that your destination is so far away from home & family. But I'm not in for a long tirade, as I'm sure you both have given the matter serious consideration and decided on it as best. You two are those most interested, and must do what [you] can towards another start in life, under conditions & surroundings that appeal to you most. But I'm wondering about your Mother, Daddy too for that matter, how are they meeting this move? I'm almost sure you have by now a letter from Roy. Suspect he did or said everything possible on the subject. To use slang [he] "went up in the air" as soon as he heard of your decision. "Can't see why they will go to such a country, where they will freeze six months or more in the year when a country just as fine for sheep [is] so much nearer and only two or three months of winter"...I know in a way you regret leaving your first real home for you loved it. But in many ways you'll be glad when all is over and you are rid of such crowds to be entertained almost constantly.... With dear love to Stan and sincere wish for success. A heartfelt Godspeed to you both. Lovingly, Grandmother

One has to admire the Coxes for their courage in making such a sudden and decisive life-style change in middle age. In the West Boulder in winter, no neighbors would come calling. Staff would be difficult to find and those who were available would expect a measure of equality. They'd want to call Bab "Bab," Stan "Stan," not "Mrs. Cox" or "Lieutenant." Equally, Stan would have to learn to treat ranch hands as equals, not with patrician airs. In Montana, ranchers sharing the same valley are inclined to "neighbor"—that is trade work between themselves. He would have to learn to help others, swap tales, and tell "windies." It wouldn't be sufficient just quoting from Will James's novels. Stan Cox would have to develop his own Western narrative, one that could be understood by any cowhand living between Livingston and Big Timber. Stan had a long way to go.

It's a shame there are no letters of the Coxes' first years in the valley. John Hoiland, who today lives five miles away at the crossroads, remembers their ways. Ramrod straight, his face handsome for its economy, John has evolved into a local celebrity, playing the squeeze box in Chevy commercials and supplying the Dorothea Lange look for Bruce Weber photographs. John is the real thing. His father, Emanuel, came from Norway, age 23, and this only son has never lived outside of the valley in all his 73 years. He has also never married. He still farms with his father's implements and is devoted to all General Motor products, especially those manufactured before 1980.

When the name "Cox" is mentioned, the corners of John's eyes crinkle as he shakes his head with the pleasure of memory. He remembers every car they owned—a '32 Ford woody, which they exchanged for a '34 Ford woody, followed by a '41 Chevy station wagon. When John's memory explodes with facts, punctuation goes to hell: "Cox was nice as he could be. Awfully fussy about his firewood. Wanted straight kind of fir tree. Only the best. So Dad snaked out some wood for him. In return he'd bring up the mail for us and Cracker Jack for me, but he didn't care for stopping at our place since the gobbler got a little on the cranky order and chased him around the yard. Tough old turkey, both of them, then one day when Stan came out from Montgomery Wards he got a set of snow tires, but he forgot them and left his chains behind and we had a hell of a snow and when they went down toward the river, and just before the next raise, they got stuck and Dad had to pull them out from a snowbank the next morning."

It might as well have been yesterday. John's eyes twinkle for we both know only a fool would go out in winter without chains and snow tires.

In 1933, the Coxes paid $9,000 for the core 1,000 acres of land along the river—a bargain price even then for nearly two miles of good river and an adjacent forest of unlimited grazing. The balance of the land, summer pasture, Stan would buy separately. At the time of purchase, improvements included the old stagecoach barn, a horse barn, a chicken coop, and several cabins across the river. The ranch had once been known as the "Hough Place," but several decades before, the Houghs and their cattle left the country and they leased their land to Big Timber bankers who ran sheep. After a night of poker, one of them renamed the place the Rum Dum Sheep Outfit. "Nesters" or homesteaders who had lost their own land moved into the vacant house. The day they left a fire untended, a stove pipe burst into flames and the house burned to the ground. The year was 1931 and when the Coxes first settled here in 1933, the house site must have have appeared a forlorn place—just a foundation and ashes.

Stan got to work immediately, possibly even before the deed was signed. He found the best builders in the country—Don Hindman (who later worked for the Molesworth Furniture Company in Cody), Paul Christensen (Ginny's husband) and Paul's brother, Tork. The chimney, still sound to this day, would be built by another Norwegian, Tosti Stenberg. The team of carpenters felled lodgepole pines on the slope beneath the escarpment, skidded them down the hill in winter and then, after curing them for a few months, hoisted them into place with a horse and team. Ginny recalls Tork riding home one day. "He was a man of few words and in nods and mutters he told me Don Hindman hadn't cared for his work on one of the house corners, so Tork just up and left. They never worked together again."

The Coxes kept photographs. It appears the core house was built as soon as they arrived, again possibly before the deed was signed. It consisted of a large kitchen with pantry, a dining room that also served as living room and one large bedroom with adjoining bath. In one set of photographs, presumably taken by Stan, Bab is escorting several stylishly dressed ladies around the building site. One wears a rakish Austrian hunting hat and her coat is trimmed in silver fox. Bab, dressed for the West in jeans, carries a box of dog treats. Don Hindman remembers building the large extension—a room that would become the formal living room, as well as Stan's office, between 1933 and 1934. He spent the winter living on the site, setting the logs with his team of mules, raising a roof, and paneling the interior. For him, "Old Stan Cox" was a good enough fellow, but "talked a lot about the Navy."

Nineteen thirty-four would shake the Coxes. In later years, ranchers would refer to the decade as "The Dirty Thirties." By most standards, it began in 1934 when rains failed and the effect of the world's depressed markets began to erode the livelihood of even remote homesteaders all the way from Oklahoma to the Texas Panhandle. John Hoiland remembers 1934 as the year only cheatgrass grew. "And it got to sticking all over your legs." Unless you fed your cattle expensive supplements, they withered from a diet of weeds. Stan had promised his in-laws a windfall in the West. Instead, he inadvertently timed his arrival to an environmental calamity. The lush West Boulder Valley turned from green to brown. The river still flowed, but even in June when it regularly breaches its banks, the river was just a gentle trickle. Every day in summer the sun scorched meadows and neighbors called each other on the Forest Service party line to share worries about the imminence of forest fire.

Stan Cox had a scheme that didn't involve hitting up his in-laws, the Reiersons. He would encourage others to buy shares in the Bar 20. In return they'd be allowed a building site as well as access to the entire property. Proportionate with their interest, they could share in profits (if there were any) and losses (a certainty). Similar arrangements had been attempted at dude ranches like the HF Bar in Saddlestring, Wyoming. In time, the owners of the cabins lost interest and ownership of the buildings reverted to the rancher. What a wonderful way to enlarge the Bar 20 infrastructure. Stan knew just the right person to purchase such a share.

On the Eastern Shore, he had befriended Larz Anderson; and, while about ten years his junior and a bit of "an egghead," he thought him a decent enough chap. Over cocktails they talked of the West and Larz had expressed deep regret he had not chosen to settle in Jackson Hole, where, at a dude ranch in 1924 and 1925, he had enjoyed the happiest days of his life. Immediately Stan shot off a letter, telling of the paradise he and Bab had discovered in Montana and the opportunity awaiting any fortunate person with discretionary funds.

Twice a week for the next three weeks, Stan drove the dusty track, past the Hoilands' gaunt Herefords, along the overgrazed banks of the West Boulder, to the McLeod post office. There he checked for Larz's response and, at the general store, filled Bab's grocery list, which apart from flour, sugar, and the usuals also included a fresh supply of Cream of Kentucky bourbon. Chatting cordially with the locals, he would listen intently and tell them circumspectly about progress at the Bar 20. Since his big radio at the ranch wasn't adequate to pick up national news, he often sat a while to listen to the McLeod Store radio, to determine what was happening elsewhere. "I can remember Bab's telling my mother about their hundred head of livestock," recalls Happy Elges, John Hoiland's uncle, "And she replied: 'Dammit, Lucille, how can you say that? You know you've no more than a milk cow, some chickens, and a few broken-down saddle horses.'" Stan knew better than to boast about livestock among these second-generation ranchers. At the store, he was known for his careful silence.

Larz's reply to Stan has been lost from the records, but we know he agreed to Stan's proposition. He said he had always dreamed of the log house where he summered in Jackson Hole during the twenties. He had kept a photograph of it, and from it, he would draw up plans for a house on the Bar 20 Ranch. With luck, he would travel out by train, without his wife, Connie, for a quick selection of the site.

I spent a year attempting to locate a descendant of Larz Anderson. Apparently, he had been raised in Cincinnati. Assuming he might have named his son after himself, I searched social registers, the Internet, telephone directories for anyone with the common surname, Anderson, and unusual first name, Larz. Finally I located a Nils Anderson, living in Vero Beach. While he wasn't related to Larz, he knew the name and directed me to Moorhead Vermilye, the president of a bank in Easton, Talbot County, Maryland. Moorhead returned my call with the phone number of the man I was seeking: Larz's only living son, Larry Anderson, a school teacher in Texas.

Larry Anderson who had recently changed his name to Larz seemed puzzled by anyone interested in his father who had lived, he kept repeating "such a quiet life." Worn down by a career teaching humanities at St. Mark's, a private school in Houston, Larry and his wife now were counting the days to retirement in the mountains of North Carolina, not far from where his sister, Consi, now lived. He hadn't thought about Montana for a long time. "I was only a year or two old at the time." All he could remember was a snatch or two of infant moments—something about a snake—woven into a hearsay hodgepodge that made up family legend. Now Larz was no longer sure of the strands—whether they originated with him, someone else, or out of the myths of siblings.

"My parents didn't talk about their past lives." He believed his grandfather had been a Cincinnati lawyer who died when Larz, his father, was 16. "My Dad must have inherited from him, but we never talked about money." His father had gone to Harvard, but World War I had kept him from ever obtaining a degree. He worked briefly in a Colorado gold mine before buying Dorsey Farm on the Eastern Shore of Maryland. He would never work again. "He called himself a gentleman farmer," recalls Larz. "He was able to live a life of leisure. He did a lot of reading, and he dabbled in photography."

There is reason to believe Larz Anderson intended to raise silver fox at the Bar 20, but the plan came to nothing. Building occupied his mind for most of 1934, even though he remained back on the Eastern Shore. Logs were cut by Tosti Stenberg, Noah Ball (who went on to build a total of 56 cabins during a lifetime on the Boulder Rivers), skidded down the hill to the house site, which now had been cleared of glacier-strewn boulders by Emanuel

Hoiland and a team of horses. John remembers his father "having a devil of a time," since the boulders were enormous and only heroic efforts by the horses made progress possible. The Andersons would have enjoyed a cellar, but with only man and horsepower, such a luxury was out of the question. Stan Cox lent his woody to the roof-raising efforts. The car was jacked up, a belt attached to its drive shaft, and a band saw connected to the belt. In the spring and summer of 1934, logs were milled and laid out according to Larz Anderson's elaborate plans.

For many years Grouse House would be the most luxurious dwelling in the entire valley. It contained master bedroom, children's bedroom, another for the registered nurse, modern indoor plumbing, a dining room, kitchen, massive living room, and a sunny porch. In addition there was a separate cabin for more help, as well as a garage. The Anderson Cabin, as this cluster of buildings was then called, was laid out like a pavilion and its position on a windy slope was, for this epoch, revolutionary: the house had been sited for one purpose alone—to make the most of the view, perhaps the best in all the valley.

During the summer of 1935 and 1936, the Andersons occupied Larz's dream house. Connie Anderson, 13 years her husband's junior, was at best indifferent. While the Andersons had honeymooned in Jackson Hole, the West didn't hold the same attraction for her as it did for Larz. Housekeeping, even with Lottie and Edward, the black couple who drove the 1932 Auburn out West each June while the Andersons took the Northern Pacific, was a hassle. Proper grocery shopping could only be undertaken in Livingston—an outing that, even with a chauffeur, was a bother, requiring an arduous drive on a mountain trail, thus wasting almost an entire day. While young Ken Presley was hired jointly by the Coxes and the Andersons at $10 a month to do chores, there was never enough help.

Connie made the most of her time in the West Boulder, planting flowers in window boxes and looking after her three children when the nanny wanted time off. From photographs, Connie appears an attractive, sometimes stunning, woman, given to wearing tweed skirts, while her bespectacled husband wears jeans. Her children were also richly clothed—Little Larry in a sailor outfit and Consi in a set of angora chaps in the fashion of Annie Oakley. In one photograph Connie is seen sitting on a river boulder, West Boulder water swirling around her. In her wan look, there's a touch of the Greta Garbo—her face perhaps suggesting the appeal of loneliness yet the fear of being alone. In another shot, she is dressed exuberantly in polished cowboy boats and silver spurs. She holds a pan filled with native cutthroat trout caught by her or by Larz. She smiles defiantly, perhaps saying to the bemused photographer: "I caught these fish. Don't listen to Larz."

Nineteen twenty-six would be the Andersons' last year. Larz had wanted to stay year-round, but Connie knew there wasn't adequate schooling in the West for the children. Ken Presley remembers Larz as being "ignorant of all things Western but quick to admit it, unlike Stan Cox. Both the Andersons were a lot more outgoing than the Coxes. I liked Larz because he treated me as an equal.

"Connie wasn't enamored of that remote living with dirt-poor communication. She was a wonderfully attractive woman, but, in retrospect, she never seemed to be particularly thrilled to be in Montana."

That year the Andersons left the ranch early and stayed one week in Livingston, possibly at the stylish Murray Hotel, while the help were accommodated at Willow Park Camp, a motel, for only a day. The plan was for Edward and Lotti to set off immediately so the Andersons, traveling later in luxury on the Northern Pacific's North Coast Limited, might arrive in Maryland simultaneously. In a photograph, Larz poses outside Willow Park Camp with his staff. Smiling, Edward holds Consi, while Betty, the registered nurse, clutches Larry. In between, and very erect, stands Larz, dressed in a three-piece wool suit, his hands clasped behind him, his back arched.

"My father never returned to Montana, but he always kept a photograph of the view taken from the porch of the house. He had it blown up to four-by-six feet and it was in his study for many years.... I think he felt he had lost something in the West, but I'm not sure what it was. We never talked about the West, or much else, again. Then World War II came along and everything changed. My father sold Dorsey Farm and moved closer to town. At boarding school whenever my friends asked me what my father did, it was always difficult because he didn't do much of anything. His life was a bit of a mystery, and I didn't feel comfortable asking him about himself. I was almost embarrassed he didn't have an occupation.

"In 1973 a few years after my father died, my mother went back to the West Boulder for a last look. It was very important for her to be there once again. But the visit was all so strange for she was then clinically blind. She was led to the banks of the West Boulder River, her white cane in her hand, and there she stood and stood, taking it all in."

What is strangest to me is the discontinuity between the Coxes and the Andersons. When Larz and Connie were in residence at their home, there seemed little association between the two couples. Larz often crossed the river to watch horse activity at the corrals. One photograph shows him with one of Bab Cox's Norwich terriers. But no photograph exists of the Andersons and Coxes together in the same frame.

Once the Andersons left the Bar 20, the Coxes never mentioned their name again. Henceforth the building Larz had designed so lovingly would cease being called Anderson Cabin. Now, the Coxes renamed it Grouse Creek Cabin. Many years later, in our time, we would know it simply as Grouse House. At first Bab turned the house over to her parents, Mr. and Mrs. Charles Reierson. The beautiful pole and wicker furniture, leather couch and matching chairs, glass and parchment lamps, Larz had designed, stayed with the house. Ken Presley remembers Mr. Reierson as "a real Southern gentleman.... He once bought me a new fishing rod when mine broke."

It may be mean-spirited to suggest the Coxes now achieved what they had originally sought—financial assistance as well as a free guesthouse—

one that was gracious enough for their in-laws, prime backers of the great Montana adventure. Mrs. Reierson was inseparable from her one child and hardly a summer month passed when she didn't arrive on the Northern Pacific for a visit.

By 1936 Don Hindman had completed the addition of the extension to the main Bar 20 house for the Coxes. Now there was an ample drawing room as well as an office for Stan. How would he spend his time? I asked Ken Presley.

"He'd buzz around. Seemed to be busy. In winter he'd carry logs. He killed chickens, I suppose. He was a nice guy but totally inept on ranch matters. Stan hadn't a clue what was going on, but he never could get himself to ask questions of the people who knew the answers. I think both he and Mrs. Cox had previously only dealt with enlisted men.

"Anybody who bought cows in Texas to calve in February just wasn't a cattleman. Stan did just that. And he rode like a squaw on a buckboard. As the cowboys would say: 'There's them that fit in and them that don't.'

"Come to think of it, I never saw Mrs. Cox on a horse. Goddamn if I know what she'd do all day. Sometimes she'd get me by the ear. Take me to the old Hawkwood post office where all the Cox family furniture was stocked. She took out this antique table and I refinished it under her supervision. I did all the sanding—five layers, then Pratt and Lambert rubbing varnish. Each time with a finer grade of sandpaper. Finally pumice stone. I decided at a tender age that I would never again refinish antiques.

"Stan must have planted the garden. They grew carrots, lettuce, root vegetable, asparagus, peas, radishes, onions, corn, which wasn't too successful. I think we watered the garden out of that spring behind the house. Canadian thistles were rampant. I spent most of my time chomping them as she watched. "I don't think Mrs. Cox left the Bar 20 more than six times."

In time, Stan would install a generator at the Bar 20. Until then the ranch was without power. But the Coxes overcame the most onerous inconvenience of their gas-lit world by buying a Kelvinator refrigerator running on kerosene.

I asked Ken about it. "It was the first time I'd seen such a thing," he said. "The Coxes bought it so they could make ice for the highballs."

I spoke with Hazel Ewan, a spirited lady of age 83, now retired to Big Timber. I had been told the Ewans had preceded the Coxes, to the West Boulder Valley, having settled there as homesteaders in response to the Enlarged Homestead Act of 1909. In the Coxes' first years at the Bar 20 during the Depression, they would have ridden by it and remarked at its "simplicity." Amid considerable hardship, this rude set of buildings supported at the time a large and undemanding family. These days, unlike the Bar 20, the Ewan Place is just a few molding timbers. A passing horseman might not even notice it.

Hazel remains lively. She leads an energetic social life within the senior citizen community of Big Timber. Between her many engagements, she spared a moment to tell to me her mother had cooked for Mrs. Cox over several years, and she, Hazel, had often accompanied her on these visits to the Bar 20. The Coxes, she made clear, "Were 'Eastern people' and they had 'Eastern ways.' I only knew them as Mr. and Mrs. Cox. I never did hear my mother call her anything but Mrs. Cox."

I asked Hazel what she meant by "Eastern." "Well," she recalled, "they dressed for dinner. When Mr. Cox would come in from work, he would always wash up and put on clean clothes—not just work clothes, but clothes he'd like to wear on Sunday. Good clothes. And Mrs. Cox would put on one of her nice dresses and fix her hair. She would set the table with good china and crystal, even if just the two of them were alone eating dinner.

"Mrs. Cox had beautiful dresses. They were all the latest styles. She would order them in mail-order catalogs from back East. You see, during those times not many of us had clothes that came from a store. Most things were homemade. Mrs. Cox always looked like she had just stepped out of a fashion magazine, and she had lovely under things, as well. You know—panties and such. Mother would launder these because Mrs. Cox wouldn't trust them to anyone else. Mother was very meticulous, and Mrs. Cox was very particular about her clothes.

"My mother and Mrs. Cox exchanged favorite recipes. I still use Mrs. Cox's coleslaw dressing recipe. It's the best I ever tasted." With that, Hazel made me a copy from her recipe book:

3 tablespoons brown sugar,
1/4 teaspoon dry mustard,
1/2 cup of vinegar,
Sweet or sour cream ("I always use real farm cream. It doesn't taste the same with store-bought Half and Half.")
Mix first three ingredients and add enough cream to cover cabbage.

The year the Andersons left the house on the hill, never to return, so too did Earl Presley, Ken's father. Unlike the Andersons, Earl Presley entertained a few grievances. One involved a winter incident. During the epic February 1936, when the temperature never rose above zero, while Earl Presley struggled to keep the polled Hereford calves alive, Stan announced he and Mrs. Cox "were out of grub and short of whiskey," remembers Ken. "My Dad was designated to go over the hill to Mission Creek to resupply the Coxes' pantry. One pack horse was dedicated just to Cream of Kentucky Bourbon. When my Dad returned, he was not a happy camper.

"In the evening," recalls Ken, "after their cook had prepared dinner, those two would sit alone at their beautiful dining-room table, drinking from those thin goblets. And every night they went through one quart of Cream of Kentucky. At the end, Mrs. Cox's eyes would roll. I was 14 and I remember."

The Coxes left behind one photograph of the dining-room table set for dinner. In this rustic log room, the extravagance of the furnishings is arresting. A polished mahogany table is dominated by a white vase of delicate paper whites, ready to burst in bloom. The mantel glows with silver candelabra. The chairs, American Federal-style shield backs, are set in place. On the table: butter plates with molded butter patties, silver sugar and salt salvers, and a delicate silver bell to ring for the cook. As always, the table is set for two.

One afternoon in the summer of 1999, I decided to corroborate Ken Presley's memory. I took the Radio Shack metal detector to the back of the Bar 20 buildings, with the intent of conducting amateur archaeology. Laying the device close to the ground, I swept a wide swath of brush going from the cabin where long-ago cooks lived to our drainage ditch, excavated by the Huggins after the Coxes had departed the Bar 20. About 50 feet behind what once had been the cabin, the detector squealed. Everywhere I went the ground appeared alive with metal. In the end, I dug exactly where Ken Presley had said I would hit pay dirt.

Metal lay only half a foot from the surface, some of it astonishingly free of rust—an oil pan from a car, a pipe fitting. Most pieces were crushed beyond recognition. I imagined the drainage ditch had been excavated through the middle of the garbage pit, the rubbish thereupon reinterred to either side. I dug deeper. Soon I was into old cans—I suspected corned-beef hash—and what appeared to be the remains of a pickle jar. I began to wonder how I would ever distinguish one bottle from another if all labels, after 60 years, had perished. Then I found them—a bed of brown shards spreading to either side of my pit, mixed in with a broken door handle. Nothing was complete. I grabbed a pair of leather gloves from the house to look more closely, and, scratching in the dirt, I picked up one piece after another. All color of glass was jumbled together with brown appearing to be the Cox midden color of choice. Soon I spotted a glass bottle finger hold, the type still found on jugs. I continued my scratching until, at last, I located a large piece of glass, reasonably intact. I brushed off the dirt. While incomplete, still clearly visible were six raised letters: O F (space) K E N T.

I now feel eerie. Sitting in the old log house, the light fading, I am awash in images of Coxes, living not in the past but as my guests. I have told

Kathryn a lot about the two, about my recent discoveries with the shovel while she was away. "I felt unspeakably nosey," I explained, "rifling through their refuse. A scavenger—that's what I've become."

I had discovered the refuse of long-ago lives, and it had not buoyed my spirits.

At first Kath was puzzled by this monomania, which extended to ferreting through other peoples' garbage. She kept asking what it was about Cox ghosts that so captivated me. I never gave her much of an explanation, but soon, after more revelations began to emerge, she began to make sense of my fixation.

"In spite of everything, I still like them, the Coxes," I confessed one day. "I probably shouldn't be so forgiving, for all their failures—abandoning kids, boorishly living lives without reference to anyone else, but what the hell, everyone's free to do as they please and who am I to judge?

"Stan and Bab knew they needed something special to help them survive day to day. We all make decisions like that. For about 18 years, the Bar 20 was that special place. It saved their asses, and, most of all, their spirit. They needed this place a whole lot more than it needed them, but that's the way it always is, isn't it? Stan and Bab didn't murder, steal, or poison the river. They were secretive, they drank like horses, were standoffish and arrogant seigneurs, but so what? They were originals and that works for me."

Kathryn studies a photograph of Stan on a horse. "I just hope you don't turn out the same way."

"Me, too."

CHAPTER 13

Winter in the Bulls

L iving year round in the West Boulder Valley, cut off from other communities, would have been no mean feat. Winter, especially, would have tested the Coxes. With just a few hours of sunlight each day, whole weeks when the roads were blanketed in drifts, a drafty log house and numbingly repetitive chores—the Coxes must have relied heavily on their delight in each other's company, memories, books, and occasionally big band music played on a wind-up gramophone. In thinking about the price they paid for privacy, I recall a Montana winter of my own.

The year is 1979. Nearly a decade will pass before we acquire the Bar 20, some 150 miles to the west. For the last few months I have given up a life in the East to be at our ranch in the Bull Mountains. One day we'll build our own home here in a draw near an abandoned schoolhouse, but in the mean time, I camp in the spare room deep in the cellar of our manager's house.

Floyd Cowles, in his mid-60s, came with the ranch. All he claims to know of the world is cattle ranching ("Don't talk to me about sheep: I'll walk off this place so fast it'll make your head spin."). It has been his fate never to own his own operation but to spend a life ramrodding ranches for others. When we first met, he had been laid off from another job and was biding his time, caretaking this ramshackle operation until he could get back on his feet. When we acquired the ranch, he offered himself up as our manager. He appeared hard-working, knowledgeable, and already more informed than me of the ten rough sections of country that comprised our ranch. He even had a horse of his own. A cowboy of the old school—snap-button shirts and tobacco juice spilling from the edge of his mouth—Floyd Cowles seemed the classic cowboy to launch this dream of ours.

Floyd and his wife, Ruby, have never before had a "boss" who lived with them in their own house. This winter they'll have to endure my company—their first Easterner ("Furthest east I've ever been is Bismarck, North Dakota," Floyd once proudly told me). My aim is to serve as apprentice; from Floyd I hope to learn the ins and outs of the cattle business, the niceties of calving, maybe the truth of Montana's harsh winters. Along the way I hope to meet our neighbors, all two and three generation ranchers.

Prior to winter I had attended two schools. One was in Fort Collins, Colorado—a course in pregnancy testing, where I learned to palpate cows to determine whether or not they were worth keeping or selling.

The other was a New York City cooking school. This evening course seemed a sensible idea since I had already tasted Ruby's cuisine—unremitting steak and potatoes, both overcooked. I should never have bothered. Regularly at 5:30 each afternoon, Ruby would beat me to the kitchen, my offer of charbonnade a bierre with broccoli or coq au vin with leeks, all in vain. I may own the ranch, but Ruby commanded the stove. Now, the smell of fossilized rump steak would seep into every corner of Ruby's house. Meekly, I would await the clock to chime six times—the appointed hour for me to appear at the kitchen table, ready to bludgeon a side of beef.

I kept notes of these months—Floyd's mentorship, my awakenings, and the pleasures, doubts, and discoveries of a winter in Montana:

Many Montana ranchers chew a brand of tobacco called Old Copenhagen. They drop a thumbful of it behind their lips and then punctuate their conversations with gritty streams of spit. Copenhagen is symbol of the raw-boned life in the modern West, and it, along with the Tony Lama boots and the Stetson, is essential camouflage for the newcomer.

I'm not yet ready for Old Copenhagen, although I have plunged as deep as any neophyte should dare in the West. A cousin, my family, and I bought this working cattle ranch in the Bull Mountains last summer. We made our decision despite well-meaning counsel from fellow Easterners. Financially, I'm now about as deep in cattle manure as I can afford. Every month there are new demands on our strained budget, and according to the accountant, another two years must pass before the seesaw of expenses and income will settle into the horizontal.

Owning land, I've always felt, is *to belong;* and to work it, I hope, is *to become.* I wouldn't like to be thought an absentee landlord. I promised myself when we drafted the earnest-money payment that I'll get to know this rough-and-tumble place intimately.

We bought the ranch in August. It encompassed more than six thousand acres, most deeded. It possessed no attractive rivers or buildings to inflate the price. "Improvements" were careless and forlorn, surrounded by a laager of old car bodies. Since it hadn't been grazed in a year, the grass was high and endless. On the other hand, the fences, corrals, and barns needed immediate attention; and the hay meadows would have to be redeveloped. For a comparatively small dry-land ranch, the price was, as the real estate agent assured us, "realistic."

Talk about country both wild and productive, here was the place of my dreams. To the east: open meadows and high cliffs. In the middle choppy hills, studded with sandstone rimrock and stands of black and yellow pine. To the north, land so isolated it could only be reached on horseback. In a purple dusk I began to imagine Africa: a mule deer grazing a forest break became a bushbuck, the yip of a coyote at dawn, the cry of hyena. I studied the enormous tumbles of rock, reminding me of Serengeti kopjes, for signs of lions.

However exquisite the ranch, I at first, hesitated, to commit. Soon my intended partner, a second cousin once removed, agitated for a decision. "Let's strike," he said, "When the iron's hot." When I closed my eyes and forgot all risk, the iron seemed to sizzle. I kept my eyes closed, and with a sweep of the pen we bought the Bull Mountain Ranch, mortgage and all. Unexpected changes, I sensed, lay ahead for me. We decided he would look after the finances as long as I managed the cattle.

This new role meant, first, a change in patterns of speech. Born an Easterner, I would have to learn to say corral, not paddock; jog, not trot; outfit, not vehicle.

I'm not certain I ever really understood the Westerner. Binding oral contracts out here are said to be twice as good as those on paper. Still, every one of these cowboys, it seemed, loves a deal, especially at your expense. Robbery may be frowned upon, but getting the best of a sucker is an honored Montana sport. In the end, my neighbors seemed to combine horse sense and frontier courtesy in a precise formula, always to be cracked. Should I try to tinker with it, I suspected, all hell might break loose.

When the Cowleses came to work for us the day we signed the contract, I detected Floyd was nonplussed by the concept of self-promotion: "Will you need any extra help?" I asked, testing the waters.

"Naaah, any help I need, Ruby can do."

"How about if I signed on as your assistant from time to time? For unskilled labor, I give a good day's work. And I come cheap."

He studied me carefully, and, for a moment, I seriously wondered if he was going to decline the offer. Finally, begrudgingly, he mumbled, "Yaaah, OK." There's no doubt he considered himself my superior in cattle matters, as well he should. But it also appeared Floyd wanted to work solo, far from the boss. He was the sort who would have preferred if I'd told him: "Just call at the end of the year."

It's now autumn and my language has suffered a prairie change. Instead of "Yes" I have begun to say "You bet." Hereford no longer has the second e, and once I found myself improvising a Western metaphor to describe a multi-colored herd of cattle. I said, "Them cows resemble my grandmother's stew." A frightening notion, for my grandmother couldn't boil water.

November winds have plucked the last leaf from our three lone cotton-woods. I still ride bareheaded, contrary to Western custom. Nor do I have boots with pointed toes or ornate tool work; and when I yearn for tobacco my taste verges not on Copenhagen but on a brand called Walnut, packed into the bowl of a pipe. I'm not even a fledgling cowboy. Just a raw transplant, and as they might say of a dog, still to be blooded.

Winter in the Northern Rockies is the blooding time. What lies in store are four months that some will compare to the notorious winter of 1886-87 when almost all Montana cattle starved. Admittedly, during the intervening century, range management has improved and this winter's death loss will be negligible, thanks to fencing and supplemental feed. Still, the weather will humble us all.

Autumn is seductive. During October and part of November crested wheatgrass, undiscovered by the newly arrived cows, turns the color of a lion's mane. Clouds race above buttes, too preoccupied by flight to worry us. Small herds of antelope graze our meadow, lulled by the abundance of grass left fallow.

This November 9 the first snow falls. It settles heavily on the ground and even the next day, when the sun timidly reappears, mats of it cling to the ground. Two days later, more snow, and this time, goaded by a wind, it set-tles in drifts in the lee of rimrocks. Every morning after dawn, in the two highest sections where our heifers and cows are pastured, Floyd and I chop an inch and a half of ice from the water tanks. By November 16, Floyd notes, breathing heavily, the cows have a "'please don't snow look' in their eyes."

On an impulse, he decides to move them to lower pastures where grass is still visible above snow, rather than risk them in this remote locale. The next morning we saddle horses and drive our 117 cows and 37 heifers nearer to the ranch house. "Sometimes," Floyd notes, "You get a storm like this and a few weeks later the weather does a turnabout and again it's fall." But the snows continue and Thanksgiving is decidedly white.

The weather has come to dominate conversation. One evening, sitting around the kitchen table, Floyd rings one of his daughters and opens the conversation with "That horse of yours died of winterkill yet?" If November was bad, December is sure to be worse. All our ranch cleanup projects have been terminated. Our big hay shed, scheduled for completion in November, will now not be ready until April. All the neglect that had overtaken the ranch preceding our tenure will have to be stomached in favor of more pressing needs. Like hay.

Hay. The word now is uttered with a baleful sigh. In October Floyd had vowed that 80 tons (half a ton each cow) will see us through winter. "Last year was the first time I ever needed to feed a cow in this country more than half a ton. But last year—hell, you'll never see another winter like that again." By the end of November, thinking we might be acquiring more land and cattle, I purchase additional hay. While we never manage to strike a deal on the land, in December my misjudgment saves our cattle from starvation. Well, almost. In mid-January we begin hunting yet again for hay, this time at inflated prices. From November 16 until the end of March, our cattle will survive exclusively on purchased hay, inspite of our grass-rich meadows, useless beneath the snow. Had one blade of grass protruded, our cows might have come upon it, but for nearly five months our fortune in ungrazed land will remain hidden, while we pay over a dollar a bale for somebody else's industry. Throughout this winter I've vowed our foremost priority next summer will be development of hay meadows. Someday, I say to myself, we'll become self-sufficient.

By the beginning of January the drifts will bury a truck. Floyd has now admitted this winter to be as severe as last year's, possibly worse. Old-timers, interviewed by the Billings Gazette, claim that neither the winters of 1917-18 and 1935-36 had begun so early, nor had their blizzards been so persistent. For weeks the temperature hasn't risen above 20° F. On a few nights, it drops to minus 30° F. "Sometimes," Floyd deadpans, "You get a January thaw. But there again, it often doesn't get here until March."

I worry most whenever I'm away. How can a cow survive such cold when I'm not around? I ask myself idiotically. During January, film assignments had kept me in the East. The best I can do is call Floyd a few times each week. A steady hum on our connection is further evidence another blizzard separates me from Montana. "How're you doing?" I yell over interference.

"Fair to middlin'."

"Don't like the sound of that."

"Well, damn cows got into the pines and started eating needles. We had two, maybe four aborts. Hard to say."

I had been warned the greatest threat to winter calf crops can be the toxins in pine needles. No matter how well fed a cow she can't resist the allure of a pine tree browse. Pitch will cause her to abort the fetus.

"We got it under control now. Me and Ruby sawed off all the lower branches in the west pasture. Took us two days. The snow was up to our butts...."

We had purchased a total of 154 pregnant animals. Had we a perfect score, our calf crop will have been 154. I subtract four. Now the best we'll do is 150. An ominous premonition during our first year's operation, before one cow has calved.

A few days later when I telephone, Floyd dispenses with overtures about the weather.

"Started calving yesterday."

"That's three weeks too early."

"You're damn right, but that's the way it goes when you buy a bunch of someone else's cows."

Our herd, purchased in September from a rancher located in a more temperate corner of Montana, was guaranteed to calve in February. I had heard our neighboring Bull Mountain ranchers prefer their calves to drop during the more manageable weather of March and April. Our calves, two months early, would thus enter this world in time to be thrashed by the Northern Rockies' most extreme weather. What newborn can survive unremitting temperatures of minus 20°?

The news launched me towards Montana. I flew to Billings, hitched a ride from a friend to the ranch, and arrived there after dark.

Within our floodlit corrals, pods of cows are huddling for warmth, ice caked into their coats. Their backs are luminescent, their faces, streaked by icicles, clownish. Floyd and Ruby have just returned from one of their regular checks of the "heavies"—cows on the verge of calving. Our twelfth calf, just born, they carry, trembling and wet into the basement, and for the last two hours we have fed it a formula of colostrum from an old vitamin bottle. When, at last, it totters on twig legs to explore the room, skating across the tiled floor, Ruby declares it ready for the night and its mother, pacing by the gate of the corral.

For the next month our corrals are as intense as a municipal emergency room. Here Ruby and Floyd practice folk veterinary medicine—heavy on hunches, short on nomenclature. When a heifer ("damn bitch") tries to kill her calf, we adopt it and let it suckle it from a bottle. When an afterbirth remains lodged in the cow's uterus, we scare her in the steel "squeeze" so we can extract the blockage by hand. Another time, a cow's udder becomes gummed with caked milk; her calf might well have starved had I not been taught to massage her teats until milk flows. One day, Floyd's horse and mine, Minnesota Fats, fight. The outcome: an angry gash across Minnesota's shoulder. In the barn I hold the lantern while Floyd dresses the wound and, without anesthetic, binds the two slabs of flesh with stitches of monofilament taken from his fishing rod ("He'll have proud flesh the rest of his life").

When there's a breech birth, we pull the calf, with chains and harness, from the womb. During the entire winter the only bill we'll receive from the vet ("goddamn crook") is $2 for a bottle of scarlet oil.

Neither Ruby nor Floyd have been able to leave the ranch since early December. Their groceries were stockpiled in early fall, stored in the basement deep freeze. During our most apocalyptic weather, mail and newspapers arrive, with luck, once every two weeks. Over 90 percent of the ranch is snowbound, inaccessible even to a man on horseback (One day I saddle Minnesota for a visit to our future home site. Not halfway there, we turn back, the snow blowing over my saddle, Minnesota's head invisible under the snow). Our life is confined to a short radius extending a few hundred feet from the manager's house. Meanwhile, corrals, deep in manure, have become a feedlot. After we haul hay to the cattle at dawn, I pause to study the solemn Floyd as he appraises priorities: where to place this bunch of cows, ready to calve, where to locate those with calves at their side. I shadow him, opening and closing gates, pitchforking manure from sheds, learning how to spot incongruous behavior, making certain horses are ready at instant notice to be saddled for cattle cutting.

"The romance of the West," New York friends had suggested, trying to explain my exile in the Bull Mountains. They're sure winter will expose my fantasies.

Two years before when on my search for farm property, I had stopped on the roadside beside a New Hampshire dairy farm and asked the owner why he enjoyed doing what he did. "I guess," he said, removing his Caterpillar hat and scratching his bald head, "It's because I never grow tired of watching things grow."

Maybe one day I'll grow weary of big hats and the smell of saddle leather, but I doubt I'll ever become tired of birth, such as I witnessed on my second night, when a calf, its face still bloody from the womb, explored the darkness of the shed, searching for its mother's teat. For 15 minutes I watched this sub-zero dance, whispering, "To the right. No. Now back up. Cow, for God's sweet sake, don't kick, OK, now move in, little guy," until finally (no doubt because I willed it) the calf began jabbing fiercely. He had found the udder and I could hear him slurping colostrum, his foolproof indemnity against a short life.

On the third morning, a howling wind exposes the corpses of the unlucky. They appear where Floyd had discarded them—black legs akimbo in the snow. One lies in the woodpile behind the horse barn. Another, at the bottom of a coulee, gives our pickup enough footing to race up the incline. Coyotes have finished off the premature victims of the pine needles—as well as those, born far from the barn, dead from winter kill.

"Had a set of twins born two nights ago," Floyd remembers laconically. "Tiny little things the size of cats. When we found them in the morning, they were both froze tight." So it goes in February. Birth, I'm learning, is a lethal time to be a calf.

On very cold nights we pull on overshoes every three hours to check corrals. One time I join Floyd, and we come upon a calf's head and an afterbirth protruding helter-skelter from a cow. Heaving on the calf's chest, Floyd explains, "The cow's got to lick it off as soon as she can, but sometimes she doesn't get there in time." We hear an occasional sigh from the calf and then all sound ceases. Its lungs have collapsed.

For me each birth is one step in our slow march toward spring. Progress becomes an obsession with numbers. In one day we have six living calves—a proud leap forward, so I figure. But the morning of February 6, Floyd is poker-faced. After a painful silence, he mentions seeing one of our cows lying in the meadow, immobile. Ruby spotted it first and since there's nothing for us to do, they only mention the setback, already relegated to the scrapheap of history, after hotcakes and elk sausage. The death of a cow is more than simple subtraction, I agonize. It's trigonometry. "What killed her?"

"Hard to say," Floyd responds, his eyes staring out the window, following a scrub jay alighting on the fence. "Maybe heart attack, maybe a bad clump of hay."

"We'd better call the vet for an autopsy. Whatever she had might be contagious. What's to stop the whole herd from keeling over?"

Even before I have finished, I see Floyd disagrees. "Naaauh. That's usually not the way it goes. Hell, if we get the vet up here, I'll bet you a buck he'll say she had a piece of mold in her hay, and then he'll slap us with a bill for $50. That's all. Naaauh, I think we ought to leave it. There isn't a cow outfit in this country that doesn't lose a cow or two each winter...."

By mid-February, the epidemic of deaths I had predicted has never materialized. I still haven't worn my expensive cowboy hat and elk-skin boots. I must be a jumpsuit kind of guy. My drab-brown uniform works fine as protection against midnight cold, mud, and loose hay, even though Floyd disapproves. According to him, ranchers don't wear coveralls. "You look like one of them damn beet farmers," he tells me, trying to be helpful.

The infernal cowboy code, I think. Who cares as long as you're comfortable? Frankly, most of a cowboy's winter work is feeding his cattle—a numbingly boring task that bears little resemblance to the hallowed legends. The 70-pound bale of alfalfa, not the horse, is the true symbol of the Montana cowpuncher. Every morning, before anything else, we must load a ton of hay, bale by bale, onto the pickup, call the cattle with singsong *kabobs* and then scatter it in long snaking lines through the west pasture. Throughout, I stand precariously on ice-slick bales, cutting, kicking, stooping, kneeling until our load is gone and I've earned a welcome stretch of the back.

Floyd, who was born before the automobile reached the Dakotas, resents his dependence on the pickup. "Damn machines," he often mutters. He has his heart set on a team of mules that he promises will simplify our feeding operation. "We won't have to make a lot of unnecessary trips back and forth to the stacks. A wagon can carry up to 100 bales, and then if a guy gets a good team, he doesn't need an assistant to off-load. He ties up the reins, calls to his team to 'giddyap' or 'whoa' and throws off the bales himself. Makes a whole lot more sense."

It does make sense. On the six o'clock news, Energy Secretary James Schlesinger has just predicted a precipitous gasoline price increase by the end of the year. A team of mules might be the sensible strategy to cut our costs. So, the moment the weather breaks, I tell Floyd he is to drive to South Dakota to inspect a likely team of mules.

On the road up from town there is a dangerous corner known throughout the country as "Mildred's," named for a widow lady whose cow camp is set in the valley nearby. Everyone knows Mildred and treats her with respect. She goes her own way, talks her mind and nothing, not even the cantankerous cow that broke her shoulder and several ribs last year, can mellow her. On February 12 I knock at her door, ostensibly to inquire about a pony I bought from her son-in-law. "How're your calves doing?" she launches in.

"Pretty good for calves born in January," I say. "We've got some scours [intestinal infection], but I suspect we'll have that under control in a few days."

Before I can protest, she begins ferreting through the refrigerator, conveniently located dead center in her living room. "Got just the thing here," she says. She hands me a $2 packet of pills for the calves.

"Thanks, but I'm sure we've got these on the ranch."

"Take them. You'll never know when you'll need them next."

"Kind of awkward. I don't have any money on me."

She fixes me with plowshare eyes. "I don't know if back in the East you people think being neighborly is weird or something, but it's the way we do things around here."

Stung but refreshed, I soon discover myself using the word "neighbor" as a verb. When another neighbor, George Snider, deposits a posthole digger at our barn without being asked, I refer to his unsolicited loan as "neighboring."

When still another's car breaks down and he walks four miles through the night without bothering to wake us up for help, I am free to characterize his behavior as "unneighborly"—in fact, downright insulting.

I now begin to revel in chance encounters with neighbors. Two pickups stopping on a lonely road will initiate landmark friendships. So it is one cold Sunday when I spot Haven Marsh, our nearest neighbor, three miles distant. He is driving his tractor along our road, pulling his two young daughters, seated on trays, through the snow. When he sees me, he stops and instantly begins a singsong monologue that, in retrospect, becomes the sonnet of Montana. It is a free-flowing commentary on the pleasure of spotting a well-fed herd of mule deer on our mutual boundary, the mailman's conspicuous absence during these last two weeks of blizzards, the deplorable state of the economy if gas prices are to rise, and the certainty that Mildred, the purveyor of calf scour medication, has a boyfriend. Small talk admittedly, but in the end we assure each other that although the world might be going to hell, all is well in the Bull Mountains.

On February 16 Floyd and I count 60 calves. I am infatuated by the big red ones, but soon Floyd treats me to a lecture about the folly of animal attachments. There can't be room on a cattle ranch for sentimentality, he points out. Every creature born here has a dollar value, so it's best to imagine calves as bolts of cloth or cans of nails. Floyd's own dog is no pet. In fact, Beau has never seen the inside of Floyd and Ruby's house. He is merely one member of our production staff, trained to yap at the heels of truculent cows whenever they're driven to new pastures. When Beau's services are not required, he's expected to retire to his flimsy dog house, even as temperatures plunge to minus 30° F. Forever auditioning for human attention, only twice would I see Floyd pat him.

Even more bewildering, at first, is the constant stream of abuse Floyd would heap on the cattle. No doubt they're stubborn, stupid, even suicidal, but an occasional "How you're doing, old lady?" might have made everything right. Even the successful birth of a calf—for me a miracle—is for Floyd business as usual. As the calf stumbles toward its mother, Floyd mentally weighs it, judges its configuration, and then gives it a shove with his boot in the direction of the shed.

"Was working a bunch of cows east of here one winter," he recalls one evening at dinner. The memory has turned his face into a puckish smile. "We did our calving then just about anywhere we could, and one day I sees eight cows and calves lying up against some pines. Thought to myself I'd get them out of the wind the next day. That night the temperature dropped to minus 45° and in the morning when I rode out, they were still lying up in the same place, all of them froze solid." End of story. "Can I talk you out of them potatoes?"

As winter advances, I begin to understand more of Floyd. The old unlettered man and these truculent, mindless cattle have somehow formed a marriage contract so enduring it is no longer worthy of discussion. Only circuitously will he talk about the bond. "As a kid in Dakota," he recalls, the day after the frozen cow tale, as we ride along breaks, checking calves, "I had a chance to do a lot of jobs, but all I cared about was punching cows. Never made much money at it, either. But it's what I know and now I'm too damn old to do anything else." Floyd is slumped in the saddle, his earflaps pulled over the scars of long-ago frostbite. In this frozen face, the eyes dart like a youngster's. "Look at them little bastards," he says, pointing to a bunch of calves skittering through the snow. "Tell me if there's anything as pretty."

By the end of February, with calves now numbering 70, my stockpile of profanity for obstinate ones is rich and colorful. Temperatures have moderated slightly, rarely dropping below zero, and finally that much-touted thaw finally warms the Bulls. "Think I'll use the break in the weather to drive down to Rapid City for a look at that team," Floyd announces one evening. During his two-day absence, he will leave the calving to Ruby and me. "She knows as much as I do about calving. Only thing—she occasionally needs a husky fellow to pull a calf."

Within one hour of Floyd's departure, a mantle of cloud skulks over the hills. As Dunne Mountain disappears from view, the temperature tumbles. The morning was 40°; in two hours it will plunge to minus 12°, pasting the north side of corral posts white.

"Got a calf out in the pasture," Ruby mutters, peering through the kitchen window with binoculars. "We'd better be bringing him in or he'll freeze tight." I saddle Ruby's horse. Bundled against the cold like a 19th-century fur trader, she and the old paint plod into the drifts while I follow on foot.

Newborn calves often can be confused by a horse. They may try to suckle it and will wander in and out of its legs with impunity. Only a great horse will resist lashing out with his hoofs. So Ruby's job is to worry the cow toward the barn, while, flat-footed, I prod its calf through drifts, in the same direction. Nudging it only makes it more eager to suckle my jeans. It stumbles, falls, and then returns to the place of its birth. I run after it and repeat the process. At last, in frustration, I gather it up, lathered from the afterbirth, and the two of us flail through a coulee until it slithers from my arms. The cow, dazed by the wind and disoriented by the storm, now rushes back to reaffirm this spidery wet bundle in my arms is indeed hers. So we advance—20 feet forward, 10 back, while my ears, toes, and fingers slowly turn senseless.

This mindless advance toward the corrals tests my will as a rancher. When finally I drop the 70-pound package inside the calving shed, the blizzard has reduced visibility to 20 feet. For the next day we will relive January.

With their day's ration of hay buried from sight, the other "heavies" bunch up in a coulee, looking as joyless. We spend the balance of the morning shifting them on horse and by foot into corrals. When the last one slips inside, I close the gate with relief bordering on jubilation. For this one day, they may have to go without much feed, but at least all their newborns will be safe from weather.

Throughout the night, the storm sings through fence posts, while granules of snow thrash my window. I can hear Ruby's alarm distantly ringing every six hours, while mine chimes on the intervening three. When it does, I rise, throw on my jumpsuit, open the door into the wind, forgetting that condensation on my glasses will instantly freeze me blind. Steam from the cattle lies over the corrals, a weather system all its own. Their bodies, racked one against the other, resemble one solid organism. When I approach, one or two rise awkwardly, to watch me with dazed ennui.

On my midnight shift, I spot a round trace on a patch of ice. The calf is immobile. I carry it to the best accommodation the Bull Mountain Ranch can provide—a stall in the converted racehorse stable. Miraculously, I spot the calf's mother—the only one visibly agitated in our herd. "Damn bitch," I mutter amiably, mimicking Floyd. I hurry the cow into the warmth of the stall and stand, breathing heavily on frozen fingers, until I hear the slurp and grunt of a feeding calf.

By dawn our storm is in Nebraska, and the skies are clear. Floyd has returned with news we now own the finest team of mules in the state of Montana. Ruby, the "brains," and I, the alleged "brawn," show him our modest accomplishments, pointing out, especially, the new arrivals. Floyd says nothing. Just a nod, which today I suspect is high praise.

Now that March has arrived, the snow has turned to mud and our calf crop numbers 110, with another 30 still to go. If we are lucky we will have lost only 14 calves and one cow out of 154. The road to town is now totally impassable and at times the only way to move through the ranch is on our hay wagon, pulled by Jerry and Jim, our team of mules. Even I can tell the grass is beginning to "green up." At almost any time of the day my heart skips a beat at a sight of unimaginable beauty—cows, heads lowered, grazing for the first time in five months, on the bounty of the Bull Mountain Ranch. We have squeaked through winter with a gambler's margin—ten hay bales—enough to feed 40 cows for one day.

A melancholic and beautiful Connie Anderson, during one of the two summers she, her husband, and their children occupied the Grouse House, the homestead they built on the Bar 20 ranch. Shortly before she died she would return to the West Boulder River for one last look, even though she was clinically blind (LEFT). Stan Cox in yet another uniform on one of the few horses, according to Ken Presley, that didn't terrify him (BELOW).

Greasy Bill Smith, the purported murderer who spent his life hiding out in the West Boulder Valley, telling one of his many bear stories to Lucille Herbert at a rollicking post-World War II party that Stan and Bab Cox would probably have chosen not to attend (ABOVE). Guests in the West Boulder River during the Bar 20 heyday as a dude ranch, late 1930 (OPPOSITE, ABOVE). An unnamed friend of Stan and Bab Cox at one of the Bar 20's elegant dinners (OPPOSITE, BELOW).

Photos (both) courtesy of Jean Reirson. From the collection of John Heminway.

Hard-bitten dudes attending one of the regular Sunday rodeos at the Link Bar Ranch up the valley. Stan advertised these rodeos as a Bar 20 fixture (ABOVE). Bab Cox's menagerie at the Bar 20's screen door, still in use today (OPPOSITE, ABOVE). One of the many pictographs near the Bull Mountain Ranch. This narrative of combat was probably carved shortly after the arrival of the horse onto the Northern Plains around 1740 (OPPOSITE, BELOW).

Photo courtesy of Jean Reierson. From the collection of John Heminway.

Photo by John Heminway.

Photograph from private collection.

Photo by John Heminway.

Photo by John Heminway.

A Mountain Fastness: a 1905 Edward Curtis photograph showing Crow warriors in a river that might well be the West Boulder, a short distance from present-day Bar 20 (OPPOSITE, ABOVE). Bill Bryan, one of my companions in Yellowstone when the temperature was nearing minus 45° F (OPPOSITE, BELOW). The Grouse House view that first enchanted Larz Anderson, later Bob and Dorothy Huggins, Paul and Monica Payne, and now us (ABOVE).

Kathryn at home in Montana, not just in summer
(RIGHT). Register Rock: an 1891 Frederic Remington
that speaks about the bafflement, fear, and melancholy
of the Native American noting the relentless advance
of outsiders into the West (BELOW).

Photo by John Heminway.

Painting from private collection.

I tried some Copenhagen, and, after a walloping headache, I've decided to remain an Easterner. But yesterday when I ride my gelding to renew acquaintance with some of our northern sections of land, I notice I'm beginning to ride differently—seat glued to the saddle, slight slouch, reins in left hand, right arm hanging at my side. For much of the way I ride along the base of rimrocks, my eyes searching for deer in the pines, eagle pinpricks amid the clouds. All I find are fresh tracks of elk and bobcat, and the spring's first western meadowlark. It stands on a fence post and sings with the gusto of a rooster.

Freedom is not just about land and space but also about seasons. Today I think of all the simple things I discovered this winter and how they bond me irreversibly to Montana. My delight in good neighbors and fat calves is proof I'm in the business of letting things grow.

Spring is the only reward I will need.

CHAPTER 14

~

Wilderness, War, and Remembrance

While she rarely was observed in the company of a horse, Bab Cox loved animals. Apart from her pack of dogs, she also raised at least two orphaned antelope and one deer. A surviving photograph would suggest she fed them her dog's Milk Bones. It's possible the Coxes had been given these wild animals by one of their builders, Noah Ball, famous for his gentle way with animals. His most celebrated pet was a deer, "Bucky," which he raised from the time he discovered it as a fawn. Fully grown, it became so attached that when Noah lay sick in bed, the deer rapped on the door of his cabin, brushed past Noah's wife, Dimple, and lay his head on his master's chest "like a Labrador, until Noah convalesced."

Visitors to the Bar 20 all remember the Coxes' favorite antelope (also called Bucky). One photograph shows him alongside the dogs and a cat, waiting at the front door for admission. What became of Bucky was never recorded, but when we acquired the ranch there was a distinctive antelope horn and skull over the door to my office. Don Hindman, the furniture maker, saw it and confirmed it had indeed belonged to Bucky.

Bucky may have been one of the few wild animals a visitor to the valley would have seen in the 1930s. The homestead era had not been kind to wildlife. Most nesters, lacking income to buy groceries in town, relied on deer, elk, antelope, in fact anything that moved, for protein. For those struggling to stay alive through brutal winters, a wild animal was, simply, meat. Happy Elges, John Hoiland's uncle, remembers how in the 30s wildlife was almost invisible. "It was kind of a big deal if you saw a deer, say, in those days. Then late in the 30s the night hunters would come in after jackrabbits, with the rabbit buyers shipping them out of Livingston. They killed them off by the thousands." The last wolves had been extirpated from nearby Yellowstone National Park in the early 30s and at the same time throughout the Boulder valleys bounty hunters were using strychnine to kill mountain lions and coyotes.

In 1938, the Coxes were again feeling the pinch and, with help from a Mr. Brown of the Northern Pacific Railway, they published a brochure, advertising the Bar 20:

> Get any visitor's reaction to the West Boulder country of Montana. It has the real ranch atmosphere—cattle grazing in the valleys and on grassy slopes, pine forests stretching steeply up, impressive mountain peaks piercing heaven, crystal streams and waterfalls plunging downward towards the Yellowstone. Every summer nature adorns its with a myriad of flowers, berries and native shrubs.

Photographs of the ranch show a gracious Grouse Creek Cabin surrounded by dashing horsemen. "Mr. and Mrs. Stanley Cox" pose gallantly with their mounts; nothing would give away the lie that Mrs. Cox, in fetching hat, flowing kerchief, was anything but an accomplished equestrian. On the back side of the brochure Mrs. Cox reappears, this time cooking a steak on an open fire by the river as Bucky watches ("The pet antelope enjoys picnicking"). Just below, Stan, donning a cowboy hat, fishes the West Boulder for trout—a romantic figure who might have been a fitting subject for sporting artist, Ogden Pleissner. When I showed the photograph to Ken, he shook his head and said he had never seen Stan fish once during the two years he was at the Bar 20. Ken also bemoaned the sight of the cattle roundup and the boast that the Bar 20 maintained herds "numbering from 300 to 500 head and usually around 100 horses."

"That's b.s.," announced Ken. "Stan couldn't make it with cattle of his own, so he sold out his herd and leased the place to a Wisconsin fellow name of A. B. Dickenson, who ran his own cattle—at best, a mere one hundred head. What's more, Stan rarely kept more than 20 horses." In fear of further explosive revelations, I didn't dare show Ken another claim in the brochure:

> The proprietors of Bar 20, Mr. and Mrs. Stanley Cox, are still young people [in fact, 47 and 45]. They are easterners with long experience in practical ranch management (4 years) and have an understanding of people and living conditions elsewhere which contributes to their rating as excellent ranch host and hostess.

The Bar 20 was open from June 1 to October 15. Rates were $65 a week "with discount for long stays." A total of ten guests could be accommodated at one time. There is no record of how the Bar 20 business fared. One suspects that any high-end enterprise during the latter years of the Great Depression, at the onset of a World War might have been precarious, at best.

Still, the Coxes made much of their business. While they never promised their guests wildlife sightings, the Bar 20 possessed other attractions—the Fourth of July Livingston Roundup, for one, as well as once-a-week calf roping in August—actually not theirs, but up the valley at the Link Bar Ranch, a professional dude operation accommodating eight guests and staffed with seasoned guides for wilderness pack trips. The Link Bar was, by far, the more successful of the two operations, and, no doubt, Stan and Bab regularly encountered its contented guests. The Coxes must occasionally have longed to be with people of similar backgrounds or pedigree; it was said that whenever Stan spotted someone who appeared suitable, Stan often offered them a Bar 20 dinner invitation.

One set of guests who would have seemed eminently suitable were Charles and Lucille Herbert. "Charlie" was a famed filmmaker for Movietone News. Except during a month in summer, the Herberts traveled extensively on foreign assignments. After a stay at the Link Bar in 1935, like others, they fell for the valley. Harry Kaufman, a dedicated district ranger of the U.S. Forest Service, helped them secure a long lease on a small holding of government land, adjacent to the Link Bar. On it, in 1936, the West Boulder's acclaimed carpenter, Tosti Stenberg, built them a cabin (the one that I viewed, riding Dewey and encountering a bear)—a stylish rustic house, featuring logs with sculpted butt ends, horn door handles, and a high, peaked living-room ceiling.

In the valley, the Herberts were always active—making films of ranch activities, documenting the work of forest rangers, taking publicity stills for their neighbors. Once the Herberts hosted a Chinese general for several weeks at their house. There would be many others—all a rich mix of friendships made during their world travels. In the valley, the Herberts were all-embracing. They often entertained Greasy Bill Smith, the West Boulder's notorious fugitive from justice ("Before dinner Lucille Herbert would often dangle his overalls in the river to loosen the soil"). During winters, Greasy Bill occupied one of the Herbert cabins, as caretaker, and, in time, he would figure in many Herbert photographs of the valley. Some of these would suggest lively parties, extravagant merriment with Greasy Bill, designated teller of tall tales, the life of the party.

Did the Coxes ever attend Herbert parties? The record goes particularly quiet on this point. The Herberts' arrival in the valley coincides with Stan Cox's membership in the Freelance Photographers Guild. One wonders whether Stan was encouraged to join by a mentoring Charlie Herbert or whether Stan simply observed Charlie at work and thought he could do the same. Nonetheless, it's unlikely the Coxes would ever have warmed to the society of Greasy Bill or even the free-spirited Herberts, who lived lives without walls. Betty Ball, Harry Kaufman's daughter, recalls: "The Coxes didn't know much about country life. They were standoffish. Both he and his wife were not too neighborly and didn't associate with the people of the country. They might have felt they didn't fit in."

In October 1941 Hildegarde Hard visited the Bar 20 as a guest. Her stepfather, Francis Thorne, Sr., an old friend of Stan's, had responded to news that the Bar 20 dude ranch was in distress and that the Coxes needed support. While the United States had not officially entered the War, many able-bodied men had already enlisted or were waiting to be called up. The middle-aged Francis, Stan's fellow veteran from the Great War, thought he might respond to Stan's muted cry for help by performing several good deeds together—aid his old friend by supplying paying guests while looking after his step-daughters, whose husbands were in uniforms overseas. Clearly the Cox-Thorne friendship reached back to free-spirited days when they were unencumbered by marriage. It was a time when men never addressed friends by real names. Stan knew Thorne only as "Pops" or "Bilge Rat," Julia, Hildegarde's sister was called "Dee" and Hildegarde was "Babs."

This party of three stayed one month. Staying at the Bar 20 was a spectacular escape from their concerns at home. Stan looked after them exceedingly well, and when he wasn't up to one of their energetic rides, he left them in the capable hands of his dude wrangler, Ed Weber (who, recalls Babs Hard, "my sister fell flat for...but when he took his hat off, he didn't have a stick of hair."). They rode every day—Dee on "Sundance" and "Sunny," Pops on "Little Dog." They witnessed the Bar 20's first autumn snowfall, and, with Stan, they enjoyed a road trip to the national park: "On the way to Yellowstone in the old station wagon," recalls Babs Hard, "Stan had a guitar. My

sister had a voice, as did I. There was always music in Stan's life and his voice was beautiful. We sang all the way and I can remember the words to every song. 'Moonlight in Kahlua' was one.

"I can recall sitting in the car in Livingston, waiting for Stan to finish his shopping in the bottle store. I looked at the mountains and I began to hum 'America the Beautiful.'"

Bab Cox never accompanied the others when they went to Yellowstone. In fact, she had as little to do with the girls as was possible, never riding with them, only occasionally visiting Grouse Creek Cabin, even when Stan lingered over evening cocktails ("That generation called them 'tappies,'" remembers Babs Hard) with his old friend, Francis Thorne.

"Bab was a green-eyed monster," explains Mrs. Hard. "She always was very jealous—jealous, even, of my mother. You see, in Connecticut, years before, when I was about ten, Stan used to come down to see my stepfather. He was a bachelor and it was all great fun. I used to ride around on Stan's shoulders; he was my horse. But that all stopped when he married Lucille Fay. I think Bab Cox was a nasty, jealous woman—jealous of anything female."

Later in life, after the Coxes left the Bar 20, Virginia friends remembered Bab as "nettlesome, waspish, hoity toity, uppity—that sort of thing. She always thought she was better than everyone else. That's why the Coxes had so few friends."

"When we stayed at Grouse Creek Cabin," remembers Babs Hard, "She never once invited us into her house. Still, I remember liking her very much. I was brought up to like people. That was my parent's way. If you found they weren't so great afterward, you simply paid no attention. Of course we didn't see too much of her."

Within a few days of the Thorne party's departure for the east, letters and cards from the Coxes began arriving at the Hards' house in Bay Shore, Long Island. "Miss you like the devil," wrote Stan on November 4, 1941. When Babs sent Stan some photographs, he thanked her and replied: "Never expect to hear from that Bilge Rat ever again after the indignities I and 'Little Dog' subjected him to." He added: "Wish I could really have talked with you over the telephone."

Unaccountably, on the same day Stan wrote, so too did Bab. "What is so remarkable," recalls Babs Hard, now nearly 60 years later, "is her sweetness when she wrote me letters. Hard to imagine. In person she was perfectly nasty."

Bab Cox began: "Sister dear, Your [thank you] letter touched my heart very deeply. What a darling you are and to have found you, again, all grown up, married and the mother of two boys, still the sister that I loved as a child, only sweeter somehow, is a wonderful thing to me. I mean that, every word and I hope you know it." The letter ends on a note that is both preposterous and painful: "Don't forget you and Dee are partly my children, will you? I wish you were both walking in the door this minute. Ever so much love from us both."

In between, Bab thanks Babs for presents and reports on ranch doings: "Our joy in having those records was great. I like every single one of them, but some, in particular: the Duchin, the Brahms lullaby and...the Bing Crosby 'You and I...' Clora (the cook) had a heart interest coming home on furlough and told Elinor (the Grouse Creek Cabin maid) that she wanted to leave the first week in November. It seemed simpler to move Elinor down to our guest cabin than anything else.... But night before last neither Elinor nor Clora took the weather into account, had practically no fires all day, both being away, and lighted only tiny ones that night. They chose the coldest night we have had and pipes being merely pipes, two froze...."

It's clear Stan Cox has become restless with his life at the Bar 20. Quite possibly, the visit of three old friends had opened a void in his life. Suddenly, he might have realized he was cut off from equals, in bondage to a wealthy, controlling woman. Needy for recognition but compulsive about privacy, Stan Cox must have felt secluded at the Bar 20, even oppressed by Bab's possessiveness. He could never have missed noticing how others treated the two of them with kid gloves. Even during his month visit, Bilge Rat never dared mention, chum to chum, the changes he had spotted in Stan since marriage to Bab. Stan, in turn, couldn't have been blind to his friend's forced politeness or to the girls' careful avoidance of all things Bab. While Stan would never challenge the comfortable equanimity of marriage to a woman who looked after his every need, he must have winced from time to time at Bab's instinct for exclusion, at her distrust of equals, at the distance she kept, especially from other women.

In his first note to Babs Hard, Stan spoke of his yearning to leave: "Just put in another application for active duty." In another, he says, in Will James jargon: "It's certainly hard to be way out here fooling with a lot of white faced doggies and wondering how in hell to get back in the Navy."

In March 1942, even Bab had come to understand Stan's malaise. In her rambling letter, she wrote: "Stan made a model sub chaser and I think did a wonderful job…and now he is working on a model whale boat and it's a beauty…. Everyone is in something or other and each mail brings the news of someone else. In a way, I dread those mails, too. Stan got awfully depressed in the middle of the winter, simply frantic because he was not being recalled, and it all made me as miserable as it made him…. 'Blues in the Night' fascinates me and I listen to anyone and everyone singing it over the radio. I thought Bing sang it better than anyone until we heard Kate Smith, and she managed to get more of the Negro tone in it, more of the rhythm than Bing. You know that 'clickety clack' in 'Blues in the Night'? Each time we hear that part we laugh, because in Maryland we had a darky who spoke of rabbits running 'lippity lop' and that was as descriptive as the clickety clack. No one but a darky could think up such a phrase…. Ordering clothes long distance is dreadful. In some Vogue I saw a green tweed suit with something in Chartreuse—blouse or sweater I think and thought of you with your hair…. With snow still scattered in blotches on the mountain sides, and very deep on the ground, I am deep in flower and vegetable catalogues…. In a way it seems so silly to plan for months ahead and yet, it's nice to be able to forget that the world is in this state, even for a little while, and concentrate upon how much asparagus you are going to have this year and the new varieties of flowers you are going to try. If only I had six children to plan for and think about, that would be a help...."

Beginning in October 1940, Stanley Cox set about to be called up for active military duty. There's no doubt, he was fiercely patriotic—from political clippings in his album, one might suspect his patriotism was of 19th-century vintage. And after the Japanese bombing of Pearl Harbor in December 1941, his resolve to serve his nation became even fiercer. Over serious naval objections to his qualification, these efforts were determined, tenacious, relentless, even to the point of flagrant dishonesty.

In his first application, he claimed he had completed two years at Amherst College, he spoke of "30 years experience in yachts and fishermen, coastwise and deep water," listed his four references as Francis Thorne of New York, as well as the owner of a hardware company, plumbing company, and grocery store, all of them located in Livingston, Montana. Suddenly his date of birth appeared as March 22, 1894—three years distant from the truth.

Cox even arranged for Senator Millard Tydings, presumably an acquaintance from Maryland, to send Rear Admiral Chester Nimitz an appeal to consider his candidacy in the Navy. Stan's campaign included a trip East to visit his mother, who he had not seen in over five years. Now living at Bass Rock, Massachusetts, age 77, Lauretta Cox was not in good health and one can only imagine the awkwardness of the meeting, since Stan had washed his hands of his family after marrying Bab. He wrote of this meeting: "I found her in a state of great mental confusion due to illness, the shock of my father's death [Stan hadn't attended his funeral two years before] and, I suppose, old age." Stan had orchestrated this mother-son reconciliation for one purpose: to obtain his mother's compliance with a new date-of-birth record, not 1891—the date, until now,

Stan had consistently used—but 1894—the year that would conveniently allow him to comply with naval age requirements. Stan was successful. He obtained from his mother, suffering from severe dementia, a sworn affidavit saying he was born in 1894. He also secured another affidavit from his surviving uncle, William Cox of Sag Harbor, Long Island, to support the erroneous date of birth.

Handwritten naval comments on Stan Cox's 1941 application notes: "obvious alteration of age...You may desire to overlook but I recommend he be challenged. He is apparently 50 years old but wants to be only 47." On Stan's physical report, conducted in Seattle, Washington, in February 1941, the doctor notes 12 missing teeth and both a captain and a commander "certify that he is not physically qualified for appointment."

Stan would not be deterred. While he would accept a commission in the Army or Marine Corps, the U.S. Navy was his first choice. In time, the intervention of Rear Admiral Nimitz was effective, because by 1942, handwritten records suggest the Navy was willing to forgive inconsistencies in the Cox record. "With his experience, believe services could be used to advantage at this time," a nameless officer writes in longhand.

Spring had been difficult at the Bar 20. A blizzard had blown through on May 11 and many of Bab's early seedlings had frozen. "Our calves," reported Stan, one day before the storm, reverting to his Will James voice, "are giving us hell now days trying to find all the larkspur, camas, lupine, and what have you that will poison them. We have lost two and nothing but lots of hard riding keeps the rest from becoming little calf angels."

On the Fourth of July 1942, Frank Knox, Secretary of the Navy appointed Stanley Myrick Cox a lieutenant commander in the U.S. Naval Reserve. "Dear Sister," Stan writes Babs Hard on July 26, 1942, "From now on if and when I can write, you will probably not be getting much news about the spot where the deer and the antelope play.... My orders to the Pacific Coast will be on their way in a few days. Well—as the guy says, that kind of cooks it. I would not take anything on earth for the chance to get back and maybe snare me a Jap or two.... Lord how glad I am, in view of the future and all that it may hold, that we had last summer. It's going to be something to look forward to doing again and now I never go over the divide to town without remembering the day we started to the Park."

By August, with the river just beginning to clear up after torrential June rains, Stan was ready to leave for active duty. On August 10, he posed outside the Bar 20. Dressed in the uniform of a lieutenant commander, 51 years old, 5 foot 8 and a half inches tall, weighing 140 pounds, his dentures, replacing 12 missing teeth on the right side of his jaw, artfully concealed, he is an altogether impressive figure. He holds his pipe and stands before the old woody in which Jess Gile, his manager, and Lucille Pearson, the cook, would soon drive him to the Livingston Depot. His jaunty smile would suggest joy his two-year dream had at last been realized. If there is sadness at parting, it is thoroughly disguised.

One must be awed by Stan Cox, at this threshold of life. Now he will be able to prove his mettle, to overcome the stigma of a rich wife and life of ease. Until now he may have suspected others sometimes wrote him off as "an inconsequential chap," "nice enough fellow but never did much with what he had." Now he could reverse those jibes. The U.S. Navy during a world-threatening engagement would be his final opportunity. If ever Stan awoke at a lonely three in the morning, kept from sleep by memory—two children cavalierly abandoned, a life of indecisive careers—he might have concluded one shot at valor, like the long-ago saving of a drowning boy, would be his final chance at redemption.

Perhaps Stan's wan smile may also be credited to anticipation of release from smothering routine and a possessive wife. His new life—formal, regimented and all male—would, paradoxically, mean freedom.

With commission in hand, Stan Cox boarded a troop train to Seattle, where he reported to ComSoPac (South Pacific Command). The war years would begin as a heady blur. In September 1942, he reported to Admiral Callahan and the U.S. Naval Operating Base, "Fulcrum," as Commanding Officer, U.S.S. *Receiving*, for temporary duty. And in December of that year, when others discovered Lieutenant Commander Cox was a reasonable mechanic, he was assigned repair officer for that same base. In fact, the base was a task force of convoy ships from the West Coast to combat areas in the Southwest Pacific. It was on one such mission, after Stan had met with him, Admiral Callahan was killed on the bridge of his flag ship, the U.S.S. *San Francisco*.

Stan was briefly transferred to the souh of Ireland and then, at the beginning of 1944, to Camp Bradford, near Norfolk, Virginia, where he served as executive officer of the amphibious training base. Naturally, Bab and her recently widowed mother followed, renting a house convenient to the base. Just prior to his departure from this assignment, he bucked up his men with some rhetoric that summarized his chest-swelling devotion to naval service: "But the log of naval warfare that is being written today by our forces is the most adventurous saga of courage and sweat, brain and muscle in the history of any people."

By the end of the year, Stan Cox found himself again stationed in the South Pacific. On November 10, 1944, while attached to the U.S.S *Mindanoa*, a mother ship for PT boats, berthed beside other naval vessels in Manus, capital of the Admiralty Islands, to the north of New Guinea, he left his ensign and solemnly walked the deck, saying good-byes prior to assuming a new command. At 4:13 p.m. that afternoon, the *Mount Hood*, a nearby ammunition ship, accidentally exploded. Shrapnel flew in all directions, and Lieutenant Commander Cox was one of the first to receive a direct hit—in the right knee and leg and, more significantly, in the right temporal region of his head. He fell to the deck unconscious. Others were less fortunate.

Before being flown back to the States, a young deck officer visited Stan in the hospital. His name was "June" (for Junior) Ewan, his mother having been Stan and Bab's cook at the Bar 20. "We talked a bit of Montana. Nice enough gentleman but, in spite of the Montana connection, I could see he wanted to keep his distance. That was the last I ever heard of Stan Cox."

Stan was transferred to Fleet Hospital 105 near San Francisco. There he complained of frequent periods of amnesia and a loss of hearing. Henceforth his handwriting would change subtly, its former bullishness and self-confidence now less apparent. Throughout this three-month hospital stay, Stan's spirits appear to have been temporarily buoyed ("I am doing wonderfully well and expect to be on the job soon.... The head wound except for the concussion healed very quickly. One hole in my right leg got infected but penicillin and sulfur beat that so now...I'm better than ever."). Bab Cox, now in Tyrone, New Mexico, again with her mother, wrote Babs Hard in December 1944: "He tells me not to worry, that everything is healing very well and [he is] expected to be hospitalized about five weeks. But how can anyone not be worried is beyond me...."

Stan wrote Babs Hard: "I have a picture of you (framed) that has been with me ever since the war started. It was one of the few things I did *not* lose in this last little "spot of trouble" and it's still right with me even though it's a bit battered and smelled like death and destruction 'til I got it aired out. My love to *all* your family and you know there is always a very great deal for you."

In hospital, Stan received word he had been promoted to full commander ("with seaweed in my cap"). These war years, so far, had indeed been good for Stan. He had found how to contribute, had rediscovered reserves of leadership and courage, untested since the days of his youth, and now his peers had rewarded him. The satisfaction of Navy life, in many ways, overwhelmed his former existence at the Bar 20. He spent two and a half weeks of sick leave with Bab in a cottage outside of Tucson, Arizona. On February 6, 1945, he was formally released from hospital in

Oakland and, after a brief stint at Yerba Buena Island near San Francisco, was ordered to report to the U.S.S. *Hamul* for further assignment. It appears the next few months would be some of Stan Cox's most challenging. As executive officer on board, his task was to rescue battle-damaged destroyers. In doing so, his ship was attacked, he claimed, on 105 occasions and weathered five typhoons, most in the South China Sea. He wrote to Babs Hard: "You've heard all about the fighting out here so I won't bother trying to write any more about it. It was simply beyond belief. We got through it somehow by getting all the breaks. The ship was cited for the Navy Unit Citation and I am supposed to get a bronze star and some other medal [the Purple Heart]. Neither means much since practically everyone *should* get them. The one thing that we all have—better than any medal—is knowing we went wherever we were sent and got the job done whatever it was." Indeed the *Hamul's* tendering services to other ships and specifically Stan Cox's role in its leadership was credited by many other captains as pivotal in their ability to remain seaworthy.

Even with the Japanese signing of the formal document of surrender on September 2, 1945, for Stan, the war was still not over. On December 7, four years to the day after the bombing of Pearl Harbor, he wrote, "It took quite a while for peace to penetrate to some of the Japs here. As a matter of fact, we [the people on the beach] are still knocking off a few each week."

As far back as February 1945, Stan had been considering the sale of the Bar 20. Bab Cox wrote Babs Hard that when Stan and she were together in Tucson he was "very nervous, tired and not up to anything, wanted only peace, quiet and rest." She continues with this ominous note: "Among the things we did talk about was the ranch. He thinks we should sell it and that about breaks my heart. If only we could retain our own house, small corral etc, and a small amount of acreage on our side of the West Boulder, I could bear it. At least we'd have that to go back to, a couple of saddle horses, and be able to look at the mountains. I know how he feels about it and realize that he will never again be able to lead as strenuous a life as he did there. But, it is a terrific wrench. I've put off the evil day of going about the selling but shall get at it before long, now. I had thought of your coming out, with the boys, and what fun we'd have, showing them the valley and all of that lovely country...."

Later, in December, while onboard the U.S.S. *Hamul*, Stan, now uncertain whether or not to sell, wrote Babs Hard: "Don't know what we will do with the ranch. Have had several offers for it, but hope we can work out some way to keep it. Bab's mother is still a problem and she can't seem to make up her mind to go and live by herself. We have no end of horses out there now—most of them absolutely tops—so I'm anxious to get back and get them started right."

On August 8, 1946, Stan Cox was finally released from active duty. He returned directly to the Bar 20. One picture tells much of the story. The smiling warrior that left the ranch exactly four years before in the summer of 1942 had returned a much older man. He stands next to a pole fence, sternly facing the photographer, the surface of his face resembling the weathered post. The lines around his mouth are drawn and his hat is raked to conceal the concavity of his right temple. His ears appear almost too big for his face and his hair, recently trimmed, has turned perfectly white.

If the Coxes had lived apart from others prior to the War, they did so with intensity now. Loren Brewer remembers Stan's stubbornness one winter when he insisted on driving his Jeep to the Bar 20, only to be stymied by an enormous snowdrift. For an entire day, he never gave up, rocking and digging, only to be halted by night and cold. So in blackness, he abandoned the vehicle and hitched a lift on the Brewers' wagon. John Fryer of Sax and Fryer Book Store in Livingston remembers how one cold night in winter, Stan called Albert Nicholson, the sheriff, on the Forest Service phone and said he and Mrs. Cox were running short of supplies. The next day a plane was diverted to drop their grocery order: a couple of loaves of white bread and two bottles of whiskey.

"When Stan returned from the fighting he had become bipolar," claims John. "You'd notice he had intense black moods, then he was euphoric, then he panicked. He had, I think, become severely depressed. I believe there was even a time when the Coxes left the Bar 20 so Stan could be hospitalized. Naturally, they kept it a dark secret."

By 1949, Stan would report to the Navy that "following my release from active duty, I have suffered continuously from injuries sustained during my active Naval service, manifested by disabling illnesses, which have increased in frequency. During the last year and a half I have been unable to pursue my usual normal duties of attending my ranch in Montana."

The Bar 20 staff was now considerably reduced, and, at one time, Bab Cox was herself forced to cook. The cattle, belonging to A.B. Dickenson out of Lake Geneva, Wisconsin, were not Stan's responsibility, and the few remaining horses were, mostly, left to their own devices. Stan never broke another horse as he once had claimed and Bucky, the antelope, had not been seen since the end of the War.

The ranch had now become a serious drain on the Coxes, and at the end of 1947 they borrowed $3,000 from the Citizens State Bank of Big Timber against it. Nine months later they repaid the bank and satisfied the mortgage by selling off parcels of the Bar 20 Ranch. In one sale, several non-contiguous pieces of what once had been a 1,640-acre ranch were sold to a neighbor. Soon all that remained were about 500 acres as well as the buildings along the river. Now Stan and Bab were mostly housebound, waiting for the final sale. Winter 1950 found them still at the Bar 20. Stan, hearing of the death of his old friend, Francis Thorne, "Pops," "the Bilge Rat," wrote Babs Hard in a frail hand, not saying what the old boy had really meant to him, but diverting from the subject by telling that Bab had bought land in Lancaster County, Virginia. There they would move as soon as the last piece of Bar 20 was sold. "What a lousy mess it all is!!" he ended, "I'd like to get some place where I could go fishing & shoot a few ducks or just stay put." This letter, written Christmas Day would be his last to Babs Hard.

One can only guess how it must have ended for the Coxes at Bar 20. Six months later they would sign over the ranch to the Hugginses, but as early as spring they had begun to move on. One can imagine their last day in August—the two walking from room to room, collecting framed photographs, the dressing-table silver, including the crystal powder jar with the enamel top, telling the "chore boy" to be careful with the paintings, especially the portraits, checking off from the list those tables (the drop-leaf Chippendale) to be sent East, those (the stinkwood and the Molesworth) to be left for Bar 20's next owners. Stan must have boxed up his Will James's novels, the ones he knew almost by heart. They would live out their days in Virginia. As for his 200 NATIONAL GEOGRAPHICS—he would have thumbed through a few of them and decided they would probably be of greater value to Bar 20's next inmates. Maybe Stan believed he had already been to all those places on far shores, had seen too much and now didn't care to travel anymore. Perhaps he said to himself, the only shore he now cared about would be his own. "They stay," he told the chore boy.

Perhaps Stan took the old Remington 7 millimeter from the gun rack in the living room, put two shells in the magazine, and ambled out to the barn. The younger horses like Star Baby and Sundance had already been accounted for—sold to neighbors, but the others—Sunny and Little Dog—weren't sound. He might find a buyer for them at auction, he supposed, but it was no secret they would both end as "canners, feeding Frenchmen," he imagined. No, he couldn't do that—not to these spirited "critters," old friends who served him all these years. Perhaps Stan recalled Pops on Little Dog—and what a sight that had been. No, friends deserve better. Perhaps he brought the horses some grain from the barn, scattered it in the meadow, and then hung back in the aspens, watching them gallop over to have that first mouthful. Perhaps he watched them as long as he dared.

Even with the medication, the memories kept Stan awake at night and haunted him, as well, in daylight. Too damn many of them—of little Babs and Dee, looking so perfect as they rode with Ed Weber up to Nurse's Lake, or Stan's first view of Lost Lakes or the time he hiked to the top of Shell Mountain and found the obsidian blade (How old do you suppose it was? What tribe had fashioned it?). Stan had been so much younger then. Strong, invincible, tougher, it was said, than even his brother. Since then, there had been changes—hills transformed into unscalable peaks and two fingers of Cream of Kentucky doing more damage than an entire bottle.

Damn the memories—that waif Edward always staring him down, accusing, sniveling. Just like his mother. And the girl—they called her Lucille—so small, almost too small when she was born and, unlike all other infants he'd known, never crying. Astonishing, but then she was taken away and you never know. Who's to say how she would turn out? Probably married now with a family of her own and it doesn't matter anymore. They'd never meet, thank God. Still, it was a shame.

What matters now anyway? Nothing lasts. Bar 20 dreams. Good health. At least his ticker still works and he can hold a rifle steady.

So there, by the barn, Stan raises his rifle, steadies the bead, knowing he's still one hell of a fine shot, but not caring as he once did. This job is too damn easy. It isn't meant for him or for anyone. Damn. Stan fires. Little Dog goes down. Perfect. And then he spins on his heels to catch Sunny just beneath the ears, before he bolts to the far side of the meadow.

Just hope Bab doesn't hear the two shots. She won't understand, and it'll be so like a woman to blame him.

Stan Cox avoids a last look at the heavy bodies. Instead, he returns to the house for his final meal. Inside those cozy Bar 20 log walls, the table is set with four silver candlesticks, silver salvers, crystal goblets, and flowered Royal Doulton plates. Once again Bab hasn't let him down.

The records show Stan and Bab first used Oxford, Maryland, as a staging point. By the time they had closed on the sale of the Bar 20, they owned land overlooking a tidewater estuary of the Rappahannock River near Kilmarnock in the northern neck of Virginia. Here beside this sleepy community filled with other retired naval officers, the Coxes would build their final house. Painted white at the end of a serpentine driveway, it was set on one level and featured several fireplaces, a handsome library, and a secret door. Disguised to look like clapboard, the house was instead built of cinderblocks coated with cement. "Very strange," said a neighbor "because I always thought the Coxes were filthy rich."

At the edge of the Cox estate, a small cottage rose. It was for Mrs. Reierson, Bab's mother, the source of all funds and Bab's second-best friend. From the screened porches of their house, Stan and Bab could sit and watch their dogs bound across the lawn onto the dock to bark at passing gulls. The shield-backed chairs and all the other family heirlooms, once at the Bar 20, followed them here to this land that amounted to a few acres. In Kilmarnock, Commander Cox occupied himself, according to his testimony by "selling farm and home properties" under the leadership of Captain H.C. Robison, another retired naval officer.

A child of one of the Coxes' friends described Kilmarnock in the 1950s as "a sea of conviviality. Every social occasion was an opportunity to drink, and it's hard to remember when one conversation ended and another began." While Bab might have dealt with it, Stan appeared "insecure."

The son of a friend recalled: "Stan may have worked as a real estate agent, but I can't imagine him selling anything.... Babs kept a short leash on him and didn't let him ramble, and he in turn was dependent on her. While he was perfectly amiable, he wasn't very assertive or aggressive, in fact, highly suggestable. It was always a puzzle to us why he never rose above commander. Most of the people in Kilmarnock were captains and admirals.

In 1960, Stan Cox was admitted to the Stuart Circle Hospital for a minor circulation problem. During a short operation on September 1, his heart played out, and he died on the operating table. Bab made sure her husband was given full military honors at Arlington National Cemetery. She then sold the house on the Rappahannock and moved closer to town, where she died on November 29, 1965. She is buried beside Stan at Arlington.

It is still remembered that Commander Cox always spoke about Montana "in the most glowing terms. He never could stop thinking about it." He told one friend that when he lived there he often rode into canyons that "he thought had never before been visited by a white man."

Mrs. Cox, on the other hand, said not another word about Montana.

In 1996, near our restored barn, we found two horse skulls covered in mud. They each had been pierced by bullet holes and, from the teeth, the horses looked as if they had both lived very long lives.

Some believe it is macabre that I keep the skulls on a shelf in the barn. Kathryn, however, understands. When I put them there, each facing west, she knew my search for the Coxes was done.

CHAPTER 15

Escape

I went through a bad patch toward the end of 1997, and by summertime had been alone for nearly a year. In the heat of July, held captive by perennials buzzing with bees, the Bar 20 had rediscovered its calm. At night fireplaces glowed and crackled while the dogs laid claim to an old wicker couch on the screened porch to guard the house from the soft gurgle of the river. The anxiety that had dogged my life was now gone. Gone too the girlfriend's angry silences over morning coffee, afternoon slamming of doors, squealing of tires at night.

Naturally, there were days when I was lonely, but loneliness held rewards. Without someone to question my every move, I was liberated, but I still felt indulged by this mountain fastness, spoiled by an excess of Bar 20 isolation. Big rooms turning gloomy at night needed the anticipation of arrival, the rustling of feet in another room, someone else's choice of music and clutter. The haunted ranch by itself was sometimes company enough, but I needed more. I began to suspect my rooms smelled of dried cork and I wondered whether I might be getting old.

I'm convinced dogs note such moods, that they're the first to detect loneliness. Mine made a point of staying close—Chui, most of all. One person was all she needed, and now, as my constant lover—so she thought—I could be manipulated by her alone. Just before light, when I was still in bed—she would nuzzle the door, pad toward my face, put her head on the pillow, and, at a distance of two inches, drill me with amber eyes. Either her gaze or the rank smell of her morning breath awoke me each time. My dog's day had begun. I was expected to take her and Duma for a run and, over the years, I learned to be religious in these duties. So, too, once returned, was I expected to brush and feed her. She must have reasoned, I now had earned the right to some of the day for, generally, while Duma prowled the outer rim of the Bar 20 in hopes of encountering a half-witted ground squirrel, Chui rested beneath my desk, the only interruption from the solace of desk time her do-or-die bark upon hearing an interloper. Her duty, above all else, was to protect me and the Bar 20 from outsiders. Deer, bear, telephone linemen were all guilty without trial.

To this rule of trespass, Chui made an exception for three individuals: the indomitable Lark, who supervised horses and grounds; Rhea, who cared for the interior of the buildings, and Kathryn, my friend from New York who had discovered Montana first on a road trip, and now through regular visits to the Bar 20. Tall and gentle, Kathryn thought nothing of lying in the hot sun on the lawn reading a book, her head on Chui's shoulder. Once she spent an hour combing out the knots among Chui's feathers. Either the gentleness and the calm that Kathryn brought to the Bar 20 or—perhaps I am stretching—the change in me that Kathryn had masterminded made this thoughtful, sometimes zany friend, Chui's ally. Kathryn loved four-mile jogs along the open road leading to the wilderness, and Chui and Duma would shamelessly forget me to join Kathryn.

Nine years before, I had acquired Chui as a puppy. A researcher, helping me with a book, had introduced me to her own golden retriever—a gentle matriarch with a fine head and swollen teats. Her puppies were expected in a few days. I was impressed by her engaging demeanor, but what captivated me was her instant affection for me. I fell for the flattery and asked to have the pick of the litter.

Eight weeks later Chui arrived in a small crate. She was anything but a docile puppy. She arrived during the last year of life of another devoted dog, and I believe Chui's high spirits and affection extended that dog's life. By the time Chui had evolved into my sole companion, she acquired queenly airs. She was highly protective, ruled houses with a sense of laisse majesté and insisted upon accompanying me to all social gatherings where her soulful eyes made everyone succumb to her gaze. When, at the age of five years, Duma arrived, Chui viewed the intrusion of another dog—a mere puppy would you know—as a personal slight. The equanimity of her rule had been rent, and there were moments when she looked at me, her mouth drawn, a hint of gray on her chin and a look, pleading: "Please, please remove this pill from our lives...."

Dogs are much like me. For them the prospect of change is more horrific than its reality. Within a few months, growls had become toothless, and as long as I wasn't watching, Chui would occasionally deign to play with Duma. In time, the two became partners. Duma found Chui a tad arch and majestic, she never went anywhere without her.

At the beginning of summer 1998, Lark was the first to say what I kept to myself: Chui was slowing down. When Chui ran with Kathryn, she often lagged behind. At the house, once she had given her warning bark at the first sound of a stranger, she then slumped to the floor without enough energy for further outrage. One Sunday when I was alone, I took Chui and Duma on a fishing trip into the wilderness. Halfway to the meadows, heavy clouds rushed into the valley, lightning struck the far wall of the valley, and thunder echoed throughout the canyon. I had seen the storm approaching, and knowing Chui's fear of thunder, I brought her to me, squatted on the ground, and let her bury her face in my arms. Once the last echoes of the thunder had echoed into the maw of the valley, all three of us ran along the trail to the Forest Service bridge. I could see the storm was traveling fast and the wooden span offered the only safe shelter from rain. We climbed down the embankment, working our way into the bridge's shadow. Eighty pounds of Chui then sat on my lap, her shoulders quivering, her eyes watching the river, dark as blood. Once the storm had rattled past us, down the valley, I climbed the embankment and whistled for the dogs to follow. Duma passed me at a gallop. Chui remained at the foot of the slope, seemingly confused. It appeared the climb was too much for her, and for the first time since she was a puppy, she began to whimper.

The next day I took her to Dr. Johnson, the vet in Big Timber. Even after he studied her eyes, took her blood, he couldn't be certain. He gave me some pills. The next day, Chui stopped eating. Three days later, Chui lay on the porch rather than run with me in the morning. I retraced my steps to her. Her golden coat, auburn in the early light, had lost its luster; her eyes, perennially sad, were clouded. I lifted her head onto my lap, stroked her behind her ears, feeling a knot, playing with it and then rubbing her neck until her eyes closed. "Chui," I whispered in her ear. "You are not allowed to. No. Never. Forbidden. Do you hear?" Even with her eyes closed her tail beat on the cool cement as if she had an answer.

Dr. Johnson was prepared to do everything known to veterinary science to reverse what he now diagnosed as autoimmune disorder. "Happens in this breed from time to time. She just can't produce enough red blood cells. But I haven't given up and I won't. Leave her with me."

While I was away in Florida, recording voice-overs for a film, Chui stayed with the vet, Too weak to eat on her own, she was now being fed on a drip. Each day Kathryn, now back in New York, called for news and Lark drove Duma to the vet's for a visit. After once seeing Chui, so still on the floor of her cage, Duma chose never again to leave the car. With every visit, Chui, too exhausted even to lift her head, welcomed Lark by thumping the floor of her crate with her tail.

When I returned to Bozeman late on a Saturday, Lark said it probably would be best I not visit Chui. She had just received a complete blood transfusion and needed to marshal her strength. Dr. Johnson, each day losing the red blood count battle, had undertaken his final strategy to save Chui's life. I was later to describe his weekend vigil as heroic.

Sunday was Chui's kind of day—sunny and quiet. I had been told there might be an outside chance, if the operation had been successful, that late in the afternoon Dr. Johnson might release Chui for me to bring home. Even in her state of exhaustion, she would do well on the warm grass and, later, in the shade of a tree. I would carry her there just as I had carried her from the bridge up the embankment and had toted her down the trail on my shoulders.

That Sunday morning, Duma foreswore her morning hunt to stay with me. In my office, she lay for the first time on the spot where Chui once had lain.

The call came just before noon. It was Wayne, Lark's husband, for Lark was unable to speak. This strong manly outdoorsman had considerable difficulty with the message: Chui never survived the night. Dr. Johnson had found her dead in her cage in the morning.

Late that afternoon, Wayne arrived in his station wagon, his cargo, covered in a blanket, lying in the back.

We buried Chui beside a grove of aspen, in sight of the old wicker couch on the screened porch where she always lay. The spot is a place favored by the deer Chui barely tolerated, and it marks the periphery of the territory she once called her own. Nearby, at the edge of the river, I found two round rocks that now lie on her grave. On them I have inscribed my farewell.

Duma engaged in a different sort of farewell. She never joined me at the burial, and to this day the only spot at the Bar 20 she avoids is Chui's grave. It took nearly a year for her spirits to be restored, but even now when we ride or walk, she skirts the place where she saw her companion vanish forever.

For a while after Chui's death, I found solace in a teepee. Ours is to the south of the buildings, and during late August and all that September, I began spending late afternoons in it.

It must be said that teepees in the northern Rockies have assumed the nature of a fad. Wherever one goes, it seems there are teepee B&B's here, some one's "folly" there. If the buzz is to be believed, one might suspect the traditional dwelling of the Plains Indian has become the preferred guesthouse for a new wave of Western homesteader. Local papers report how Jane Fonda once gave Ted Turner one for his birthday. Jeff and Susan Bridges keep one near their ranch on the Yellowstone River. Bruce Weber and Nan Bush have six. Fashions are having more and more impact in the West and one would assume that after teepees, there will be igloos, yerts, geodesic domes.

Odious as I find the buzz, I discovered qualities in the teepee that might escape celebrities. Not only did I note that the teepee mastered climate, wind, and smoke, but also its calm, soundness, and history moved me. In time I learned something about its role in the history of the Bar 20.

We came into possession of the teepee almost by accident. Hilary, my sister, had been frequenting a trading post on the Crow Reservation, a few miles from where, in 1876, General George Armstrong Custer met his end. Here she bought one of the teepees abandoned after the filming of "Son of Morning Star," a made-for-television re-creation of the Custer debacle, at a knockdown price. "It will look a whole lot more appropriate in our valley than the house," she explained. A winter passed, while we awaited someone, perhaps an Absaroka Indian to show us how to erect it.

In 1990, no Native American at all, but a cowboy, known locally as "Teepee Don," walked stiff-legged into our lives. He provided lodgepoles, tripod, pegs, door cover, lacing pins, *ozan*, lining and within a few minutes the teepee was the evocation of all our valley's glorious past. "Hell of a teepee," muttered Don, surveying the mutt. "Part Crow, part Cheyenne with an odd mixture of Blackfoot." He took off his hat to rub his forehead.

He had noted that its canvas had been purposefully darkened to give the effect of many moons of smoke and weather. "Show biz," Don said shaking his head, grinning.

That was the extent of my association with teepees for another year until my niece, age 11, and her au pair began conducting their summer tutorials in the teepee. They reported its "remarkable brightness" and "unearthly calm," that it was "not at all like a tent."

So, one early autumn evening, I hived off for the teepee, set in a meadow and protected by stands of trees along the river's edge. I stooped to negotiate the door and, once inside, I lowered its cover to make the effect of the interior complete. Lying on a sleeping bag to read, all I could see beyond this world was through the smoke flaps, a trapezoid section of bitter sky and frantic cloud. Colored tribal streamers laced to lodgepole tips, snapped indolently in the wind. Even from this womb, I sensed the aspen had begun to shift from yellow to amber, their reflection adding candlepower to the dusk. Was I inside a giant parchment lampshade? And might there be more than just normal reflection?

Sounds, too, were magnified. Two sandhill cranes were passing the time of day with each other, yammering rude *gar-oos*, as they flew formation, on their return to Lost Lake for the night. A Canada jay alighted high on a lodgepole and never looked down. Within this living hologram, anonymous bird shadows flitted past in more than two dimensions: were they meadowlarks, nuthatches, pine siskins? Much later, when the sky had turned the color of eggplant, I sensed—but could never be sure—a great horned owl alighting overhead, calling to a mate in the canopy of trees along the river. The mountain mournfulness stirred me to gather kindling. This would be my first open fire under canvas.

But even without adjustment to the smoke flaps, the fire drew as well as any chimney. Had there been mosquitoes, few could have penetrated this atmosphere. The evening chill soon vanished and my sweater began to smell like green roasted spruce. I lay back once again, this time beneath the ozan, a partial canvas ceiling intended to trap warmth; here I dreamed of eggshells brimming with long-forgotten faces. Look at any campfire and it is possible, after a fashion, to levitate. But when I studied this fire, it became the aorta of teepee life. The crackling drowned out the rush of the glacier melt tumbling through boulders nearby. My normally ordered mind conducted a wild filibuster of memory, reaching back to days on either side of birth.

Soon it was too much. I wasn't used to this unanticipated frolic with the subconscious, this calm, massive introspection. I checked the fire to make sure it was safe, then straggled back to more familiar ground—a square house—looking back once to note that the teepee had now become a giant luminaria, and that a ceiling of smoke had settled into the high branches of trees, cathedral-like.

Was it me or was it the teepee? A few days later, Teepee Don set me straight. His wavy gray hair was slicked in place, snap-button shirt taut as a spinnaker. He welcomed me to his house in Livingston with a smile that spread seamlessly from ear to ear. In his yard there were sheep wagons that hearkened back to the days of range wars and a totem pole from British Columbia; on the walls of his "conversation pit" living room—beadwork and headdresses. By tradition, cowboys are not champions of the Indian. But this cowboy, modest, laconic, a modern "Virginian," was in the business of teepees not just because he liked them, but, perhaps, to right a few wrongs. Here every artifact was a yarn. Yes, he said in cowboy fashion, he knew a thing or two about teepees and, by the way, would I be interested in a Manhattan?

Don Ellis is arguably North America's most exacting producer of teepees. Even though he is of Swedish descent, he is a champion, of sorts, for Native Americans. One of his tents is in the St. Labre Museum on the Cheyenne Reservation. Dowanda Little Coyote Backbone, a prominent member of the tribe, owns four of his teepees, including one of Crow design (ironic because the Crows were traditional enemies of the Cheyenne). "I'm real pleased," says Ellis, "To be able to give back to the Indian some of the heritage we stole."

Don Ellis's fascination with all things Indian began at age four when his father, a rancher, ran a couple of bands of sheep on the Blackfoot Reservation near Browning, Montana. During that 1933 summer, at the time of the tribe's encampment, the small boy slipped into one of the teepees. "I can remember how cool it was. It may as well have been air-conditioned, and there was a stillness there—quite different from the bustle outside." The impression lasted a lifetime. In his thirties, when he acquired a ranch of his own, he discovered his land encompassed a buffalo jump—a *pishkin*. Here he could recreate the path on top of a plateau where Indians—one dressed in a wolf-skin to harass the herd—had tallyhoed the bison into the glaring sun of dawn, until they plunged over the precipice. And at the base of the cliff, he found not just remains of buffalo but also stone rings that had marked the perimeter of teepees. Here long-ago hunters had feasted.

Like many a cowboy, Ellis sashayed through more than one career. There were nine years spent owning a guest ranch near Cooke City at the northern end of Yellowstone Park (naturally, a teepee was one of its features). Later Ellis and his family moved to Livingston where he built log cabins for others. Where was he to house his crew? How about in teepees? The rub for Don was that, at the time, industrial teepees were inferior. They bore little resemblance to their historic counterparts and they were so flimsy their seams split after a day.

Don Ellis, entrepreneur, spotted an opportunity. He and his team began manufacturing them. The result was a small cottage industry. His work attracted acceptance, and soon Don became the sole source of teepees in Park County. With Marcy, his wife (formally married to Sam Pekinpaw), and Wendell Cooper, an expert sailcloth cutter, he launched White Buffalo Lodges. Within months, his reputation spread to all corners of the West. Today he has made over 700 teepees, of varying tribal specifications, some illustrated by Marcy with shadow stories. He prefers the Cheyenne and Sioux designs—those set around a tripod of lodgepoles—but he is happy to accommodate anyone partial to the Crow or Blackfoot style—those based on four supports ("the homeliest teepee you ever saw").

Ironically, Ellis's teepee intelligence comes not from the Indians themselves but from other white folks. In 1957, Reginald and Gladys Laubin wrote the seminal work on teepees: *The Indian Teepee—Its History, Construction, and Use*. A laboriously researched book, it's illustrated with curious photographs of the Laubins decorated in war paint, and it offers odd teepee tips: "To really enjoy the teepee you should wear moccasins inside. Shoes just will not do. Indians despised hair on the face.... They referred to white men with whiskers as bear faces, hairy faces, or old buffalo bulls. So, even when camping in the teepee, I shave religiously every morning."

The Laubins took up the Indian cause long before *Dances with Wolves*. They became authorities on Indian dance, the Indian sweat lodge, Indian parfleches (rawhide bags). Even today, from their home outside Jackson, Wyoming, this elderly couple still live according to an Indian ethic. "May the Great Spirit travel with you," they said to me once when I called. Their Sioux teepee, decorated with a massive bison is their summer home; they swear by its calming power.

My first misconception, corrected by Don Ellis and the Laubins, is that the teepee is a perfect circle. Wrong. Its shape is oval on the ground, above ground a tilted ice cream cone, steep side to the rear. Indians traditionally chose to live in the round, their encampments circular, their lives symmetrical, each a continuum, beginnings commingled to ends. Any one point of life is but a moment in the infinity of existence. Look wider and a human life imitates both the cosmos and our earth, each the shape of an egg. Only white men think in square blocks.

The teepee probably existed long before 1600. Teepee rings, dated to Pre-Columbian times, generally suggest that, prehistorically, they were small—

on average not much more than 14 feet across. A teepee's size was limited by transport technology. The horse, stolen or feral, only reached the Northern Plains between 1740 and 1750. Before then, the dog had been the Indian's beast of burden, dragging the pole platform known as the travois. The arrival of the horse was liberation for the Plains Indian. With a horse, larger travois were conceived, longer lodgepoles cut. With substantial lodgepoles, the teepee could grow—some as large as 30 feet in diameter. Soon, the teepee became more than the hunter's shelter, but a substantial dwelling, large enough to support an extended family throughout the year.

Originally, the wall of the teepee was made of buffalo hide, rubbed clean of hair. But hardly any 20th-century Indian recalled seeing such a teepee, for by the 1840s steamboats had negotiated the Missouri and white traders were swapping bolts of canvas in exchange for buffalo hides. To the Indian, canvas was another form of liberation. "But," Don Ellis says, shaking his head, "they paid dearly for it. The exchange of skins for canvas was always weighted heavily in favor of the white man."

What a sight those 19th-century encampments must have been! In 1832, the artist George Catlin described the speed the Sioux broke camp: "...in one minute 600 lodges (on a level and beautiful prairie), which before had been strained and fixed, were seen waving and flapping in the wind, and in one minute more all were flat on the ground. Their horses and dogs, of which they have a vast number... was [sic] speedily loaded with the burden allotted it, and made ready to fall into the grand procession."

By the end of the 19th century, the Northern Plains Indians had been exiled into ghettos, reservations. All things Indian were discouraged—principally, the Sun Dance and the teepee, both of which were deemed "savage." Instead, Indians were issued the eminently civilized wall tent, an awkward rectangular structure, hot in summer, cold in winter, with limited headroom anytime. In the 1930s on the Standing Rock Sioux Reservation of North and South Dakota and on Montana's Crow Reservation, the first teepee seen by most Indians belonged to Reginald and Gladys Laubin. Black Elk, the holy man of the Sioux, in the memoirs he dictated at about this time, noted: "The Wasichus (white men) have put us in these square boxes. Our power is gone and we are dying, for the power is not in us any more. You can look at our boys and see how it is with us. When we were living by the power of the circle in the way we should, boys were men at 12 or 13. But now it takes them very much longer to mature. Well, it is as it is. We are prisoners of war while we are waiting here. But there is another world."

I suspect my experience in the teepee had much to do with the imperfect circle. Maybe the Native American, at pains to consider a straight line, perceived an earth shape in the teepee. He saw sky, stars, horizon as circular. The wind never traveled directly; it whirled. The sun and the moon and the seasons formed circles and even a human life began where it ended, one childhood leading to another. The teepee reflects Indian reality. In the words of Black Elk, "our teepees were round like the nests of birds and these were always set in a circle, the nation's hoop, a nest of many nests where the Great Spirit meant for us to hatch our children."

I see no reason why the teepee cannot reflect others' reality as well. I spend lots of time in mine, not only alone but, I hope, in company. I take to heart the Laubins' claim that "it's near-impossible ever to have a fight in a teepee." I view promises about the teepee's effect on mood as convincing as those once made about pyramids.

Evenings in the west, I can one day foresee many teepees, illuminated—conical lanterns—to form tight circles over plains and river valleys. The big circle will not just be the one visible, but a graceful arc through time, evoking an era before the West was "won." Who knows—the teepee may one day come to embody a new form of frontier justice.

~

CHAPTER 16

Indians on My Mind

In the kitchen of the Bar 20, there's a calendar I think was left behind by Stan and Bab Cox. No one since their era has dared remove it. Published in 1933 by the Great Northern Railway, it features a portrait of a Blackfoot warrior named Turtle. The lines on his face run deep, and his half-shuttered eyes appear to convey both pain and wisdom. It is so easy to dismiss him with banalities like "the noble savage" or "last survivor of a great race." But it all seems so sham and inexact. Must the American Indian forever be condemned to clichés? Every morning at breakfast, I stare fixedly at this Winold Reiss calendar and wonder what the Coxes made of this warrior. All I can summon are nonsense lines. Did they spend any of their time contemplating the Bar 20's Indian past? Hardly half a century before the Coxes claimed this ranch, it possessed no boundaries, no title deeds, no seigneur. It was part of an enormous territory loosely described as Crow country.

What about these Indians? What about all these people who lost their land to outsiders? Could their descendants tell me anything of those who once wandered this valley?

Impulsively, I call my friend Bill Bryan, author of *Montana's Indians*. With his wife, Pam, and his help, I discover an astonishing geographic coincidence: history has isolated most Northern Plains Indians to the Hi Line near the Canadian border; and right through its center runs Montana's last rail passenger service. Trains that plied this track were once the pride of the Great Northern Railway. Today, operated by Amtrak and still cunningly dubbed the Empire Builder, this occasional service beads together reservation, battlefield, encampment, and fort in a kind of historic necklace. Say I was to board the Chicago to Seattle train in Williston, North Dakota, and disembark in Whitefish, I could sit in the lounge car and see nearly 600 miles of Montana while witnessing a cavalcade of Indian history. And whenever curiosity gets the better of me, I can disembark, rent a car, and then reboard the westbound train the following day.

Before joining the Empire Builder at Williston, North Dakota, on Montana's eastern border, I pay another visit to Fort Union. It's been on my mind ever since the road trip—this remarkable site, so pivotal to Western history, yet so little visited. From a distance the structure resembles those Lincoln Log forts I played with as a child—high ramparts to thwart unwanted visitors, corner turrets for lookouts. But Fort Union was built for commerce, not for war. Begun in 1829 by John Jacob Astor's American Fur Company, it was strategically located near the confluence of the Yellowstone and the Missouri, to serve the trade in beaver skins. Later, when Eastern fashion declared silk hats the rage, Fort Union didn't blink: instead, it began supplying the nation with buffalo robes to keep Eastern bodies warm. For over three decades, every trader, trapper, scout stopped here. Fort Union was a traveler's caravanserai, the gateway to the Rockies and the Northwest—the new territories reconnoitered by the Lewis and Clark Expedition. Everyone of consequence dallied here, before embarking for *terra* barely *cognita* to the west.

I arrive an hour before sunset and warden David Dufficy, locking the great stockade doors, appears little inconvenienced to delay closing hours to escort me, the only outsider he has seen all day, on the catwalk along the towering palisades. In 1966 when the land was acquired by the National Park

Service, he explains, all that remained of Fort Union were two mounds, remnants of original corner bastions. Much of the fort had been cannibalized shortly after the Civil War, to build a proper military establishment— Fort Buford—better placed to serve the army during a time of mounting hostility with Indian nations. Paintings made in the 1830s by Karl Bodmer and George Catlin as well as modern archaeology helped the National Park Service restore Fort Union. Today, within its stone and log walls, one can readily visualize its long-ago bustle. As many as 100 men—a cosmopolitan mix of Easterners, Blacks, Russians, Italians, English, French were employed here, many of them married to Indians. The large interior courtyard, filled with stores, barracks, bell tower and kitchen, was dominated by the bourgeois' house. Here distinguished visitors dined, eager to gather intelligence about surrounding tribes and the frontier that lay to the west.

The treeless hills that surround the fort and the banks of the Missouri, heavy with cottonwood, are much as they were 160 years ago. Today, the only sign of life is cattle; then the valley floor was awash in teepees. Assiniboine, Mandan, Crow, and, briefly, even Blackfoot engaged in active trading at the fort. Skirmishes were rare, and, for a while, white man and Indian might have prospered as partners.

In 1837, the first of many outbreaks of smallpox struck the Northern Plains Indians as well as the inhabitants of Fort Union. Some claim virus-infected blankets were knowingly given by whites to the Indians, lacking immunity. Of 1,000 Assiniboine, only 150 survived and in one year—1857— as many as 80 percent of the Crows, bivouacked near the fort, also succumbed. Traders had begun smuggling illegal alcohol into the fort. Addiction to "firewater" became yet another virus for which the Native American peoples of the Northern Plains had no resistance. For alcohol, whole cultures were pawned, ancient tribal alliances bartered, and the clock sprung to record a cycle of self-destruction. By the end of the Civil War, the Indian Wars would commence with fury.

The last time I was here I thought about how Indians had been marginalized at centers such as this. Today I'm thinking of ghosts; here on these prairies, decency, good intentions, parity were left to die. With gates flung open, Fort Union once might have appeared an invitation to anyone happening by. Closed, it became a laager against the West. Today, too late, the gates are open once again, but now swallows outnumber visitors.

I've not made this trip as an act of penance. Rather, I've come to Northern Montana to learn about some of the people who might once have lived around the Bar 20, to find out how they have survived the experience of being marginalized, demonized, trivialized and, recently, eulogized. I must confess I wasn't always so curious. When I first came to Montana, I was swallowed whole by the cowboy legend. I must have been a slow starter for only later, and then in slight increments, did I sense there might have been other inhabitants—ghostly presences bereft of legend factories. Everywhere I hiked or rode in the Bull Mountains and at the Bar 20, I felt myself in the shadow of others. The teepee I struck by the edge of my house *they* had consecrated. The mountains, the game, the river, the white fish were mine because of *them*. The arrowhead I found by the gravel pit had delivered some long-ago deer into *their* spirit world, now woven into the fabric of *my* life. Still, Indians remained theories exiled to reservation and lore.

During the early Montana years I stopped regularly at the Little Big Horn Battleground, where General George Armstrong Custer made his "last stand" in 1876. Here is the site of the most celebrated of all Indian engagements, the largest battle ever waged between white man and Indian. As a child, I was raised to judge Custer one hell of a guy—swaggering leader of 170 men willing to take on 10,000, savagely cut down at the peak of his illustrious career. Now history has, mercifully, come to its senses, and today the National Park monument bears witness mostly to Custer's recklessness. Every time I stopped at the site, I'd poke among the whitewashed headstones of the army's fallen, asking what went wrong, how could such a leader make such a frightening miscalculation? I also discovered the cruel irony of the battle, that it was indeed only a pyrrhic victory for Indians. They may have won this battle but their future was forever sealed. The Indians of the Northern Plains would never win again. They had, in fact, irreversibly lost the war of their lives. For me, this battlefield is an anomaly, an aberration of history. Truth must lie elsewhere.

The morning after Fort Union, I board the Empire Builder. I knew it would be no better or worst than most Amtrak trains, probably, in fact, fairly spartan. Instead, I am modestly surprised. For what charm the top-of-the-line staterooms lack through institutional design, they make up for in comfort and roominess. I am given a modest roomette, exceptionally cozy for the single traveler; next door, I spot a woman working feverishly on a yellow pad. It's a screenplay, she reveals. "And I hope to have a first draft by Seattle."

The bar steward, conductors, and baggage man are unanimous in their apologies that today's antiquated equipment is not representative of what an Empire Builder can really be. "Just wait until you see the new lounge cars." Still, I'm not disappointed. On the observation deck, windows are enormous and reasonably clean. *Die Hard* is playing on a series of monitors, but no one is watching. They're all looking at the landscape.

An altogether American atmosphere pervades each car. Friendships are formed with reckless abandon. Two pairs of strangers who met each other on the platform at Williston now are a chummy foursome in the dining room. The bar steward's job is to serve as a kind of fertilizer for good fellowship— a task that evidently gives him license to barrage us with a series of groaners on the public address system ("Ladies and gentlemen, on the right you'll notice some round bales. Next year these'll be outlawed since cattle need a square meal, too.")

Most passengers on this Empire Builder appear to be retirees, content to sit, watch, sigh as one landscape after another fleets past their windows. Those under 60, the minority, all have defined missions. A cluster of Mennonite women, faces shuttered in bonnets, dark skirts trailing the ground, are traveling from Canada to pay a social call on another Mennonite colony. A seed salesman has found the train the most efficient form of travel along Montana's endless Hi Line. And a Portland psychiatrist is heading home after a weekend spent with Assiniboine friends, at a "wiping of the tears" ceremony remembering their deceased son.

Young, old: no one is immune to this scenery. This is not opulent Montana, the sort the new dot-com billionaires might covet. As recently as the late 19th century, it was described as "the great American desert." Today it's still saddle-sore country—now vast farms cobbled together by enterprising homesteaders from single landholdings, each 160 acres. Onboard this train, I needn't be an expert to read its 20th-century history. I can see where hills have been flattened, boulders shifted, bottomlands squared by teams of muscled mules. Where once buffalo roamed, I can spot where drills, discs, and harrows then played. From my comfortable perch, it's a snap to imagine how it must have been for those hardy pioneers—in summer the heat twanging their tin roofs, in winter, snow and ice shrouding them. Today, autumn and progress has made the land downright benign.

Plenty is a sometime thing. Where there is wheat, the fields are geometric and the grain storage elevators cathedrals, even though the price of wheat is at a record low. But on cattle land, silos teeter, corrals are manure wallows, calving sheds look abandoned. Small oil wells, pumping metronomically, appear to give the lie to wealth. But who might they benefit? Possibly, I wonder, bankers in Billings or Denver. Certainly no one here seems to be getting rich. At 80 miles an hour we pass memories of towns, now all rusted "Sinclair," "Oasis Bar," and "Dancing" signs.

Nature remains certifiably virgin only in the draws, adrift with willows and cottonwoods, on the rim of the Sweetgrass Hills and in that peculiar purple light, a sparkle with star bursts between nursery-rhyme clouds—a light and a shadow and a glow that reminds me of Africa.

We rocket past a herd of bison—some rancher's folly. Once they numbered as many as 50 million west of the Mississippi—so many, in fact, condensation from their breaths created early morning fog across entire counties. The repeating rifle, a voracious demand for hides, and blind greed led to their extermination. En masse, bison were not especially wily: often men on horseback could shoot half a herd before the survivors, milling idiotically about the carcasses of their friends, realized something was amiss. By the beginning of the 20th century, buffalo numbers had dwindled to 3,000. To see them today, on the rebound, restored to Indian country, makes my heart skip a beat.

Indian towns are unfathomable at speed. No more than a gathering of frame houses, each distinguished from the other by color not shape. Their yards are landscaped with satellite dishes, doghouses, rusty pickups, little grass. If I am struck by anything as the Empire Builder (gasp!) charges through the Fort Peck Indian Reservation, it's that Indians have something else on their minds other than housing.

In Wolf Point, I detrain, rent a car, and double-back to the town of Poplar. Bill Bryan has arranged for me to meet Curly Youpee, a Sioux so I might be introduced to the sweat lodge ceremony. Curly's "sweat" is in the shape of an igloo, framed with willows, roofed in blankets. Since dawn, river rock from the Poplar River has been roasting on a nearby fire; it will be my task and privilege, as guest, to carry these stones on the end of a pitchfork into a pit at the center of the "sweat" while Curly and his friend, Ben Greyhawk, wait inside.

Sweat lodges are only materially like saunas. Inside, I will engage in a religious ceremony that reveals something of Native American spiritual thought. What I didn't expected is the ceremonies' impact on me. With each load of stones placed in the sweat's interior, I have been instructed to intone "for my relations." Once inside, all of us naked except for towels, sit upright on a carpet that climbs the walls. Curly tells me that here in this sweat, we shall all meet our ancestors, become reattached to earth, animal, plant, and landscape. Together we three form three points of the compass, reaching not merely to the ends of the earth but the quadrants of the universe. So far, I find the process interesting.

The door closes; blackness is now absolute. "Don't be surprised if you feel something brushing against your forehead. It's just the Creator touching you," says Curly.

"Sure," I think. As soon as Ben pours water onto the hot rocks, the humidity soars. I may as well be on the Red Sea during monsoon season. Now Ben begins his song to the Creator while I struggle for breath. Curly has told me tales of other guests unable to cope with the discomfort, who bolted across the white hot rocks for the door. Will I be such a one? No way, I think. I'd rather suffocate than be found a wimp. Ben's chant, its words incomprehensible, soon subsumes all other thoughts; it possesses an astonishing hypnotic power—a kind of mantra whose effect must lie in the very monotony of sound, capable of tapping my animal brain. I find myself edging past consciousness toward some inner quiet, immune to tickles of sweat pouring from my face into the cheap carpet or the furnace breath scalding my face. Later, I will wonder whether this state of calm approximates the serenity said, on occasion, to proceed a violent death.

Suddenly the door is opened and a cool prairie wind brushes my face. The sweat ceremony is divided into four acts, called "doors," also representing quadrants of the compass. Each will remind us, we're told, of the debt we owe our ancestors, our lifetime bond to nature. "Sit straight up," admonishes Curly, "so you can look the most pitiful to the Creator."

Curly is a big man with a face ravaged by childhood smallpox. After a self-described youth of dissolution and rootlessness, running with other displaced Indians on the West coast, Curly has spent the last decade reaffirming his Indian soul and reinforcing, as he says, his "pitifulness before the Creator." When he returned to the reservation, he started performing the Sun Dance ceremony—the most brutal ritual of all. For years this "barbarous" ceremony in which the participant must hang from a tree by ropes laced into his chest, was outlawed by the Bureau of Indian Affairs. Now, I can't keep my eyes from his proud flesh, angry in the heat of the sweat lodge. Of us all, he sits the straightest, hair varnished to skull, one long braid falling straight behind, so long it brushes the carpet. I'm in awe—struck by the grace with which he reveals to me, a perfect stranger, the secret faith of his culture. By giving up drink, reaffirming his roots, he is, I suspect, reflection of an Indian renaissance, but I wonder is he alone?

On the third "door" I very nearly come unglued; I reach my apparent outer limits for discomfort and panic. My own pitifulness is apparent, I know, not only to my Creator but to me. But soon after this door begins, I discover my only escape lies in flight within—to a private, refrigerated world of nonsequential dreams. In it, there's no measure of time and I can do anything—even fly.

After the fourth door, when we return to the original points of our compass, the door opens for the last time, the lodge fills with the smell of sweetgrass, sage, and cedar and I'm shown a path to the cool waters of the Poplar. Here I wallow in muddy water, restored to simplicity.

Late that afternoon on my return to Wolf Point to catch the next Empire Builder, I meet Oliver Archdale, an Assiniboine. Tall and heavy-boned, Oliver, like Curly, is another who's recently reclaimed an Indian legacy, determined, like Curly, Native American culture won't die. To that end, he's erected a reproduction of a 19th-century village on the banks of the Missouri. He intends to show outsiders like me what he calls the "Indian gift of living," in other words introduce us to a traditional life in a village. I look at the river and ask him about Lewis and Clark. They must have passed this very spot in 1805. "Was their journey the beginning of the end for Indians?"

"Never," he responds vehemently. "Our culture is only dead if you let it die…. For some of us it's going to live forever."

Framed by willows, the encampment is composed of six white teepees. In one, a fire has been set, its heat sure antidote to the sudden dusk chill along the river. Oliver and I sit on the ground, brainwashed by flames. I tell Oliver about the teepee at the Bar 20 and the solace it's brought. "Why does it have this affect on me?" I ask him, playing with the kindling.

"Because here you're close to the Creator. You sleep on great-grandmother earth from from where you've come.... It's an energy source, a human battery."

Traveling west, the railway hopscotches and helixes beside Highway 2. Occasionally, I spot roadside crosses where young bloods, high on drink or drugs, have careened off the road and met their Creator—a problem of epidemic proportions on reservations. Far to the south are landscapes that recall Charlie Russell—sere buttes, long rolling mesas. To the south, in the winter of 1886-87, he painted "The Last of the 10,000," reproduced on countless postcards. It illustrates the fate of the last surviving cow of Jesse Phelps, an absentee cattleman. In this almost childish drawing, the drifts are overwhelming, the temperature subzero as wolves move in for the kill. During that epic winter some 90 percent of Dakota and Montana herds perished. The catastrophe was the seminal moment of pioneer history. In spring, most ranchers called it quits. Those who stayed probably would become better cowmen. Almost all changed businesses.

For Native Americans 1886-87 was just another bad winter. Recent years had all been demoralizing. After the Civil War, the white man began expropriating Indian territory with a vengeance. Treaties were signed reallocating one reservation for another. Sometimes the ink wasn't even dry on one treaty before it was revoked for another, in each instance, the Indian take severely reduced. Most paper treaties the Indians were shown they never understood. Since Indian authority was diffuse, chiefs arbitrarily shifting roles within the tribe, white negotiators had no difficulty in exploiting a seemingly indecisive and vacilating command. For Indians the pale face's lust for individual land was enigmatic, for, to them, no one person could possess it. The landscape belonged whole to the tribe, in trust. It was never theirs to buy, sell or barter. But during the late 19th century, Indians, lashed by war, disease, and the loss of an economic base, were essentially rudderless, and, in exchange for firewater or guns, they would submit to coercion and sign deeds they never fully understood. They were subjected to a ruinous cycle of hypocrisy and deceit, and, for them, there was no recourse to justice—at least in white courts of law.

As my Empire Builder tackles the run between Wolf Point and Havre, I am transformed from Charlie Russell images into the world of Indians. To the south lies Snake Butte, a towering remnant of the earth's granite mantle. Locally, it is recognized as a sacred site. Here, for hundreds of years, Assiniboine and Gros Ventre warriors have sought exile. Five days, five nights prior to battle, they retreated to this plateau for self-denial, fasting, meditation. This ritual is called "vision quest" and, even today, as a rite of maturity, young men from the Fort Belknap Reservation come here for mortification of the flesh.

I detrain once again, this time at midpoint. Havre is through and through a railway and cow town, its pioneering days preserved underground in a remarkable labyrinth of saloon, bank, and bordello. Interesting, but my mind is elsewhere. I leave town by rental car to drive 40 miles southeast, to the Bear's Paw Battlefield, sacred to the Nez Perce ("nezz purse"). Here in everyday hills, I will come to feel the bitter and the sweet of people displaced by history.

Through the mid-19th century, the Nez Perce lived in the lush lands of Washington, Oregon, and Idaho. Traditionally, they had been at peace with the white man until gold prospectors, in contempt of existing treaties, invaded their territory. In 1862 and 1863 new treaties were drawn up, but these were signed by only a few chiefs, without tribal consensus. Many Nez Perce simply refused to sign. They resisted all directives from the federal government in Washington, choosing instead to stay where they had been born—in the Wallowa Valley. By the 1870s the dissidents' position had become precarious since a new wave of interlopers—this time farmer-settlers—had displaced them along the valley's lush bottomlands. The year was 1877 and these noncompliant Nez Perce begrudgingly accepted their fate and agreed to the odious move. They set off for their new reservation, but en route, a few young bloods, simmering from loss, took revenge and killed a handful of settlers. Now all "non-treaty" Nez Perce, knowing the U.S. Government would seek revenge, took flight into the "no man's land" of the West, their route lying in an easterly direction. For four months of constant pursuit and attack, warriors, women, children, horses endured a forced march through Idaho, Montana, Yellowstone Park, and back into Montana. In October 1877, 40 miles short of sanctuary in Canada, an early winter set in. The Nez Perce were exhausted, ill-prepared for snow and cold. They were also demoralized by their betrayal by fellow Indians—Sioux, Cheyenne, and Assiniboine, serving the U.S. Army as scouts. After six days, the Nez Perce chief, charged with the welfare of women, children, and horses, surrendered to the U.S. Army. He was given Colonel Nelson Miles's solemn oath his people would be allowed safe passage to the treaty reservation west in Idaho. Instead, the Army broke its word and exiled the Nez Perce east to Oklahoma where many of them were to die, some say of broken hearts.

Here on the surrender site, the sense of tragedy extends to me. My notes are revealing:

"I am standing on benchland in Northern Montana surrounded by 15 school children still dozy from an all-night drive. Dressed in his regulation National Park Service Smoky the Bear uniform, Otis Half Moon, hair cropped like a pageboy's, olive skin, axe-sharp features, tells the tale of the 1,170-mile retreat followed by battle and surrender. At each ridge he invokes another chief's name. His voice carries far on this crisp wind of autumn that makes cottonwood cotton scatter like mayfly hatches and brings the clouds of Canada thundering overhead. The names he intones are illusory—to me, pagan church bells: Chief Looking Glass, White Bird, Eagle Necklace and, most celebrated of all, Thunder Traveling To Loftier Heights, best known as Chief Joseph.

"'This is sacred ground,' says Otis. 'All along this embankment lie human beings. The remains of *our people*. And being an Indian and a National Park Ranger, I am torn.'

"I'm wrenched. Otis's monologue has levitated me like a time machine, to a harrowing event that virtually reworked relations between two races. I have been made to conjure Indian women and children burrowing into earthworks where they would be pummeled by 12 pound howitzer shells until death. They're still here, covered by ground they dug, in this place so little visited, so easily ignored. The minuscule Bear's Paw National Park seems to me ground hallowed not so much by war and death but by the rights Nez Perce and so many other Indians lost here. Along featureless coulees where blades of prairie grass are ceaselessly rewoven by wind, a way of life yielded forever to brute greed and the pomposity of a ruling nation. At this site, after nearly four months of fearful marching, Chief Joseph capitulated with words that still me make quake: 'Hear me, my chiefs, I am tired; my heart is sick and sad. From where the sun now stands I will fight no more forever.'

"Blood-frying words: with them the freedoms of the Northern Plains Indians were decisively subverted to the will of others—namely, that of *my* ancestors."

So it was, as well, with the Bar 20 and the mountains, forests and plains surrounding it. Five years after the battle of the Bear's Paw, with the U.S. Government feeling vindicated throughout the West, the Crow Nation said goodbye to the Boulder Valleys and then were shifted east to far less salubrious lands. Their words of farewell have been lost in the great maw of Western history. At the time, the Crows had only Plenty Coups, but no Chief Joseph to lead them, nor were there hotheads to question authority or dramatize their betrayal. Submissively, they packed up their lodges, loaded travois and horse, and began their trek toward the so-called Custer battlefield, where, at least on paper, they had once won their greatest battle. And around this place, hallowed for bluster and vainglory, they would, so ironically, live for another century, perhaps forever.

"Today, I accompany young Nez Perce pilgrims, just arrived from their homes in Idaho and I'm not feeling altogether comfortable with what I've just learned. In fact, I'm distinctly awkward. Some of my companions can trace their ancestry to the chiefs invoked by eloquent Otis, one straight to Chief Joseph. Handsome, pensive kids: girl's hair glistening like petroleum, boy's tumbling in long braids between their shoulder blades. They are here this weekend to celebrate a so-called "time of healing" between tribes, between Indians, between whites. Only one other fellow white has shown up. Still these Nez Perce are not embittered people and the atmosphere of the pilgrimage is exhilaratingly free of rancor. With hands dug deep in pockets against the chill air, several generations of perfect strangers adopt me as a friend as we ponder the moral slaughter my ancestors wreaked on their forebears."

Otis Half Moon and I have been joined by Jim Magera, a white schoolteacher from Havre, arguably one of the best-informed scholars of the battleground. I ask him why outsiders, such as he and me, are so affected by this place. "Well, there were 22 soldiers killed here...and between 23 and 30 Indians...but you know, that's not the really important thing that happened here. You lose your freedom here, you lose your culture, you lose everything that is important to you as a human being. At other more famous battlefields...that really wasn't lost.... But it was here."

At the Bear's Paw Battleground, geology seems to conspire with the wind to speak after all these years and to say that the limbo that was the Nez Perces' lot after this battle is, in truth, the same emptiness all Northern Plains Indians have endured in the chaos of 19th- and 20th-century history. This spot marks where one sovereignty was terminated, another begun, where old ways would end and new ones, famous for compromise and equivocation, start.

"Why," I ask Otis, "are Indians so forgiving?" We're now under fluorescent lights in a large school gym in Harlem, east of Havre, for a powwow to continue our celebration of "healing" especially between the Nez Perce and those who betrayed them. Large drums, eagle headdresses, ankle bells, and brilliant beadwork, dazzle me, filling me with longing for the clarity of an unhomogenized culture. Still, I know that tomorrow all these dancers will be wearing jeans and cowboy hats.

Otis is staring at three elderly women, dressed like birds of prey, marching in tandem to a beat so slow it's beyond recognition. "We're all going to die some day, go back to Mother Earth," he replies, now turning his eyes to a beaded child no more than six, whirling to his own rhythm. "She won't spit me back because I'm an Indian or spit you back because you're white.... We walk on the same Mother. We have one sky above us. We're one people."

We roll out of the Shelby station with a new train crew. As soon as we move, I begin to pick out the Rockies emerging through a phosphorescent dusk. After this flatland trip, they are, in every way, a shock. Soon we'll be in country that belonged to the once-feared Blackfoot. In Browning, I leave the Empire Builder once again, this time to go fishing with a descendant of these blood-thirsty warriors.

Joe Kipp is unlike other Indians I've met. He's outrageously cocky, full of chutzpah, never in doubt he's a member of a chosen race. Shortly after dawn he takes me to Kipp Lake, named after the white trader who adopted his grandfather. "The Crows," he announces matter-of-factly, "wet themselves every time they heard the name 'Blackfoot.'" Not only were Blackfoot supreme as warriors, controlling two thirds of Montana, much of Alberta and Saskatchewan, but, according to Joe, they were the best-looking. "You see," he says, "When we took prisoners we always kept the best-looking for ourselves as wives. It shows in our breeding. There's no such thing as pure Blackfoot for we were always raiding others."

Being a Blackfoot helps, but Joe Kipp probably has come by his self-confidence from guiding pale faces. His bonhomie seems a certain ticket into the promising world of ecotourism. He is dedicated to introducing visitors not only to catch-and-release fishing, but to a culture stunningly different from their own. According to Joe, of the 24 fishing lakes in the million-and-a-half-acre Blackfoot Reservation, Kipp Lake, naturally, "is the best." Here, with snow lying in the shadows of banks and western grebe and whistling swan watching us from far shores, we cast long lines for "giants." In the too few hours we're able to fish, these would elude us. All we could claim would be a few unremarkable 16-inch rainbows. Still, I find in Joe a refreshing spirit: "You know, we Indians can't just use any commercially tied flies. We have to tie them ourselves. We pray when we tie them, and we have an elder bless them for us." I study his eyes to see if he is pulling a fast one. His expression tells me nothing. "This is called the Kipp Special Fly, blessed by the best. Use it. You'll see."

Nothing happens except Joe changes the conversation. "My father and a lot of people of that generation were taken away from their families at a very young age by the U.S. Government. They were put into boarding schools and disciplined every time they spoke native Blackfoot tongue. They had their braids cut off, their moccasins taken away.... They were forced to be assimilated.... To this day every time my father tries to speak Blackfoot, he just stutters. He can speak English very fluently but not his native tongue.... I'm not bitter.... We can't change what happened yesterday, but, by golly, we're changing what's going to happen tomorrow."

I choose not to overnight in Browning, the seat of the Blackfoot Reservation. Instead, I catch the evening Empire Builder. I stay onboard long enough to cross the Continental Divide and to chat with the conductor, an acquaintance from a previous leg. In Essex, I hop off for dinner and bed.

This flag stop, home to 18 stoic residents, is beside one of the prize hotels of the entire route—the Izaak Walton Inn. Here locomotives idle, waiting to assist freight trains across the Marias Pass to the southeast. The inn was built in 1939 to house railroad crews and to serve as a gateway to Glacier National Park. The gateway was never built and today only railway buffs, fly fishermen, and cross-country skiers descend upon this large rambling Tudor hotel, as eccentric as its name.

At dinner, listening to the howl of freight trains, I ask about Glacier National Park, a few feet to the north. Today it's known for views, hikes, grizzlies, and mountain goats. Once it was the western edge of the Blackfoot Nation. At the time of their encounter with the white man, these nomadic Indians depended largely on buffalo ranging east through the plains. Glacier was where the tribe retreated in summer. But it was never enough to sustain them. Once the herds on the Plains had been extirpated, the Blackfoot began dying from malnutrition, smallpox and, some say, grief. Soon the tribe had all but been annihilated.

In 1895, a white friend of the Blackfoot, George Bird Grinnell, cajoled them into releasing their summer range for mineral exploration. In 1910, the mining caper never having come to much, the mountains were set aside by the U.S. Government as a national park. Thereafter, the Blackfoot would only be allowed inside by "invitation only," usually for the entertainment of tourists.

The next evening I board the Empire Builder for the last time. Because of bad planning, I realize the most beautiful leg of the journey will be cast in darkness. What a shame to reach my final stop, White Fish, with its Tyrolean-styled station, under arc lights.

By morning I've recovered from my disappointment. I'm staying at comfortable Grouse Mountain Lodge for one final visit—this to the Flathead Indian Reservation. Its 1.1 million alpine acres belong to a few white settlers, but mostly to the Confederated Salish and Kootenai Tribes, historic enemies of the Blackfoot.

Today while their range is a shadow of what it once was, the Salish and the Kootenai control land that is the envy of all—the southern shores of Flathead Lake, much of the Mission Mountains to the south, and the fertile meadows west to Idaho. These Indians see their future not in casinos but in their land and wildlife. The buffalo in the National Bison Range on the reservation contains some of the bloodlines of the survivors of the 60 million that once roamed the West. Revenues from the KwaTaqNuk Resort on Flathead Lake, an attractive lake hotel, directly benefit the tribes. In this reservation everyone wants to bend my ear about culture and natural resources.

High on a hill overlooking the Mission Valley, I find the most eloquent testimony of all from Velda Shelby, who represents the tribal Confederation. She tells me that only 20 years ago at school white teachers taught her it was "'bad to be an Indian...that (as a people) we do not contribute to society....'" I quickly do the calculations in my head only to realize she is referring to the time I first arrived in Montana. It was a period of my life when I was besotted by cowboy ways and thought little of the Indian.

"Now," she proclaims, "it's our turn to tell the story." As we start down the hill, I ask her whether she considers herself foremost an American or foremost a Kootenai. She smiles, knowing perhaps that at school only one answer might have been tolerated. Looking me square in the face, she says, "Today, I am Kootenai first, American second."

After we say good-bye, as I wait for my lift to the Bar 20, I keep repeating her words. Is she being un-American? And what would she and all the others I've met think if I brought them to the Bar 20? Would they look at that beautiful West Boulder country and think "stolen property?" Would they stare at me and cry "thief"?

I think of the 1933 Winold Reiss image of Turtle that dominates the kitchen of the Bar 20. In nearly every station of this trip I've seen other calendar Indians, painted by Winold Reiss, commissioned by the Great Northern Railway. At the Izaak Walton Hotel beside Glacier Park, I saw three: Bird

Rattler, Wades in the Water, Takes the Gun Strong: looks from the 1930s and 1940s that I thought I would never witness again. In each countenance, there was a heavy-lidded impassivity that I sensed concealed a sort of totemic grief. I saw the warriors as victims of history, each still suffering, albeit atavistically, from desperate forced marches, brutal relocations that marked the history of their race in the 19th century.

The grieving, I discovered, is over. Today, if Winold Reiss were to paint the faces of Curley Youpee, Joe Kipp, or Velda Shelby, he would have to look for other qualities.

The Indian has returned to the Northern Plains and has, I've found, much to say.

~

CHAPTER 17

Portraying Indians

F rom my earliest moment at the Bar 20 I began thinking of art. It would appear the Coxes had filled their rooms with heavy oils. From her will, I learned Bab Cox treasured family heirlooms. They transported them wherever they went—from Connecticut to Maryland to Montana and finally to Virginia. Sitting alone in this house, they would have found the stare of ancestors touchstones to their past and a comforting release from the occasional brutishness of the West.

Family portraits didn't work for me in the West. I saw another opportunity for the Bar 20's dark walls. I wanted the house to reflect its heritage, not mine. And the heritage I especially valued was the one that preceded the West Boulder Reserve, the Magats, the Kahles, the Huggins, the Coxes and all those other pilgrims.

Indians. Soon after we acquired the Bar 20, I became transfixed by long-ago images of them. Joseph Henry Sharp had caught something very arresting about them. So too, on some occasions, had E. A. Burbank. As well as O. C. Seltzer and Henry Farny. The photographs of Edward Curtis—they had all sought an evanescent look that seemed to speak for history and an entire race of people.

What was it? At the turn of the century, I think artists, perhaps unwittingly, caught a privileged look into the Indian's eye. At its best, it evoked a sense of collective loss, an expression of cultural grief so powerful I would physically ache. Occasionally the artist might disguise that look behind a smile, a vacant stare but it was always there—haunting and puzzling. The pang of loss, I came to believe, emerges in more paintings than I ever expected. For nearly a century, artists—many of them European—arrived in the Northern Plains to confront people broken, betrayed, robbed, demoralized by the onslaught of Easterners and their demands. It wasn't so much that Native Americans had lost their land, their living and, so often, their lives. In works of art, I could see they had lost their way.

My taste in portraits of the Indian selected for this internal equivocation, for my aversion to stereotype, for a suspicion there was more to a face than what met the eye. Indians on the edge of the 20th century often possessed one look for the world, another under wraps. A good artist, on a good day, could avoid formula and find them both.

As soon as I reached this conclusion, I wanted to paper the Bar 20 with Indians, both sorrowful and majestic. I now lived on land that had once been theirs and, I concluded, I owed it to them not to forget. Perhaps through art, I might always remember.

While I never could afford grand art, I began to accumulate a few little paintings, often executed by unknown artists who, in my opinion, had "gotten it right." Sometimes I scored: I'd find an image of someone—mostly a Crow—who may well have hunted this very valley. One little Edward Curtis photograph entitled "A Mountain Fastness" portrays five Indians watering their horses in a river that I swear is ours. The Douglas firs and the high rimrocks seem familiar. In 1905 when Curtis created this dark and brooding moment, these warriors might actually have been within a few miles of our place.

Art can be adventure. It can take you off the road, out of your way, into uncharted country, and, like all great journeys, it informs you of yourself.

Art took me into libraries, museums, galleries as well as into auction rooms, where occasionally I discovered the outer limits of my mania.

When Kathryn entered my life, she was eager to feed my passion for Indians. She instantly fathomed their right to the Bar 20, and she readily helped me close the historic circle of our place in Montana. Soon after we first met, she began to tantalize me with auction catalogs. Later, she endorsed my decision to hang a portrait of a chief above the mantel. When we had been together for a year, she surprised me with a gift of beaded Sioux gauntlets and, later, some beaded Blackfoot cuffs.

Once, in an Idaho auction catalog Kathryn and I spotted a watercolor of an Indian on horseback. He was a solitary soul, beautifully turned out for battle without, it appeared, any battle to fight. We both loved the image and I vowed to make a very modest run at it.

Miraculously, at the moment it sold, serious buyers had left the room. By telephone, we cast the winning bid—all the more strange since I violated Kath's golden rule of never buying art without first examining it personally. When, several weeks later, the crate arrived, we found the painting even more astonishing than expected, especially because of a small label adhering to the back of the canvas.

The name on the scrap of paper was familiar—that of my great-great-uncle, once removed. I was puzzled. After a few calls, I learned the painting's provenance. In the 1930s, it was sold by my great-great-uncle's son's widow to a small Texas museum. The museum, in turn, displayed it for half a century and then, after a change in institutional policy, deaccessioned it. When I called remote members of my family in St. Louis and Djakarta, I uncovered family history no one had ever before explained.

My great-great-uncle had been one of the first major ranchers in Montana—far to the east of the Bar 20. After 15 years in eastern Montana he began incurring great losses. Soon, with awful sadness, he left, never to return. Most startling of all, this Montana obsession had occurred prior to statehood, nearly a century before my time. One of my great-great-uncle's cowhands had been the artist who painted the Indian we so admired. The warrior in the painting might well have been one of those dispossessed by my own family.

The look in the eye: it is now a passion. If someone were to ask me which artist captures it best with the Indians of the Northern Plains, I wouldn't hesitate. Winold Reiss. The work of this German-born artist, now dead for nearly half a century, was my first introduction to the bitter and the sweet. For a time, he, like his subjects, became an obsession. What endowed an artist with a passion for Indians? Here is what I found.

Nothing gives away the surprise. The mailbox on the forested lane in upstate New York is unpainted, the driveway treacherous in winter, and the converted barn at the end weathered, unadorned, defiant. The son, architect of this subtle memorial, guards against enthusiasm. When he greets a visitor, there is about him, rather, a laconic air of resignation, as if he were but the porter for history's comings and goings. It is all a front. He has, it appears, spent his 85 years trying to disguise a passion. With few words, he takes you through the minute kitchen, into an angular room adorned with hand-carved chairs and a spitting fire. Here he pauses to caution you of the cold before sliding open the door to the repository. You enter a vast room, arresting in every way. At one end, beyond a screen wall that filters the wind and the piping of bats, there is a Blackfoot tepee. The moon shines on it. At another end of the great room, in a corner, a carved table, reminiscent of a German *bierstub*, is set for drinks. For a brief second, one's eyes spot a bleached horse's skull and, high overhead, a fringed surrey, groaning in the wind as it swings from the ridge pole.

These are but diversions, for one is instantly commanded by the art. The paintings illuminate the rough lumber siding of the barn, as sunbirds will transform gray rock.

On one canvas, a construction worker, half again taller than life, wields a pick; on others, towheaded boys, players in the Oberammergau Festival, smile wistfully at each other; a great Piegan chief seems ambiguous about his own resplendence; a transcendently innocent Mexican mother cradles her infant while her man appears impatient, even desperate. Hate and ennui, coquetry, alcoholism, envy, blindness, calculation, despair, and glory. On these walls one can penetrate the face of man.

The time frame of these paintings is critical; not only does this room capture a moment before the human species opted for T-shirts and jeans, but before the bone structure of our faces softened, the fire in our eyes blew out. This last hiccup of cultural history is recorded by one artist seemingly indifferent to racial stereotypes, an artist with passion for man's variety, quirks, anomalies. Here eccentricity has become the stitch of life. And while the subject of each painting appears to be dressed with exactitude, what endures, in the end, is a kind of subcutaneous character.

The rediscovery of Winold Reiss can be dated to October 27, 1989, when the Smithsonian's National Portrait Gallery opened the exhibition "To Color America: Portraits by Winold Reiss." The show ran through April 1, 1990 and highlighted African-American leaders of the Harlem Renaissance, the Blackfoot and Blood Indians of Montana and Western Canada. Those who had recognized Reiss foremost as an Indian artist—a Depression-era George Catlin—were surprised by everything else: his portraits of Harlem blacks and his remarkable renderings for restaurant design, which heralded decorative modernism in the United States during the first half of this century.

"He came to America," explains Tjark Reiss, Winold's son, the man who presides over the barn, "to paint Indians." Even accounting for the European fascination with the American Indian, inspired in part by the Leatherstocking Tales of James Fenimore Cooper, Reiss's motivation seems today a mite romantic. He arrived here in 1913, a 27-year-old man, married just a year. His wealthy and strikingly beautiful wife, who he met at art school, financed the

Atlantic passage. "He thought there'd be Indians waiting on the dock in New York," adds the son.

To someone averse to war, the Kaiser's increasing belligerence must have been ominous. Hans, Winold's brother and fellow pacifist, had already immigrated to Sweden. But for Winold, America with its dashing Indians, held all the allure. The New World seemed as far from the scene of impending battle as any destination.

From photographs, yellowed by age, one sees a young man with high-intensity eyes, dark hair carefully swept back, a mustache. All through his life he would insist on dressing well. On one occasion, a Tyrolean hat would set the style, on another, a beret, and on still another, a trilby. Even during the leanest years of the Depression, his Hupmobile mired in muck on the roads of Montana, Winold Reiss would continue to defy the economy in his natty, fringed buckskin jacket, the best-dressed member of the group.

But while Reiss invariably faced the photographer with fixed jaw, one might detect that he did not take himself all that seriously. A letter home at age 17, during a lengthy bicycle excursion through Germany with his brother, is illustrated with cartoons in which he has cast himself as the victim of events—a bewildered, gawky youth. Indeed, this self-deprecating air, this bent for the slapstick, is what ultimately sealed his bond with the Blackfoot.

Reiss' first art teacher was his father, in Karlsruhe. Fritz Reiss was a well-established landscape painter, specializing in Black Forest scenes that are still being reproduced on greeting cards. By the time the son received formal artistic education—at Munich's Royal Academy of Fine Arts and the Kunstgewerbeschule (School of Arts and Crafts), he was well prepared for an expansive curriculum. He studied alternately under Julius Diez and Franz von Stuck, the bon vivant and celebrated teacher of Paul Klee and Wassily Kandinsky. From this association, Reiss developed a sense that art was the outline for all living spaces, whether it be represented by a woodcut, by the welcome of a couch, line of a face, profile of a mantelpiece.

This protean artistic capacity would distinguish him from many of his American peers.

As Reiss abandoned the sentimentality of German romanticism, he also witnessed the dethroning of Art Nouveau as well as the popularity of cubism and German Postimpressionism. Reiss's technique was peculiarly positioned to make use of the insightful standards of the portraiture of Hans Holbein the Younger as well as the decorative geometry of the world of ornaments, lived and breathed by von Stuck. These two divergent artistic purposes merged when Reiss focused on his crafts and, especially, the American Indian.

Winold Reiss was in the United States for six years before he could realize his Indians dreams. War and economics had intervened. Living with his wife and infant son and working out of a studio at 96 Fifth Avenue, he devoted much of his time to commercial art. His design for the interior of the Busy Lady Bakery exploited the brilliant use of light, the spareness of lines, and the bright colors that were to become his trademark. In 1916 he started his first art school and three years later he completed designs for the Crillon Restaurant at 15 East 48th Street. At first the owner of the building rejected the plans, saying they were too modern, too "circuslike," and threatened to break the lease with the restaurateur. Later this landlord become one of Reiss's greatest supporters, refusing to dine anywhere else. The Crillon was America's first Art Deco restaurant and New York's smartest. While its boldness may have perplexed the haute cuisine establishment at first, soon the lightness, order, and purity of Reiss's Art Deco became appreciated for its elegant calm. The Crillon boomed. Many of the original drawings of Reiss's interior and industrial designs are now in the permanent collection of the Library of Congress.

Above all, Reiss was drawn to people, and New York was the place to find every ethnic type. "I can remember," says his son, Tjark, "walking through Union Square on our way to Luchow's. Dad would spot someone sitting on a bench or on the curb and he'd nod to Uncle Hans (now in America with his

Dad). Negotiations would begin as Dad and I watched, and as soon as the fellow accepted the terms, Uncle Hans would nod to us and Dad would head back to the studio, lunch now forgotten. The first Indian Dad painted was a Blackfoot he found on the Third Avenue El. He had just been fired from the circus and was very hung over. Dad borrowed a war bonnet and beaded shirt from the American Museum of Natural History and was beside himself with excitement. I can remember it well.

"The first question he always asked of anyone posing for him—whether fashionable New York society lady or somebody he'd found on the street—was their ethnic origin. It was important to him to know this background and he felt people should be proud of who they were. He had absolutely no racial prejudice. He defended all races, exalting in their differences."

In the fall of 1919 Winold Reiss at last encountered his first Plains Indians. He and his student, W. Langdon Kihn, disembarked from the Great Northern Railway in Browning, Montana, at the heart of the Blackfoot Nation. Those glory days, when Blackfoot warriors were masters of the Northern Plains, had now passed. The last battle with the Assiniboine-Cree, longtime enemies, was barely recalled by a handful of elders, and after 1919 the tribe was permanently confined to the reservation. Still, in the first years of Reiss' work among the Blackfoot, few of them had entirely lost their identity. Tradition and symbol continued to buoy them.

Reiss leaped into Indian society with schoolboy gusto. On the station platform, when he saw his first Blackfoot, he slapped him on the back and then showed him the palm of his hand in the much-caricatured Indian greeting. His familiarity and enthusiasm was, for the Blackfoot, totally bewildering, the greeting "How" meaningless. Still, Turtle, also known as Angry Bull (as Reiss learned to address him), was actually more confused than maligned. In time, he became a lasting friend and much-painted subject.

Working out of one of the public rooms in the hotel, sometimes trudging on snowshoes to Indian lodges to paint by kerosene light, and sleeping in a bed that was alternately occupied during daylight hours by a cowboy, Reiss managed to complete 35 portraits in 30 days. The Blackfoot were so impressed by his industry, they initiated him into the tribe and named him "Beaver Child."

"I think their respect for him comes from something else," says Paul Raczka, once the owner of a trading post on the Blackfoot Reservation, and an acquaintance of several elders who had encountered Reiss. "There was absolutely no guile about the man. He wanted to record their greatness, not just for him but for them—and they spotted that immediately. I mean, look at these paintings, of Shot On Both Sides, for instance. He's wearing his yellow-and-red war paint, his red-horned headdress. Blackfoot don't put on finery for anyone. It represents their status and it's a private matter. Winold Reiss had, over time, earned their trust. He was, they knew, one white man who wasn't about to rip them off."

"The bond between them and Dad was laughter," adds Tjark. "For instance, they went wild with his description of an audience between the German king: how you couldn't turn your back on the old monarch even when you were leaving his chambers. Dad reenacted this scene many times, tripping over stools, fumbling for the door handle, bowing and then falling down. They adored the skit."

When Reiss returned to New York, his pastels and tempera paintings were exhibited at the E. F. Hansfstaengl Gallery in January 1920. These Indians were not stylized "redskins" the public had come to expect from the Taos and Southwestern Schools. Instead they stood by themselves: real people decoratively interpreted.

Strong and sometimes somber faces, illuminated hands, heavy with age, were highlighted by the bold lines of accessories—beads, quill work, painted tents, baskets, parfleches, and blankets.

Nearly every painting in the exhibit was purchased by Dr. Philip Cole; today, through a bequest, these constitute the permanent collection in the

Bradford Brinton Memorial Collection in Big Horn, Wyoming. Strangely, Reiss didn't return to paint Indians for eight years. In the interim, he developed his New York art school, completed many commissions for restaurants and hotels, and, in the fall of 1920, traveled to Mexico. Here he met Katherine Anne Porter, who was struck by the artist's ebullient energy. In declining Reiss's invitation to undertake a 25-mile walk that day, she noted in her journal: "He showed me some rather remarkable sketches of Indians and told an amazing story: he had tramped the states of Oaxaca, Jalisco, Puebla, and think Morelos...alone, unarmed, carrying enough food to last only from one village to another." During the next two years, Reiss illustrated several Porter short stories for *Century Magazine* as well as articles on Mexico for *Survey Graphic Magazine*, where she served as art editor.

Beginning in the mid-1920s, Winold Reiss spent time in Harlem to paint portraits of the African Americans there. It was a period of stirring cultural change, now referred to as the Harlem Renaissance. The clichés seemed to interest Reiss little; he was drawn instead to figures who, to him at least, were at the forefront of the revolution: black lawyers, black college students, a singer, a poetess, a public school teacher. In 1927, he painted black Americans in the South, notably on St. Helena Island off South Carolina Low Country.

In 1925, once a body of this work was complete, no gallery in the "heartland" of New York City showed any interest in the subject. Black people portrats were not sought after. Only the Harlem Branch Library agreed to put on the show, and when it opened, his work attracted the attention of only a small, dedicated following. The paintings were unexpected: Roland Hayes looking askance, his head lost in simple white; Paul Robeson smirking as the Emperor Jones, his handsome, powerful head still unaware of contradictions; a little girl from St. Helena, her hair bobbed and face explosive with laughter.

Black essayist Alain Locke wrote of the show: "And by the simple but rare process of not setting up petty canons in the face of nature's own creative artistry, Winold Reiss has achieved what amounts to a revealing discovery of the significance, human and artistic, of one of the great dialects of human physiognomy.... In design...he looks not merely for decorative elements, but for the pattern of the culture from which it sprang." Today, 12 of these paintings are in the permanent collection of the Smithsonian's National Portrait Gallery.

By now, Hans, a sculptor, had arrived in New York to help his brother with the art school. The muggy summers in the city, however, inflamed his allergies and he took to spending time in Glacier National Park, doing what he liked best—mountain climbing. One of his first clients, soon after he obtained his mountain-guide license, was Louis W. Hill, president of the Great Northern Railway. From this brief association, a deal was struck for his brother to paint Blackfoot Indians in Montana and Alberta on behalf of the railway. Beginning in 1927 and over the course of ten summers until 1948, Winold Reiss undertook one railroad commission after another.

In the first summer, and for many thereafter, Tjark, then age 13, served his father as scribe and crayon sharpener. Winold was now divorced, and during the school year this only child commuted between his father's studio in Greenwich Village and his mother's home uptown. And in summer, Tjark went to Montana with his Dad.

"During all those years, I can only remember Dad taking one day off—and that was to go mountain climbing in Glacier Park with Uncle Hans. Part way up, he found he suffered from vertigo and for five hours was left by the others on an 18-inch-wide ledge towering over Glacier Park. He disliked that experience so intensely, he never again allowed himself a day off."

So consumed by the details of character was Winold Reiss that he hired his son to record the history of each of his Glacier Park subjects: their lineage, their great battles, their horse-rustling forays, their first meetings with whites. Tjark's interpreter was Percy Creighton, half-Scot, half-Indian. He, too, returns to life today in paintings by Reiss, his eyes half-shuttered, feigning sleep, the cowboy hat his disguise. Besides interpreting, it was Percy's job to tell stories to the old Indians or to have them tell about their lives, to keep them alert.

"It was an extraordinary life for a boy. At the age of 45, Dad learned to drive and we reached Glacier Park by Hupmobile—long memorable drives when we stopped at as many Indian Reservations as we could. After Minneapolis, the tarmac gave out and when we weren't fighting the washboards, we were negotiating with farmers to pull us out of ditches.... After my Dad had a couple of profitable years, he bought a Cadillac. He paid $4,500 for it, and he was so proud of that car. But one year, his finances went for a loop and we had to put the Cadillac up on blocks the moment we reached the park.

"Dad, of course, never admitted he was strapped. Too proud for that. He simply said Montana roads would damage it. In the fall, once back in New York, I went up and down Broadway to used-car dealers. Dad refused to come with me. Finally I found one who offered $600 for the car. The news just killed my father. Times couldn't have been tougher."

In the summer of 1934 Reiss took his art school to Montana. He was known as a gifted teacher (among his many students in New York had been Marion Greenwood and Ludwig Bemelmans). The Glacier Park art school was located in a log lodge on the shore of St. Mary's Lake in sight of the rugged Continental Divide. "Classes began at 9 each morning," remembers Tjark. "Usually the Indians posed in their own ceremonial robes. However, if they didn't have any, we'd borrow a museum-quality one from Margaret Carberry, who ran the trading post in Glacier Park Station." In addition, Reiss offered free art lessons to the Blackfoot. "His message, whether to them or to blacks in New York," says Tjark, "was always 'Paint like yourselves, not like me.'"

Beginning in 1927, the Great Northern Railway underwrote most of Reiss's trips to the West. Louis Hill personally bought at least 80 of his paintings. Many were reproduced on the railway's monthly and later annual giveaway calendar. Today the Burlington Northern Railway, the Hill Estate, and the Anschutz Collection closely guard a king's ransom of these vintage Reiss's. Ned Jacob, a contemporary painter of Indians, knows many of the works. "It's quite extraordinary imagining one artist virtually painted an entire tribe," he comments. "I might occasionally take exception with him when he searched for a design and that design tarnished, compromised, his subject. But that's rare. Never did he patronize his subject. Never did he romanticize the Indian. He strength lies in the character he wrought from those faces. Only Karl Bodmer comes close."

Reiss's largest commission was the Cincinnati Union Terminal, opened in 1933. Here he was allowed a space of 12,000 square feet and given instructions "to come up with something about Cincinnati." Indeed he did: one year later this vast rotunda was illuminated by two 105-by-25-foot murals, illustrating the history of transportation, rise of Cincinnati, and the opening of the West. In the 450-foot-long concourse, 14 mosaic murals lined the walls, each one depicting the workers of the Midwestern city's industrial muscle. So driven was Reiss by this commission that, at the last minute, he suggested halving his fee in order to work in the material of his choice: glass mosaic.

For years this great work was one of Cincinnati's landmarks. When the days of long-distance rail travel came to an end, the station was mothballed. A decade ago, the industrial murals were moved to the Greater Cincinnati International Airport and, in 1989, construction was undertaken to transform the Union main terminal to house the Cincinnati Historical Society and the Natural History Museum. This mural commission, with over 4,000,000 pieces of Venetian glass, is the largest in the United States.

Between 1935 and 1946, Reiss's design work boomed. Henry Lustig, an immigrant whose first career had been as pushcart peddler, commissioned Reiss to design a restaurant. Lustig called it Longchamps and soon it begat a remarkable New York chain, each distinguished by an integral theme suggested and created by Reiss—one Mexican, one American presidents, and, naturally, one dedicated to Native Americans. In addition, nearly 30 theaters, hotels, taverns, offices, foyers, and cafes in New York, Chicago, and Boston were given the Reiss touch—a combination of modernism, fresh color, and clean, elegant lines to make people instantly feel comfortable.

For years Winold Reiss had dreamed of creating an Indian museum. He wanted to call it "Monument to the American Indian."

Reiss drew up plans for a spare, dignified building. He calculated he would need ten years to travel throughout the West, and he began a careful approach to sell the concept to America's great philanthropies. But, charity by charity, with cruel consistency, his proposal was rejected. By the late 1940s Winold Reiss's plan to build a museum, dedicated to America's Indians, was abandoned forever.

Reiss was less dismayed that it had been shelved than he was by the demoralization he had begun to observe among Indians. He despaired to see old friends abandon their ways, to watch the Bureau of Indian Affairs deny them access to pathways, customs, and beliefs that gave meaning to their lives. Most of all, Reiss loathed to watch the Indian drink. "He was appalled to see a human being—any human being—lose his dignity," recalls his son.

With his monument to the American Indian stillborn, Winold Reiss threw himself into other, unrelated projects. He seemed lost. On August 29, 1953, this German-born artist who celebrated America like no other, died of complications from a massive stroke. At the time, his great body of work, dedicated to Native Americans, was, except on railway calendars, largely ignored by America.

Just a few people learned of his death. After the ice thawed on Cut Bank Creek the following summer, a parcel arrived at the post office in Browning, Montana. It was sent by Tjark Reiss and was addressed to Bull Child, an old friend of his father's.

Several months later, Tjark learned through an interpreter Bull Child assembled all those Blackfoot Indians the artist had once touched. On a day when the wind played tricks, they gathered on Red Blanket Hill, at whose feet the cottonwoods were shedding. Here, with virtually the entire Blackfoot Nation in attendance, the ashes were thrown high into a hard blue sky. All watched as the wind scattered them for miles.

At long last, Winold Reiss had arrived.

CHAPTER 18

Speaking with Rocks

Everywhere I look these days, I see Indians. When I consider my predecessors at the Bar 20, I think about present-day Crows living near Crow Agency, 150 miles to the east. I think of Chief Plenty Coups who served as their titular head for nearly 40 years, living in a rough-hewn log cabin. I think of Blackfoot, once everyone's scourge, now confined to a small territory in the north of the state. But today's people only tell a partial story of Montana's past. Some of the rest can be read from the rocks.

Stark and totemlike, this rimrock is sentinel above the shortgrass prairie of the Bull Mountain Ranch. At most, this hard-angled butte made me appreciate, fleetingly, the raw bones of the American West. But most times, over two decades, I barely gave the formation any notice.

Two years ago these cliffs changed for me, forever. A team of archaeologists from the Department of Interior's Bureau of Land Management, appraising parcels of land in our county, spotted a series of anomalies on our cliffs. On closer inspection, they discovered the sandstone festooned with rock carvings and scratchings. Most of these petroglyphs they believe had been etched or "pecked" not much later than the time of the Lewis and Clark Expedition, perhaps many centuries before. The drawings feature teepees, feathered lances, stick figures said to be shamans, and, over one notable panel of rock, a foot warrior slaying a horseman. Remarkably, the warrior is a woman—the only female combatant yet to be documented among all the rock art of the Northern Plains.

Ever since, I have gotten into the habit of climbing these cliffs in late afternoon, when the lowering sun dramatizes its relief. I skirt ledges, scour rubble on the valley floor. One time I surprised a bobcat. Michael Kyte, the BLM's lead archaeologist in this region, spent a few hours with me at the site. He took me up the cliff onto the plateau where he paced the outline of long-ago encampments. He believes this spot was a seasonal bivouac for bands of Crow, even Shoshone, leaving homes to the south, probably in late fall, to hunt the great bull buffalo.

Sitting beneath the rock art, beside Duma, panting from the climb, her ears' cocked for inadvertent coyote yips, I feel the onset of night—the rush of chill air as the sun drops behind Dunne Mountain. Every time, I try to fathom why, long before barbed wire, this butte was a chosen campsite. From here, I see across sage and arroya a widening plain that on a crisp day pretends never to end. Above me are the remains of a prehistoric campfire. Nearby, there's a thin canyon at whose end a spring percolates from gray mud. Fresh water, good spotting, shelter—our butte has it all.

There's something else, altogether intimate ghosting about this place. In the evening, with the wind talking through gaps in the rock and the night star bright before all others, these cliffs urge me to float outside my skin. After an hour adrift in the illuminated black, I rise to become a nothing—phantom corpse more bird than mammal, high above sandstone, halfway to Orion.

Might rock art lend shape to the human spirit? Was this cliff's sacred quiet once canonized by these rock doodles? Is this a site where hunters invoked gods, recounted exploits, and thought of themselves in the abstract?

"There's a bundle of rock art yet to be found," claims Michael Kyte. "It's everywhere, covering so many Montana cliffs. It's just that few people have bothered to look for it."

In a warm August day, when Michael could extricate himself from government service, he helped me satisfy my curiosity by showing me rock-art sites on public land. We began at Castle Butte, no distance from the ranch and hardly a mile from the Lewis and Clark Trail.

We leave the pickup beside a seldom-used dirt track, straddle a wire fence, trudge through sage to the foot of a sandstone monolith, evocative not of Bavaria but of a shipwreck. There is no sign to tip us off we've now crossed onto land belonging to the Bureau of Land Management. Duma, panting heavily, finds the path of least resistance, precariously stitching one ledge with another. Finally, Michael, his face rimmed by black beard and shaded by an Indiana Jones hat, pauses on a promontory and then leans against a shelf. He then nods his head, as if to acknowledge Act One.

I might have missed it, for Act One is disarmingly subtle. One entire face is composed of drawings. A stick figure, arms in air, screams for attention. Nearby a bull elk is poised to penetrate a female, her sexual passage spelled out as if it were a target. The view from this art galley is unexpected. Here I am at the helm of a great prairie that ends with the Yellowstone. Not 150 years ago I might have looked out from here, across this plain, and would have seen hundreds of thousands of buffalo—numbers rivaling today's wildlife on the Serengeti. And the images on the rock face reflect the profusion. Game was then everywhere and, when this butte was a sacred site, Indians and buffalo lived, more or less, in balance. Today the images are artifacts of richer times. Beginning in the 19th century, the ground all around this butte was turned "wrong side up," and along the river today, sugar beet farmers, once the richest agriculturists of all, plead poverty.

Even experts of Northern Plains rock art can't be dead certain which tribe is responsible for which image. At the time of the Lewis and Clark Expedition between 1804 and 1806, (Captain William Clark defaced some prime examples with his signature at a site called Pompey's Pillar on the

Yellowstone) both Crow, Blackfoot, and occasionally Sioux seasonally visited this country. The carvings might have been executed by either one of them. Dating also poses a problem. While pictographs and petroglyphs (painted art) can be found throughout much of the West, researchers generally lump material from the Dakotas, Montana, Wyoming, Idaho, and Alberta in one geographic category, some as old as 5,000 years. Since etchings do not contain datable material, the epoch of their creation can only be deduced from the image. If one of the subjects is, for instance, a horse, then we may assume the work must have been completed after 1740 or 1750—the time of the horse's first appearance in this country. If there are images of rifles then we can assume the etching was done after 1820. Guns and horses make dating easy but most examples of rock art aren't narrative. Many feature totemic symbols or wild animals.

In Billings a week before my scouting trip with Michael Kyte, I tracked down Stuart Conner, a retired lawyer turned archaeologist who has spent much of his life documenting rock-art sites in Montana. In his 1971 paper, still upheld as a seminal resource for rock-art devotees, he has arranged this region's rock art into several broad types: notably humans portrayed as "shield-bearing figures," "v-necked figures," "stick figures;" animals such as horses, deer, elk, bears, turtles, snakes, salamanders, porcupines, beavers, birds, mountain sheep; teepees; human handprints, and coup sticks.

What is rock art all about? I asked Conner. I had met him at his home— a shaded ranch house near the university. Now in his 70s, this acknowledged authority narrowed his eyes and shook his head. Apart from documenting sites, he admits, he can do little more than speculate. Their significance, theme, meaning, even authorship is all a matter of interpretation. Now laid low by a recurring disease, Stuart Conner is no longer able to explore. "Only think," he proclaims. Today he sits in his living room, pensively staring at the high rimrocks girding the city. "Rock art may record," he says "the magic of the hunt," or a desire "to immortalize" events. He goes no further. "When archaeologists don't know what a cave is," he laments, "they say it's *ceremonial*. Nonsense. We simply don't know."

Native American elders, who, one supposes, should know, have on the whole been equally circumspect. No Northern Plains tribes appear to possess direct knowledge of who created rock art. In fact, as long ago as 1876, Crow Indians denied they had drawn these pictures at all. Instead they believed pictographs the work of "spirits."

The sun is now high and, below us, dust swirls across the road beneath Castle Butte. Michael Kyte and I have reached the crown and now drop onto the saddle—the most direct course to a high bluff. Along the trail, we have seen graffiti, some of it historic ("J. Cosgriff 1901," "Arkansas Traveler 1874"). Funny how white folks must always identify themselves while Indians remain nameless. When we scramble onto a high plateau and stare, Duma's tongue appears the only bright color on this monochrome prairie. Few vandals seem to have made it this high, and the rock art appears, for the most part, intact. One panel shows a herd of elk on the move, some as elegant as those on the walls of Lascaux. On another: a hunched, love sick man armed with an impressive phallus; beyond, creatures that resemble specters. "It wasn't just anybody who made these," I say lamely. "This is the work of an artist."

"Who knows," says Michael, unwilling to make an assumption. "This may have been a place where lone guys came for *love medicine*. The elk seems to have an association with sexuality. When someone had been rebuffed in love, he might come here to be alone, to seek, you know, redress." Michael stares at the ground, retrieves a stone. "Porcelainite," he says, changing the mood. "Flake from a projectile point."

We're now bound for Steamboat Butte, accessible only to those who like opening gates and challenging their four-wheel-drive vehicle. "Until recently about the most that had been done with rock art," Michael explains with his hands on the wheel, "was cataloging.... My job is only to locate it, inventory it, make an assessment. Nothing more. It's a field that's wide open."

I ask Michael my Act Two question: if he were presented with two months of paid leisure to study anything of his own choosing, what would it be? For an instant, my archaeologist pal seems on the cliff edge of a smile, my question as preposterous as if I had asked him what would he do if he won the lottery. The smile disperses and, without a word, he brakes the pickup, and nods for me to follow.

Steamboat Butte also stands alone, sandstone sentinel, evocative of many a Charlie Russell landscape. At each ledge of our steep climb, I speed-read the rocks in an attempt to be the first to spot the art. Michael, naturally, wins. He points at a shadow that instantly evolves into a shield-bearing warrior, the figure so crude it may as well have been described by a pipe cleaner. His shield is another matter: it contains all the artist's energy—as if to say the clan shield, not the individual, makes the man. At least that's what Michael asserts. "Sorry," I admit, "I don't see it as a shield. It appears to me a cow elk."

Michael smiles considerately. He continues: "It's possible this butte was, say, a focal point for a tobacco society. Crow elders belonging to this society would have come here, secretly planting seeds of Nicotiana on the plateau at top. They never smoked the stuff. The act of planting was what it was all about—a way of perpetuating culture."

As I reach the brow, I begin to understand how these sandstone rim-rocks, soft to the touch, invite all comers to make a mark. The response to this temptation has been remarkably different between cultures. While Western society sees history as the cumulative act of individualism, these prehistoric people, either unable or unwilling to credit subject or artist by name, appear quite content to heap honor upon the tribe, clan or society. It seems to me rock art is testament to aboriginal Americans proclaiming: "The River Crow (or the Mountain Crow or the Blackfoot...) were here," in stark contrast to our society where a lone "Kilroy" flaunts the implausibility of his life. For Native Americans, the unnamed warrior woman, the buffalo hunter, seem to have been icons of an entire society. Their bravery reflected not on them but their people.

We sit at the top, flanked by a rock panel featuring impressionistic horse prints. Michael has found another porcelainite arrowhead. As he plays with it, he explains that, when Indians traveled on foot, shields were originally huge—the size of the human torso. When wild horses—descendants of those brought to the Americas by Spanish conquistadores—reached the Northern Plains, large shields became impractical. The shield was thus miniaturized. The size of shields relative to the human figure is therefore another clue to the dating of rock art.

Stuart Conner told me only two of the enormous clan shields are known to exist today. Unearthed in an Idaho cave in 1925, they were made of leather. Stuart had said the colors were "fantastic. You'd swear they had been applied with Magic Markers."

"Interesting," Michael intones. His mind must be elsewhere. "You asked me what I'd do if I had two months on my hands," he says almost in a whisper. He rubs the porcelainite treasure in his hand. "Well, I'd spend it exploring this very country. I'm positive there're lots of petroglyph sites never yet recorded. Everywhere there are rocks, there's probably rock art, and here, north of the Yellowstone, south of the Bull Mountains, is the country I'd choose. I find this region's art exquisite, and it's just waiting to be discovered."

"OK," I say, challenging him with my Final Act. "About five miles from here, there's another butte much like this. It's on a neighbor's land, not far from the road. I've never climbed it and I bet you haven't either."

On the map this butte, resembling so many others, has no name. It rises in a series of terraces where stunted bull pines grow. On the top: a grassy plateau, endowed, one supposes, with astounding views.

Duma, now understanding the drill, is the first to the top. I don't follow Michael but amble intuitively, picking my way on the edge of scree, around a ledge, past trees, along a ridge, as if I were a long-ago hunter and this was my habitat. At the top, I find myself beside a towering rock wall, flat as a canvas and protected from slanting rain and direct rain.

While at high noon, surface definition over the face of the rock is muted, I begin to see irregularities. So too does Michael. I squint and look again, this time spotting two carefully etched figures: a shield warrior and an elk, both testament to economy of line and the simplicity of profile. I turn away to look south into an expanse of heat and distance. This heart-thumping view of prairie, now converted to wheat, extends without pause to the horizon. "Amazing to think we may be among the first to see these drawings over the last two centuries."

"Stunning," Michael says, imitating me. "Like uncovering a lost Holbein."

Silenced, I retrace my way to the pickup. I can't believe I heard Michael correctly.

At the bottom of the hill, pausing, the archaeologist clears his throat to correct himself: "Well, maybe not a Holbein."

Just then I see the holes. It seems someone long ago blasted the face of a large rock with his shotgun. I clamber through a thicket of rabbit brush to have a closer look at this oddity. While much of the rock is studded with pellet holes, the vandal clearly wasn't a good shot. He missed by a yard. Below and to the left of his gormless contribution to history, a collection of pictographs remain unscathed. They are as clear, as haunting as anything we've yet seen: a ceremonial lance, a buffalo skull, decorated with feathers—all of them surmounted by a bird in flight. They appear to have been flecked deeply into rock with a stone adze. Michael believes they may be as much as 600 years old. "Wow," Michael says, uncharacteristically. "A total surprise...Had no idea."

While he takes measurements, snaps photographs, and does a transparent job of suppressing a big grin, I push my way back through the rabbit brush, then stand back to admire the scene in all its fullness. Maybe not, but these carvings are good—the work of an anonymous sculptor with distinctive talent. Unseen, except by at least one armed lout, they've endured centuries of fire, snow, and indifference to speak to the two of us on this sultry August day.

In the end, I found there are no words for discovery. The experience is altogether subjective, even primitive. My heart raced, my cheeks flushed, I became tongue-tied. If I talked at all it was to myself as well as with the nameless artist speaking to me across the ether of unrecorded memory.

CHAPTER 19

In From the Cold

These winters, the Bar 20 is locked tight as a drum and I am elsewhere. All the while, I never stop thinking about it, dreaming of ice on the river, tracks in the snow.

I suppose we could live the winter at the Bar 20. We would have to tinker with pipes and I'd become a demon woodchopper, like Stan Cox, but in winter the valley becomes a canyon, and day is counted in minutes, not hours. My office would seem very distant from the house, and the house would become a garrison against dark. Like Stan, I would have to take up model building.

Instead of wintering at the Bar 20, I dream of it and skirt its edges. I know I am missing out, but I'd rather not hibernate. Instead, I feed our cattle at the Bull Mountain Ranch, ski above the Gallatin River, act like a boulevardier on Bozeman's Main Street, pay visits to Big Timber and Livingston—always on the edge, always in search of a message from mountains and our valley, but never there.

Just before Christmas recently, I realized an old dream—to cross-country ski Yellowstone National Park the world's first national park. I would be within 50 miles of the Bar 20, and perhaps I'd discover some of its secrets. Two friends, both devoted to Montana winters, and I would make up the party. The notion of a guys' event had much appeal for me at that moment. I'd been together with Kathryn for almost a year and for the first time in a long while, I felt my life shifting toward solid ground. For most, that sensation might have been reassuring. For me it was radical. Throughout my life, I had known many sudden bursts of happiness, but until this year, I wasn't familiar with the quiet hum of contentment. I had lost control of something—I didn't know what—and my heart had hit its stride. I wanted to think about my feelings, to make sense of my happiness. Four days away from Kathryn, I believed, would help.

I slide to a stop, remove a mitten to photograph and immediately regret my impulse. The cold is brittle—so intense fingertips feel inflamed, then senseless. I guide them visually to the camera. Through the viewfinder, condensation billows from the Fire Hole River, instantly drawing a curtain across the kill on the far side. I hear the chill sound of jaw breaking bone. When wind cuts the mist, I spot her, outlined against the snow of the far bank. A coyote. "Might be chomping a goose," I whisper, making the inference from a doleful, faraway honk—a survivor, I suspect, calling for a lost companion.

Bill has spotted a bloodied tail. "Muskrat," he corrects.

I imagine the scene we just missed: skulking coyote, using rising mist as cover while her unwitting victim, imagining itself secure, made a tactical slip. In a nanosecond, Yellowstone National Park is short one muskrat. Now the coyote, savoring a final gourmet morsel, looks at us vacuously. Then, when she's reduced everything to a blood spot, she shakes herself. Droplets of water, warmed by her coat, radiate like a halo and fall to the snow, ice.

An ingenuous act of violence and grace leaves me breathless, poised for more. Yellowstone under snow promises wildlife intimacy unimaginable during the easy weather of summer. I'm especially tantalized by the prospect of seeing a wolf—to me, along with grizzlies, the grand slam of North American wildlife viewing.

But Yellowstone has been infiltrated by others. Just before Christmas each year, Yellowstone opens its gates not only to cross-country skiers but to snowmobilers whose two-cycle engines, belching carbon monoxide, reign supreme over most of the park's 200 miles of winter roadways. Will I discover this vast national park, larger than Rhode Island and Delaware combined, too cramped for a winter enthusiast of my aesthetics?

Yesterday morning, friends—Bill Bryan, an expert of the Rocky Mountains, and Jonathan Wiesel, a master ski tourer—and I left Bozeman at six in the morning while the temperature was minus 12° F. In our headlights, the empty high street of this western Montana town was aglare with ice. As we crept west, then south toward the park, I snuck a glance at my companions and our gear. Hard to imagine we're not embarked on a Himalayan assault. I wear so many layers of down I may as well be inflatable. Like the others, I've attempted to outwit an apocalyptic forecast. Yesterday, in a Bozeman store, I made a beeline for the Expedition Wear section. Now, I'm festooned with tags, each talking gibberish: "Endura," "Capilene," "Mazama," "Polartech fleece," "Talus," "Synchilla." In the end, I was seduced by long underwear with superior "wicking." (Is it what I think?), made virtuous by a neck gaiter manufactured from "post-consumer recycled soda-pop bottles," flattered by "Smartwool" socks, chastened by gloves equipped with an "idiot cord." My splurge has left me conflicted.

Today at dawn we cruise Highway 191 beside the Gallatin River, in tune to the radio refrain of "severe Arctic cold." As dawn breaks, temperatures drop in increments of two degrees until they wallow at a chilling minus 28° just as we cross the city limits of West Yellowstone.

City limits? Not really. West Yellowstone, one of five gateway towns to the Park, seems an overnight impulse, a community of zealot handymen in need of an architect. Before 1970, its fabled winter weather was of marginal interest; today its predictably snowy winters have fueled an entrepreneurial bonanza. West Yellowstone now claims the dubious distinction of being

America's snowmobiling capital, its population—1,800—roughly equal to the number of snowmobiles available for rent by the noise-addicted.

As we pass a slurry of honky-tonk structures, West Yellowstone seems on fire from cold, thanks to pickups idling in front of fast food restaurants, and motel heat ducts belching smoke like iron smelters. Our stabbing breaths add to the effect as we transfer skinny skis and down-filled duffels into a snow-coach that will take us to the interior of the park. Track vehicles are all that is allowed inside the park from December to April. Jovial Jim Berry, our driver, inured to such temperatures, makes do without gloves. He tells us we haven't seen anything yet. "The record here, long ago, was a doosey: negative 62°!"

Hand on a flimsy door, Jim explains that his snow coach, built in 1978, was one of the last manufactured. "Today, everything except the steering wheel's been rebuilt." He bows with feigned courtliness as we step inside: "But still the finest Yellowstone can offer."

This yellow oddity advances where no wheeled vehicle dare go; it does so with a deafening vibrato of steel groping steel, as glacial winds whistle through leaks in the paneling. All my hollered questions will prove inaudible.

Once beyond the park gates the effect of leaving the banality of West Yellowstone is complete; I'm now in a place of astonishing rectitude—uniformly spare signs, little overt commerce, a land where the only tick of the clock is dawn and dusk. Yellowstone is athwart a volcanic plateau of plain and forest, a land fixed in no millennium, culture, time zone and protected for eternity. Trumpeter swans bob the Madison River's riffles. Having summered in the Arctic, wintry Yellowstone is their idea of warm, thanks to thermal features that keep many park rivers ice-free.

Halfway to Old Faithful, we round a corner to encounter wolves. Well, maybe not wolves. Wolves weigh about 120 pounds, coyotes a mere 30. Soon, no-matter how full-coated, these are clearly coyotes: two lone males bound on a walkabout. They barely acknowledge our presence so intent are they on predation. They pay even less heed to pintails, buffleheads, Barrow goldeneyes, and scops duck trapped at the junction of currents. These two Yellowstone businessmen pad north, bound for better windfalls.

There's no escaping the hideous scarring of the pine forests, sorry reminders of the devastating fires of 1988. "Don't be mistaken: fire's a happy story," beams Jim. "Look at all the young lodgepoles, now three or four feet tall, it brought into this world. When heat from fire exceeds 130 degrees Farenheit, resin begins to pour out of their serotinous cones. That creates a series of events which ultimately...," here Jim purses his lips to make an unexpected belch, "leads to seeds popping out. Not bad. Look at 'em—a new generation of lodgepoles brought to life on rocky ground all because of the thing we fear the most: fire. You see Yellowstone needs it—a good blaze once a century, just to keep itself honest." Jim seems buoyant.

Today in landscapes reduced to grisaille, fire is of academic interest. When we reach our staging post, Old Faithful, at the center of Upper Geyser Basin, the temperature has plummeted to minus 35 degrees. At these extremes, cold feels all the same. Now there is a new consideration: the daily crusade of West Yellowstone snowmobiles, reaching Old Faithful at noon in time for lunch in the new lodge. Trailing them: a corridor of yellow haze, effluvia of unregulated engines. I'm glad Kathryn isn't with me. She wouldn't have a kind word for snowmobiles.

Jim whoops. "That's a first," the ebullient cynic shouts, pointing out a snowmobile, crashed against a roadside sign. "A *bubblehead* who actually stopped at a stop sign." Snowmobilers circle Old Faithful Snow Lodge like swarming hornets. Because of their dress code—black from helmet to boots—they become an abstraction—dehumanized machines driven by inscrutable faces.

Now, with hardly three hours of sunlight remaining, we lunge into the cold. I'm kitted out with new skis, new boots, new windbreaker and borrowed cap, uncertain if I'll ever find comfort in this bitter cold. Jonathan's cheeks are already an angry red. Competitive Bill feels compelled to set a fast pace. I wonder whether wildlife watching with him will become an endurance contest. My first sliding steps are tentative. I try to ski-skate in hopes a burst of flashiness will disguise my mediocrity. No such luck. Bill watches me analytically. We advance several hundred yards toward Old Faithful, forsaken today by even intrepid snowmobilers. Heavy steam, rising from all quadrants of the geyser basin obscures a pallid sun. Today at this World Heritage site, elk, foraging on bare earth around the geyser, outnumber humans. Ten minutes late, the national monument explodes, belching steam 200 feet into the gloom sky.

Our goal is to cross this inflamed icescape, range north along Biscuit Basin Trail to Morning Glory Pool, Daisy Geyser, and Castle Geyser, then to return by dark. Snow is thin around the thermal features and the boardwalks make for easy but unnatural skiing. On summer visits to Yellowstone, I've paid scant attention to thermal features. Today they're a singular distraction in land the color of steel. The pools' greens, oranges, blues are unexpected. Yellowstone is a study in survival. In scalding water, heated by molten magma some 10,000 feet beneath our feet, tenacious microorganisms thrive, some prospering at temperatures hotter than boiling point. How feeble we humans: Were I to stumble into the springs, I'd be parboiled in a second. Were I to spend the night, without shelter in this cold, I'd be stiff by morning. In these environments humans are no match for either bison or bacteria. I lunge back onto the trail, chastened.

Now my companions are out of sight. I'm doing a full-bodied sliding run that would be sheer poetry were it executed by a Norwegian. Pity Bill can't see me now. Game stays distant, while thick clouds blow in from the northwest and lodgepoles turn menacing in fading light.

So far wildlife spotting has been a bust. Then I see the bison, at dusk, blacker than pitch. We halt before seven females, lumps beneath conifers. Since the trail passes within a few feet of them, to advance appears precarious. I recall: Just last summer a know-it-all hiker at Lake Lodge was left near dead when he breached a bison's personal space. Now, we must face a choice—forward or a detour. Drool on each bison's face has congealed into a mandarin mustache, while condensation has built a rug of rime on their backs. A ton of black, pierced only by bantam yellow eyes, they follow our every move.

I look to Old Faithful Lodge for support. I could do with snowmobilers just now, but they've left the park for the night. The ancient structure seems to rustle, as ravens rise, black against black, into the night's maw. At half past five, Yellowstone Park is ours to haunt.

Consciously choosing not to look at the bison—a precaution I learned while trekking gorillas in the Congo—I advance, passing within 20 feet of them. Seven bison heads rotate. Nothing more. They make no effort to rise. They may as well be pets.

"Bison in winter, bison in summer," punctilious Jonathan recaps at dinner in the lodge later that evening. "Two very different behaviors. In summer you're dead meat when you approach on foot. In winter, their mission is conservation of energy. Every unnecessary move steals calories that they can't afford to lose. Cows, especially, need to husband resources, build food reserves in preparation for dropping calves in May." Jonathan polishes off another jalapeño popper. "Punitive action" he add, "simply has no food value."

The park supports about 2,200 buffalo—some claim too many for the habitat. A number congregate around thermal features in winter for easy access to exposed vegetation. Others in meadows metronome their heads, plowing snow to reach buried grass. When grazing becomes exhausted, some migrate out of the park on packed trails, bound for ranch lands. But leaving the park can be fatal. In Montana as many as 1,000 have been shot during one winter, all because of a controversial decision by lawmakers to screen domestic livestock from bison-borne disease.

Bison migration is one hot issue we discuss this evening at the lodge— itself a tad cool, given the savage temperature outside. We sample a salad of subjects: Montana's future and the principles of effective "wicking," while my mind turns to Kathryn. I wonder where she is, whether she'd like it here, if she would find conditions uncomfortable. In spite of a gas fire spluttering in the dining room, Jonathan, Bill, and I are bundled in three layers of down. To compensate for the calories we burned in today's cold, we slurp Sonoma Merlot, wolf brie crisps, hoover New York cut steaks. Our exuberant waiter, Brent, originally from Layton, Utah, is condemned to wear the Old Faithful Snow Lodge regulation T-shirt, exposing bare arms to the cold. Rocky Mountain convert, he knows that by running between courses he'll stay warm.

Jonathan keeps warm by fulminating against cross-country doubters. "The ones who've never done it, think cross-country skiing is about competition, hard muscles, tedious work. They're wrong. Take Yellowstone: here, the sport's much more—adventure, nature's beauty, fellowship." Jonathan brushes remains of the chocolate eclair from his mustache, vindicated.

At dawn the next morning, the thermometer has broken at minus 40°. In the lobby, there's talk our temperature is the same as West Yellowstone's, reputedly minus 52°. I go outside, throw a glassful of hot water high, and watch it return to earth, hard as gravel. So, too, my spit.

Today is the big day. At ten, we board a snow coach, our intent to disembark at Fairy Falls Trail and then, return circuitously to the lodge in time for supper. Above, the sky is hard sapphire; at tree line, steam from the thermal basin turns sunlight to twilight. "You suppose we'll see much game?" I ask our driver, Matt, over the clatter of the snow coach.

"Of course," he says. "If you're blessed with my luck, you'll see plenty." Matt leans over to confide "You know I've the best job in the park." He beams beneath his wool hat. "It's a dream being here in winter: I've seen bears emerging from dens, coyotes stealing backpacks from skiers, bison charging ravens. And recently, I've spotted wolves."

"Wolves," I intone, roiling the word in my mouth for a full-bodied taste. Matt now has my undivided attention. "Here?"

"You might get lucky. You never know. But you stand a better chance to the north, in the Lamar."

"You never know:" the lullaby of the wild. I repeat Matt's refrain as we break trail along Fairy Creek Trail, following old power lines. Once across the Fire Hole River, the sound of two-cycle engines fade. Now I concentrate on the crackle and bite of cold snow beneath skis, the faraway lowing of young bisons for mothers. Gone is yesterday's knee wobble, and when I manage a steady syncopated rhythm, I fall into a reverie of wolves.

After an hour the spell is broken. "Nose, ears, cheeks, toes," invokes Jonathan, watchdog of frostbite. When he studies my cheek, I note his mustache resembles an ice flow. "White spot," he intones. "Frost nip," comes the diagnosis. "Precursor to frostbite." I rub the cheek gently with my glove until he pronounces me cured.

At noon, snookered, we retrace our trail, loping along the main road until we spot bison. Since snowmobilers seem more impressed by noise than by wildlife, whenever we leave their tracks, we're rewarded by virgin snow, undisturbed game, and dulcimer calm. We set a course between pods of bison— Henry Moore marbles—creatures so vast one is tempted to think of them as geographic features. Condensation from their breath mimics steam spewing from thermal features. I recall a mid-19th-century account that described how bison were so numerous their breaths created a cloud system spanning three counties of Kansas. By the end of the 19th-century, of North America's bison once numbering millions, only a few thousand survived. Today, while bison are no longer endangered, Yellowstone's population of 2,200 remains critical. Before me are America's fountainhead herd, the world's last wild Plains bison.

Wild? Appearances deceive. We ski between groups, their barrel heads so fixed on grazing, they give scant notice to coyotes prowling the edges, like jackals on the Serengeti. When we halt beside a fallen tree to munch on sandwiches, the herds describe three sides of us, the burden of winter weighing so heavily on them, they won't even waste a glance on us.

It's now dusk and we've just passed Artemesia Pool. Three miles of trail separate us from the lodge. Jonathan has been setting the pace with Bill in the vanguard. Seemingly intent on elegance, Jonathan cavalierly passes 12 feet from an elk. It's a six-pointer—the sort that renders a hunter delirious. Within two bounds this monster could be raking Jonathan and me with his antlers. He alternates his gaze between the two of us, his eyes somber, his breath short and stabbing. I freeze.

Not even a blink. Around the elk's ice-framed mouth, I see the sparkle of sun. His eyes shift first right, then left, unprovoked to the point of ennui. Silence, except for the thud of my heart.

When I turn to find Bill, I see another six-pointer has gone unnoticed, this one racked out in snow under timber not ten feet distant. "Behind you." I gesticulate. Bill slowly turns. Will I see him leap into the air? No, the old deft hand remains immobile, then flashes me a devil-may-care smile. Now this moment is something Kathryn would never forget. In fact, if I tell her about it, she may accuse me of selfishness.

Much later, at dinner, over Merlot, we all agree: "It doesn't get much better." But my contribution to guy talk is restrained. I'm thinking of what I miss—Kathryn and wolves.

Early next day, the winter solstice, we are met by burly Mike Bryers, another snow-coach guide, for a daylong journey north to Mammoth Hot Springs. I know better than to ask him about the prospect of seeing wolves.

By now the irritant of the snowmobile has receded. We seem largely alone once we pass Madison Junction. Following the Gibbon River east, we set a course for Norris Basin. Mike's commanding voice slices through the rattle of the snow coach, his running monologue paying tribute to a lifetime spent in lonely places. A Dangerous Dan McGrew sort, Mike tells of years spent running remote traplines, evenings satisfied by bar room brawls.

Beside Paintpot Hill, on a meadow shimmering white, rimmed by bison, Mike stands on the brakes. "Wolves," I inhale recklessly. I've spotted a glimmer of canids, dark blurs against snow. I glass them, and again my heart twists. Coyotes, always bloody coyotes.

Near Inspiration Point on Canyon Rim Trail, some 7,000 feet above the sea, we abandon snow coach for skinny skis. Mike's are patched, his outfit mismatched nylon jacket, balaclava, and itchy wool pants, yet he outwits the cold as effectively as me, kitted out with Endura, Capilene, Mazama, Synchilla, Idiot Cords, and Smartwool. His is an evocative figure—solo skier cutting trail beside the Yellowstone divide. We advance toward the Grand Canyon of the Yellowstone, the heart of the park.

After President Ulysses S. Grant designated Yellowstone a national park in 1872, it became a target for winter poachers. A book issued to officers, enlisted men, and scouts, warned: "All persons traveling through the park from October 1 to June 1 should be regarded with suspicion." Possibly the most notorious of winter poachers was a certain Edgar Howell, who made a livelihood off bison and elk. For years he evaded capture, shamelessly building a home for himself in Yellowstone. Far from prying eyes, he stocked the cabin by hauling his provisions—sometimes as much as 180 pounds— on a homemade toboggan. And with it, he ferried his wildlife booty out to Cooke City. When he was finally brought to justice, his captor, Emerson Hough, found Howell to be "a most picturesquely ragged, dirty and unkempt looking citizen. He wrapped his feet when snowshoeing [skiing] into a pair of meal sacks he had nailed on to the middle of his snowshoes [skis]. The whole bundle he tied with thongs. His snowshoes [skis]... were a curiosity. They were 12 ft. long, narrow, made of pine (or spruce), Howell himself being the builder of them. The front of one had its curve supplemented by a bit of board, wired on. All sorts of curves existed in the bottoms of the shoes.... He had broken one shoe while in the park—a mishap often very serious.... With the ready resources of a perfect woodsman, Howell took his axe, went to a fir tree, hewed out a three-cornered splice about 5 ft. long, nailed it fast to the broken shoe, picked out some pieces of resin, coated the shoe well with it.... He said he could travel as far in a day on those shoes as any man."

On the day of his capture, Howell was brought to Canyon Hotel for breakfast. In one sitting, he tucked into 24 pancakes.

Once poaching was contained, cross-country skiing slowly evolved into recreation: "I saw out of the corner of my eye the President taking a header into the snow," naturalist John Burroughs wrote of Theodore Roosevelt during the winter of 1902 in Yellowstone. It "had given way beneath him, and nothing could save him from taking the plunge. I don't know whether I called out, or only thought, something about the downfall of the administration. At any rate, the administration was down, and pretty well buried, but it was quickly on its feet again, shaking off the snow with a boy's laughter."

Today, we're alone, inoculated by quiet, comforted by our hissing breaths. Following a burly woodsman, cut from the same tree as Hough and Howell, I have no doubt I'm in the traces of history. The nonstop raconteur has now withdrawn into a personal hush, his satisfaction apparent in a lilting, loping, wool-encrusted gait. No doubt were he to be overtaken by night in these extremes, he'd survive without a hiccup.

As he crests the rise, he breaks into a guffaw. It's an odd response to a view. But once I top the precipice for a look, I choke: yellowed canyon walls, wailing river, blue ice bottling the falls—the entire landscape as chaste as if I were Thomas Moran, his paintbrush in hand, the year 1871.

Greeted by ravens, I scope the solemn canyon for sign of wolf. I see where bison have broken the far escarpment's snow to reach the river. Otherwise: no life, no smudge of silver and black, no lone howl.

Jogging from one headland to another, to find other views of the canyon, I find it convenient to escape: I think of Duma, a dhow ghosting mangroves along the Kenyan coast, Kathryn on a horse at the Bar 20, the time she cooked fusilli covered in shrimp, whether there was enough wood for a good blaze in the fireplace at the ranch and whether I really have the words in me. The view of the canyon clarifies all.

The third evening—our last—we check into Mammoth Hot Springs Hotel. Here, at dinner, three once-courteous friends—Jonathan, Bill, and I—surprise each other with imparted confidences, backhanded compliments. Guys aren't supposed to say everything that's on their minds, but I'm inclined to drop a hint. Jonathan tells about the tough times of his life, Bill about the death of his dad. I keep my confidence for last and it's not much— just about how dumb I've been all my life. Missed opportunities, the search for something I knew could never be found. They listen and I think they know. Then it's back to wolves. I speak of them as I would a casualty. Wolves, we all accept, are central to the park, a winter fundamental, pivotal to the food chain, and a kind of lullaby of the past. Well before Ulysses Grant, Thomas Moran, Edgar Howell, Emerson Hough, Teddy Roosevelt, the wolf roamed Yellowstone, refining and strengthening the order of life through predation. In the 1920s, because of its unpopularity among ranchers, the wolf was poisoned, trapped, and finally extirpated from the park. Since then, for over 60 years, Yellowstone was more or less wolf-free; as such, many biologists believed an entire cascade of interrelated lives languished through its absence.

In 1994, after long and heated debate, the wolf was restored to Yellowstone. Altogether, 41 individuals from Alberta, Canada, were released into the park. Of those pioneers, with only 12 surviving today, second and third generations have, miraculously, swelled the park's wolf population to over 140. The number continues to grow, and some claim this reintroduction to be the most successful of any animal in National Park history.

Before light we leave Mammoth. We're now confined to a car because here the snow is skimpy. We drive in silence, solemnly aware our lives are less graceful. Grand Loop Road follows Lava Creek Canyon and as early morning light transforms Specimen Ridge into a row of canines, we crest onto the

Lamar Valley. Below us, to our left and right, stretching onto a rising plateau, appear successive phalanxes of buffalo and elk, the song of the valley, the cadence of their murmurs. Snow lies in catchments high in drainages, where grass is the color of ocean-washed driftwood. When we stop the car to glass the ridges for wolves, the air warms and, for a moment, I think the adventure may as well be over.

The sight of so much life hardly touched by our presence might as well be Yellowstone's parting gift. We clamber back into the car to drive northwest through the valley, checking each ridge until the road climbs into timber on its march to Cooke City. Time now to return to Mammoth. So what if we missed wolves.

When we pause near Slough Creek, no one cries out. Nothing so dramatic: only a cough as we see elk dispersing. We follow their stares, our eyes rising to the apex. There: at first five, then seven dark silhouettes. For once, I'm positive these aren't coyotes. Even at a great distance they're formidable. They lope together, fluid like mercury, and when they intercept a beam of sunlight, their coats luminesce as if they were molded from coal. At long last, wolves.

During these five minutes, which now, a year later, I replay backward and forward in my mind as if the Druid Pack had been captured on videotape, nothing really happened. The wolves didn't howl, they didn't look our way, they didn't stay long. And when they crested the ridge, they vanished without a trace, leaving behind a vacuum quickly filled by coyotes, bickering like songbirds. The coyotes offered a cry that, in this gut-wrenching landscape, seemed comment, epiphany, and comic opera.

The moment I spotted the wolves something happens to me. I feel comforted, one question answered, the other soon resolved. I realize these very creatures could make their way, a week or month from now, to the West Boulder, even to the Bar 20. This time of year, no one may ever know. Wolves have probably been across our land many times before, but no one would see them. When they come, they follow the deer along the river, leave tracks that soon melt, cross mountains, then evaporate. And far away, when everyone else sleeps, they howl.

Ghosts—that's what wolves are; one more link to all the others.

The Druid Pack relieves me of my final burden. From Mammoth Hot Springs, I find a car, offer no explanations, and drive faster than I should.

CHAPTER 20

Search for Beginnings

Kathryn had found a patch of sun outside the airport terminal and is waiting for me, as she had once before. Her books are strewn on the pavement, and she smiles as she gathers her things and joins me in the car. She had expected I would be late and there's no need, she says, for apologies. I'm not certain if I understand. As we drive, she stares at the evolving landscape and says not another word, so glad is she to be back in Montana.

For one week, we feed cows, ski, talk, and drive fast, sometimes close to the Bar 20. On one such drive, on a slick mountain road, I finally ask her. For five minutes she is silent and I don't dare look for fear of catching a slick of ice or breaking the spell. When, finally, she finds the words, it is to inquire what has come over me, whether I'm making a joke.

I don't answer her directly. I merely tell her to open the glove compartment. Within it, she spots the small leather box and she asks me what she now must do. I say: "open it."

We are still driving fast, but when she sees the ring, I slow.

Before the Coxes, the trail runs cold and my historic clock must race faster and faster. What I learned of our place was in the form of names and occasional incident. When I searched for character, all I found were crumbs. For the entire winter of 1999, Kathryn watched me puzzle over the evidence, and she saw me frustrate myself with its gaps. She told me not to think so hard, to let the material come to me. She was right.

An elderly woman, Mary Rogers Rahn, gave an interview in 1996, shortly before her death. I obtained the transcript of it. In it, she recalled the cabin that burned, the one preceding the Coxes.' She and her sisters passed it daily, to and from school, in the early 1920s. "There was no one there at the time" but the house "could have been made livable. There must have been a living room, a kitchen and dining room combined, and 2 or 3 bedrooms, and an indoor bath of some sort, with water piped into the house. Nearby was a large barn and two long sheds. The folks who built it must have been very well-to-do." Mrs. Rahn, confined to a nursing home in Livingston, remembered, best of all, the trees near the Bar 20. "Are the quaking aspens turning?" she asked the interviewer.

"Yes, in the higher country, the leaves are fallen, but along the river they've changed color."

"I just loved them as a kid. I'd lay under the quaking aspens and I'd listen to the various things they'd tell me. They never are quiet. Even if there isn't a breath of wind, the quaking aspens are saying things. They'll talk to you all the time."

While Mrs. Rahn knew the original buildings as "the Hough Place," the deeds suggest that Fred and Gertrude Hough and Fred's sister, a widow called Sarah Hoopes, had sold out to Albert Crest in 1909. While the wealthy Crests then owned it for some 24 years, they never succeeded in endowing the land with their name.

Albert Crest was a hardworking, dour Norwegian, one of four brothers who came to the United States. Albert arrived in 1870, at the age of 18, and settled in Montana in 1884. Soon he wrote his youngest brother about opportunities awaiting him in America, especially in Montana Territory. Like his older brother, Albert was a sheep rancher, prospering in an era when wool was in demand and Big Timber had become one of the core wool marketing centers in the West.

The Bar 20 land was not free for the asking under the Enlarged Homestead Act of 1909. It had already been spoken for under a previous Homestead Act, presumably because it was so choice, with its high grass and plentiful water. Albert Crest was wise to pay cash for prime land at a time when others were claiming marginal land for free. He held the property for over two decades, and when he reached the age of 70 in 1922, he leased the Bar 20 to outsiders—mostly Big Timber bankers—who let weeds overrun the land, buildings decay. Quiet and dour, coming and going with little fanfare, Crest was a deeply religious man, said to be frugal to the point of penny pinching. For 24 years he owned the land unencumbered by a mortgage, and when he sold it to Stan and Bab Cox, he made good money while others fell victim to the Great Depression and languished. His brother, Martin Crest, more volatile by far, would die one summer day in 1936 after diving into the West Boulder and hitting his head. But Albert Crest was a sensible fellow. When he sold out to the Coxes in 1933, he was already in retirement in San Bernardino, California. There he lived until the age of 95, still remembered in Big Timber for the Hammond organ he gave the Lutheran Church.

Fred Hough, Crest's predecessor, was impulsive, a risk-taker through and through. On April 23, 1891, the Livingston Herald reports he "was among the enterprising young men who started in business here in a small way, and now has one of the finest and completest photographic art studios in Montana. He turns out an excellent class of work at popular prices. It is the place to go for fine work." Six years later, Fred was working a second job, engaged in census-taking for the county. It was on a head-count trip along the West Boulder River, he saw an opportunity awaiting a restive fellow like him. He and his brother-in-law, Pierce

Hoopes, a Pennsylvania Quaker, veteran of the Civil War, agreed to patent several 160-acre holdings, checkerboarding each other, as far up the West Boulder as was possible. Pierce was a clerk in the local superintendent's office and a man of some means. Soon he would begin describing himself as a cattle rancher. But shortly after he joined with Fred Hough on the West Boulder, he died, age 57 of "apoplexy," leaving behind a wife to operate his West Boulder holdings. In this alien valley, she held on, leaning heavily on her dynamic brother, Fred Hough.

Hough's first Homestead Patent was signed on June 12, 1901 by President William McKinley, the second, September 18, 1906, by President "T. Roosevelt." As early as 1902, Fred Hough declared he and his family—just his wife—were residing on the land, that he had built a dwelling house and other improvements, that it was his intent "to claim said lot of land." On March 19, 1904, in a document again signed by Teddy Roosevelt, the land was officially his by virtue of his having "proved up" on it. In time, Fred Hough would own 4 lots, each 160 acres, all of them abutting land that, in 1864, had been granted to the Northern Pacific Railway "to aid in the construction of a Railroad and Telegraph Line from Lake Superior to Puget's Sound."

Fred Hough was altogether an entrepreneur. Soon after acquiring the land, Sarah Hoopes and Fred began trading between each other. In 1904, Fred directed his wife, Gertrude, to mortgage part of the property for $7,950. In 1906, she paid it back in full after she remortgaged the ranch to J. E. Swindlehurst and Company for $8,000. In 1909 the mortgage was satisfactorily dissolved through sale of the property to Albert Crest. Throughout, the Houghs clearly possessed an inflated idea of their land's worth, for they only managed to sell it for $6,000 to Albert Crest. With a $2,000 loss, they must have been sorely disappointed. At this point the Houghs' trail grows faint. Whether this "enterprising young man" and his wife remained in Livingston is doubtful. It's clear the two were never again seen on the West Boulder. All they left behind was a name. Even Stan Cox in the early 1930s would have to remind people the Bar 20 was "the old Hough Place."

By spring I began to apprehend how the Bar 20 reflected the great adventure of westward expansion. It seemed my family, Kathryn, and I were living at the heart of a transcendentally American tale. Before the Coxes, the Bar 20 was not a playground for the wealthy but a landscape where industrious and creative people had attempted to survive.

With these revelations, I loved the Bar 20 all the more. Its social profile had changed suddenly, prior to the Coxes, and I told Kathryn how I gloried in that change. She, too, saw the land differently, especially when I discussed the Roosevelt connection, but at the time, we had both become distracted by something else in our lives.

Prior to the Hough period, Bar 20 land covered the site of the eponymous Hawkwood, no more than a post office and a barn, built in the mid-1880s to serve as base for loggers, dubbed "wood hawks." The post office was still operational during Fred Hough's era and, while childless, he would generously cede a small lot on his land for the purpose of building a school.

In the mid-1880s, the Northern Pacific Railway began attracting outsiders to this remote region. Possessing an insatiable appetite for ties, it dispatched burly Norwegians and Canadians up all Boulder drainages, including the West Boulder. All year long, they lived rough throughout the forest as they cut and squared fir trees to railroad specifications. Each tie would bear the tie-cutter's initials, and in spring, when the river rose—sometimes as much as 12 feet above normal—these men floated their booty downriver, to Big Timber. There, clerks tallied each logger's take-home pay, computed at the rate of seven cents a tie. A good logger on a good day was capable of cutting and squaring as many as a hundred ties a day. At seven dollars a day, many of these Norwegians, after serving the Northern Pacific's cause for a year or two, were able to set themselves up as independent ranchers.

In 1883, on the Main Boulder to the east, so many logs floated downriver in one day, they jammed together in a limestone fissure of the river, thus forcing it to change course by flowing overhead. The result was a spectacular waterfall that lasted 49 years until, in 1932, the logs finally disintegrated and, once again, the river ran free through the crevice.

In 1985 outfitter Larry Lahren interviewed George Fallat, a homesteader whose land neighbored ours. Fallat recalled hearing as a youngster how one of these early loggers drowned very close to the site of today's Bar 20. The unfortunate Norwegian is said to be buried, possibly on our property, in an unmarked grave.

In 1888 a stamp mill was hauled up the Main Boulder for the purpose of mining gold at a recently created settlement called Independence, about 40 miles from the Bar 20 on the main Boulder drainage. In 1890, the mine was purchased by Harry Le Vieux of Cleveland and gold fever became epidemic. Shortly afterwards, Le Vieux bought the Boulder Mines Stage Line to connect Independence with its two hubs—Big Timber and Livingston.

In its heyday, Independence produced as much as 5,000 ton of ore a year and had a population of 500 miners with another 300 living in outlying country. The "old stagecoach road" that passed the site of our barn "was so rough and steep," according to one account, "accidents and runaways were common. Often two horses would be placed behind the wagon to brake the load." On this road down the Bar 20 escarpment, mail, passengers, and freight (much of it whiskey) traveled to the mine camp. On one occasion, the stage negotiated our precipitous road, carrying a piano.

In about 1900, the main ore border at Independence began to play out but a few stalwarts continued mining there for decades afterward. The last, Jess Clements, was a placer miner who lived in a minute cabin in the old ghost town. He called his place "Setting Sun," and there he died in the late 1940s. Today, Independence is more difficult than ever to reach. It is now totally uninhabited.

In 1990, when we dug a well for Grouse House, we struck a seam of gold at 70 feet, before hitting water—hardly a noteworthy occurrence on the West Boulder. Throughout this country there are rare metals, including platinum and palladium, now more precious than gold, but, these days, only corporations can afford to extract them. They do so at considerable risk to landscape and river. In our valleys and towns, there are now many like us who feel this country's most valuable resource is no longer mineral but wilderness.

One day Kathryn and I drove to the new platinum mine near the pinnacle of the East Boulder drainage, about 20 miles from the Bar 20. Monumental earth-moving equipment passed us on the road as we crunched into lower and lower gears to negotiate the final incline. Once we topped a rise and passed a security guard, we saw the mine. The landscape was filled with cement holding tanks for runoff from the mine and a temporary block of office buildings had been erected on the floor of the high valley. Busy men, wearing hard hats, hurried from mine entrance to office, their activity resembling bees. No one appeared to pay attention to the occasional knee-rattling *wooompf* of dynamite exploding underground.

The entire complex had been constructed at an altitude of 9,000 feet in an alpine zone. What was most startling were the trees. There were none. An entire forest had been razed. The valley, resembling so many of the wilderness valleys above the Bar 20 had been entirely deforested. Two helicopters, carrying steel beams, chopped the air overhead. I told Kathryn this mine was possibly more environmentally sensitive than any other in the United States, but she had seen something that, to her, resembled an environmental holocaust. We drove back down the road in silence and for the next week she couldn't stop hearkening back to the valley. "The arrogance," she repeated.

In the late 19th century the federal government had not yet enacted a forest protection plan. In the year 1900, after woodhawks had removed prime timber from what is now wilderness, a devastating forest fire swept the Upper

West Boulder Valley. No doubt, fire has been a common event before the era of Smoky the Bear. It removes deadfall, transforms wood into meadow, and is central to a forest's cycle of regrowth. But what an impact it must have had on our landscape a century ago! For years afterward the smell of ash and charred wood lay heavy in the air across the valley and, in time, dead trees blew down and formed an impenetrable labyrinth for miles beside the river.

Regrowth was immediate. Within a year, lodgepole pines, germinated through the fire's intensity, rose from the devastation, and today the entire upper valley is on parade with these tall, creaking trees. In 1904, Teddy Roosevelt used the Forest Reserve Act of 1891 to place millions of acres in Alaska and the American Northwest under government jurisdiction. First known as Forest Reserves, in 1905 they were transferred to the Department of Interior and renamed National Forests. One such Roosevelt gift was ours—the vast Gallatin National Forest that borders private land on the West Boulder.

Once Ken Presley called me asking about a mammoth Douglas fir beside Grouse House. He said when he passed it on his wanders of the Bar 20 in 1934, age 14, he had felt sorry for that "damn old tree." It leaned precariously to one side and its entire crown was blackened, no doubt from a lightning strike. I told him the tree still stood, dramatically raked toward the east, just as he remembered. Ken was relieved.

His idle question prompted my curiosity and one day Kathryn and I reexamined the old tree. It's five feet in diameter—the largest tree I've seen in all the valley. Larry Lahren claims it might be about three hundred years old. Rubbing my hand across its rough bark, I think: this Doug fir was old at the time Captains Meriwether Lewis and William Clark entered this country. It has endured wind, fire, blizzard, pioneer, tie cutter and even Stan Cox's insatiable appetite for firewood. It will surely outlive us all. It is the most permanent of all living things in this valley.

Eighteen eighty-two was a threshold year in the West Boulder and adjacent country. The Crow Indians were persuaded to exchange their millions of acres lying between the Boulder River and the headwaters of the Yellowstone to the United States at $30,000 a year for 25 years or a total sale of $750,000. Once the treaty was signed, the Crow were shifted east, first to Absaroka, later to their present headquarters at Crow Agency beside the site where General George Armstrong Custer had lost his final battle.

The Crow had thus inhabited our country for 140 years, it's believed, from about 1740. In their heyday, they probably never numbered more than 2,500. As soon as the treaty for their removal was signed, there was an onslaught of whites into the Boulder Valleys. In the first year, some 1,450 mineral claims were recorded primarily along the Boulder and East Boulder Valleys. This prodigious figure hints at the extent of illegal trespass on Indian lands, when they were still sovereign land of the Crow. The Indians had regularly voiced complaints to their agents about the unstoppable numbers of whites—hunters, trappers, wolfers, and gold miners—sneaking into the backcountry. Now outsiders would never have to sneak again. The Boulder Valleys had fallen to their ownership.

When in 1883, the federal government published proclamations announcing the dissolution of the Crow Reservation, it described the Boulder country, available for settlement, as a "homeseeker's paradise." This use of land would be a novelty, for Indians had never treated this region as a homesite. The Boulder Valleys had been hunting grounds.

Thomas Leforge wrote an interesting account of those who once wandered Bar 20 land before the white man. Leforge, born in Ohio, traveled west with his parents into Montana and in the early 1870s joined the Kick-in-the-Belly band of Mountain Crow. In time, he married two of their women. His clan laid claim to the land lying south of the Yellowstone (whereas the River Crow's influence reached north). The account of these years, *Memoirs of a White Crow Indian*, describes how he and his band were based at the mouth of Mission Creek (about 17 miles from the Bar 20), how he would join others, seasonally, into mountains to the south. On one occasion he came to fell trees, but more often he and his friends ventured into this country for game. "The trapping and hunting," he remarks "were too good for me to be bothered with cultivating land." Here along our West Boulder, known to Indians, as the Little Beaver River there was "plenty of beaver and some otter."

Larry Lahren, archaeologist and packer, believes the West Boulder was probably the best of all three drainages for "aboriginal survival" because of the quantity of game, sunlight, and exposure. Here there were dependable populations of elk and mountain sheep, and until the advent of the fur trapper, many beaver. He conjures a West Boulder of 200 years ago, not deep, free-flowing and rapid as it is now, but a lazier river, broad and wide—a year-round floodplain, riven by a network of beaver ponds. Indians rarely camped on the edges of this river because of mosquitoes. Instead, according to Lahren, "their trails and encampments can be found along the escarpments, well away from rising water."

Two hundred years ago, the Bar 20 floodplain was underwater. Only once the beaver was eliminated, once their dams had rotted, the benches drained, would the river narrow to assume the course and the single mindedness we know today.

Kathryn and I wanted the ceremony to be held here at the Bar 20, but, in the end, we decided on a less private place.

Once when returning to the Bar 20, I turned the corner onto the West Boulder Road and saw, nearby, my neighbor, John Hoiland, repairing fence. For the last 73 years John has missed very little in this valley. Naturally, he spotted me. He waved and, as always, seemed to have something on his mind. I stopped, walked over, and the two of us were soon talking Indians. When John's uncle arrived here in 1889 from Hanover, Germany, the Crows had recently been relocated. John pointed into the escarpment and said, "My uncle told me there was a chief's body lying in them trees. That old bird had been laid there to his rest, you see."

He continues: "Indians," he whistles, "everywhere." He looks at the ground and begins to pace out a large circle. "See this. You're standing on a teepee ring. This is where they camped. Cattle have stomped the stones a bit, but this here's the place. Clear as day. When I was a toddler, used to play right here where Indians had camped for years. Didn't notice it at first, until I spotted the stones."

"Makes sense," I responded. One couldn't have selected a better site: to either side clear views of advancing friend and foe, no mosquitoes and sweet water from the West Boulder a mere two-minute hike. Altogether perfect. I walk into the space once occupied by a teepee, stretch my arms, and imagine.

Ghosts. Here in this enchanted valley one has a supernatural choice— Indian or pale skin. One can discern the spirits of them both. The whites, here for only a minute of history, left behind the preponderance of artifacts. They also imprinted onto the valley their brashness and presumption. They assumed ownership rights they considered inalienable, yet these rights were only transitory and, as it were, historically novel. The Indian, more ghostly by far, discarded only bones and stones, came and went with stealth, didn't draw boundaries across valleys, and subjected their rights to nature's. Stand here and you realize just how their spirit has endured.

Hardly three miles from John's house lives his neighbor, a cousin, Emma Ellisson. The two haven't talked in decades, their dispute mired in a family matter dating to the late 1920s. The rift, too gothic for the minds of non-family members, now appears beyond resolution. That didn't stop this friend of John's from paying a July call on Emma and asking her about the valley. Recently widowed, she sat in her large and comfortable living room, on the edge of a summer sunbeam, and told me how her older sister once worked for Bab Cox as a Bar 20 maid and how one of her duties had been to brush Mrs. Cox's dogs' teeth. But on this day I wasn't especially interested in the Coxes. Instead, I was after tales of an association between Emma's family and Chief Plenty Coups, the seminal Crow leader who led the fractious tribe during the late 19th and early 20th centuries. I had heard this great Indian leader had been a friend to Emma Ellisson's father, William Elges. Emma nodded, said it was true and watched me warily. She would rather talk of Coxes.

For two hours we chatted of her family, her ten brothers and sisters and the other white inhabitants in our valley, but when I gathered my notes to leave, she checked to make sure my tape recorder had been turned off before whispering. She told me the West Boulder had been Plenty Coup's favorite hunting grounds, and each autumn until about 1915, he returned here, to the Elges Ranch, where he and his followers camped in their painted teepees. He stayed a month each year, hunting and reminiscing with his longstanding friend, William Elges. "Have you heard about the knife?" Emma asked.

I admitted I had, but I knew few details. Her voice lowered to an almost inaudible whisper. She had grown up with a family legend, she explained. Plenty Coups had apparently lost his favorite hunting knife on the Elges Ranch. Each year, toward the end of his life, he returned to look for it, but it was never found. Emma's voice trailed off. The dog was barking hoarsely at a devil of dust in the driveway. A visitor was approaching. Before saying good-bye, I asked Emma to the Bar 20 for dinner the following week. If she came, she would meet Kathryn.

To my delight, Emma arrived on the appointed evening. She brought her daughter, and the two beamed with pleasure at the prospect of dinner away from home. Soon after arriving, Emma took Kathryn aside and asked whether I had told her about the knife. Kathryn nodded. "Would you like to see it?" Kathryn thought she had not heard correctly. She asked Emma to repeat herself. "The knife," Emma said once again. "Our hired man found it a few years ago—the knife Chief Plenty Coups lost, never could find. Didn't John tell you? It's been found at last, some 80 years after it was lost."

Emma removed the knife from its cotton packing. It was not as I imagined. There was little of the Indian about it. The steel was German, the handle elegantly carved from bone into the head of a buffalo. The knife must have been a gift to Plenty Coups from an outsider. It was hefty, self-congratulatory, and it felt appropriate to a chief.

Over 80 years, a bush had grown where the knife had fallen. Were it not for the sun glinting oddly off the blade late one afternoon, the hired man would never have found it. I held it, judging its gravity. The blade had been polished, but was still dark and pitted. It felt dependable and deadly. While I knew it belonged in a museum, I felt a thrill it had remained all these years, undiscovered, in the West Boulder Valley.

Later, Kathryn would say she felt Emma's determination to show the knife was her gift to us. Seeing it, holding it, was all we needed. At the time, no one could have displayed greater generosity.

In this valley, before there were Crow, there were Shoshone, often called Sheep Eaters. Their tenure reaches back to about A.D. 1000 and it is possible the teepee rings John Hoiland showed me had been theirs as well. "The Shoshone," claimed Larry Lahren, "weren't co-dependents of the whites, like the Crow. They didn't rely on horse and rifle, and, yes, maybe they were ousted from this valley by the Crow, but they could hold their heads high, boast *they* were still free, *they* were among the last totally self-sufficient Indians of North America." Larry gloats with this morsel of intelligence. Anything to do with self-esteem meets with his approbation.

The Shoshone and their predecessors knew this Yellowstone country well. Pure hunter-gatherers, they made good use of its resources. Arrowheads, dating to 1500 B.C. and carved from an outcrop of Yellowstone obsidian, 60 miles from the Bar 20, have been found as far away as Michigan.

Sunset yet again. I am with archaeologists Larry Lahren and Mark Papworth, naturalist Doug Peacock, and six enthusiastic acolytes at the foot of a cliff, 40 miles to the north of the Bar 20. The cliff curves above the Shields River, dimpled by the evening wind that dries our sweat and turns us to thoughts of beer. The cliff is midpoint on the saddle formed by the Bridger Mountains to the west and the snow-crusted Crazies to the east. For hundreds of years Indians have used this cliff as a *pishkan*, a buffalo jump, and the bones of hundreds of their unfortunate victims lie buried at our feet. But buffalo bones are not what has attracted these archaeologists to this site.

One morning in June 1968, local construction workers came here in search of gravel for a school parking lot. Operating a front-end loader, one of them scraped at the rubble along the foot of the cliff. On one of the operator's trips, loading gravel, an object dislodged itself from the cliff and fell into his scoop. It was a stone blade, covered in red ocher. There were more—literally dozens of bifaces and spearheads—enough to fill ten five-gallon buckets. Associated with them was a skeleton of a child, also covered in red ocher.

When professional archaeologists arrived on the scene, the site had been severely compromised by the curiosity of the construction workers. What was certain was that there were two skeletons, a two-year old child dated to 10,600 years of age, a nine-year old to 8,000, all covered in red ocher. The artifacts comprise the largest cache of Clovis blades ever found in either North or South America. The infant had belonged to the New World's fountainhead human population.

This site, called Anzick after the owners of the property, catches the eye for many reasons. It looks east into the rising sun of dawn and possesses all the hallmarks that hunter-gatherers have preferred for ages—a safe landscape with sweeping views of both approaching enemy and grazing wildlife. "Look at these two mountain ranges," says Larry, pointing at the Crazies and the Bridgers. "Ten thousand years ago, they were no doubt completed glaciated. Where we stand today was a corridor free of ice and rich in resources. It is practically consecrated land. This corridor brought peoples down from the north and then led them far to the south."

Imagine this place when the glacier departed—massive boulders strewn effortlessly everywhere, the ground scarred from the passage of a formidable mass of ice and, on the perimeter, pools of melt, forming ponds and lakes. Onto this landscape one can see those early explorers, padding silently amid the wreckage of the glacier, searching here and there for an opportunity. Their ghosts, I believe, are here, like all the others.

Forty miles from the Anzick site, back at the Bar 20, I contemplate the successions of life that have exploited this place by virtue of that corridor. Seemingly wild and untarnished, this valley has hosted so many souls over thousands of years, each of them with different needs, each leaving trace elements of their passage.

Today, in this valley, we are hardly changed from those early hunter-gatherers. We build our houses high on hills so we can see far, beside the the river because it provides life's essential, beneath tall trees for shade and protection. While we are no longer birds of passage, like creatures of long ago we are, once again, seasonal. We have learned how little life this valley will support in winter, how provident it becomes summer and fall. Today, humans come and go, searching, much like our ancestors, for opportunity. Today, opportunity comes in the form of a trout, a hard hike, a view.

Kathryn and I were married in June. Since then, my life has set a new and astonishing course. Others say they see it in my face. She claims she has never known such calm. I am now realizing a dream, a purpose, I never knew was mine. I may as well be a child for all I am learning. One distinctive pleasure is watching her change alongside me.

Evening once again. I study Kathryn as she pulls dandelions from the flower garden. Soon she will join me on the screened porch and we will sit and watch the abrupt shadow of the escarpment behind us creep over treetops on the eastern hills on the far side of the river, then climb, faster and faster, up the hill until evening becomes night and sandhill cranes cease calling. In this half-light, we could be at the very edge of the earth. Deer will ghost through the wildflower meadow and Duma and the new puppy, exhausted from our afternoon climb along the edge of the escarpment, may never open their eyes to notice. The last to leave will be the hummingbirds and then we will only hear river and owl. For all this time, she and I, watching, listening, may never say a word.

The West Boulder Valley has seen many beginnings like ours. I believe it treats each one impartially and forgives us all.

OWNERSHIP CHRONOLOGY
OF THE BAR 20 RANCH

∼

Present – July 21, 1987: Heminway family ownership of several Bar 20 buildings.

1987 – 1973: Eugene Magat ownership of Bar 20 house.

Present – March 1, 1972: West Boulder Association ownership of most former Bar 20 land.

1972 – 1960: Harry L. and Mable M. Brewer ownership of most Bar 20 property with the exception of the Grouse House, owned first by Paul R. Payne, later, survived by Monica M. Payne.

1973 – 1960: Ownership by Dr. Robert R. Kahle of Bar 20 house.

1960 – 1957: Ownership by Paul R. and Monica M. Payne of most Bar 20 land and buildings.

1957 – 1951: Ownership by Robert M. and Dorothy M. Huggins of most Bar 20 Land.

1951 – 1933: Ownership by Stanley M. and Lucille R. Cox of all Bar 20 land.

1933 – 1909: Ownership by Albert Crest.

April 7, 1904: Patent from the United States of America to Fred H. and Gertrude H. Hough and Sarah C. Hoopes.

September 27, 1902: Provisional homestead rights from "The Public" awarded to Fred H. Hough.

1940 (approximate) – 1885: Development of gold mines in Main Boulder Valley.

1885 – 1882: Building of Northern Pacific Railway through south central Montana.

1882: Purchase of land from the Crow Indian Nation by the United States.

1882 – 1740 (approximate): Crow Indian Nation controls West Boulder Valleys.

1868 – 1863: The Bozeman Trail, created to aid settlement in the West, passes within 20 miles of Bar 20.

1806 – 1804: Lewis and Clark Expedition.

1740 – A.D. 1000: Influence over West Boulder Valley by Shoshone (Sheep Eater) Tribe.

A.D. 1000 – 10,000 B.C.: Occasional occupation of region by aboriginal peoples, beginning with Clovis culture.

ACKNOWLEDGMENTS

∽

I began this project with some dog-eared foolscap and now the file weighs over a hundred pounds and the library fills an entire wall. Wherever I looked, stories abounded, thanks to hundreds of good souls endowed with sharp memories. Throughout Montana and especially in our valley as well as among friends and relatives of past Bar 20 residents, I was overwhelmed by generosity, hospitality, and candor. Where history is the subject, doors almost always opened, frowns turned to smiles—not just among the elderly but also among those who once listened to their elders.

I especially want to single out the following who contributed directly to my research: Mitch Alga, Larz Anderson, Teddy Annear, Betty Ball, Bud and Justine Bell, Frank Birdsall, Sue de Brantes, Loren Brewer, Sandra Cahill, Ginny Christensen, Lonnie Clarke, Stuart Conner, the Honorable Richard Danzig, Happy Elges, Jean Elgen, Emma Ellison, Hazel Ewan, Marie Mikkelson, June Ewan, William Fay, Ann Fitzpatrick and her friend in Georgia, Alberta Francis, John Fryer, Ray Hunt, Dr. Robert Kahle, Walt Kirn, Tony Kiser, Michael Kyte, Linda Larsen, Edward Lethem, Eugene Magat, Lee Niedringhaus, Dr. Mark Papworth, Scott Patterson, Doug Peacock, the late Mike Pearson, Chuck Reid, Tjark and Renate Reiss, Jean Reierson, Judy Rue, Rick Spellman, Ann Sperry, Major General Charles Vyvyan, Ed Webber, Jonathan Wiesel, John Worth, and all members of the West Boulder Reserve as well as its prescient founders.

Larry Lahren has been a friend, advisor, and prophet of this valley ever since I first arrived. I owe him much. Donna Harkness of Big Timber helped considerably with research. Judy Baumeister kept many pounds of unruly files in order. John Hoiland is the most famous resident of the West Boulder Valley. He well deserves the honor. I'm grateful for his memories. Chan and Carla Pyle took an interest in the valley's history before my time, and I owe them my thanks for the vital interviews they conducted.

Rock Ringling, Teresa Erickson, Tami Tavridakis, and Michael Reisner have all helped me understand the serious challenges threatening the health of Boulder drainages. Haven and Deanna Marsh of the Bull Mountains have been my friends and inspiration ever since my family arrived in Montana. Sharon Wolske, Bob and RaeDawn Wolske have, many times, made our life in Montana possible. Lark, Wayne, Andy Pollari, Rocky, Katie Cosgriff, and Rhea Smart have brought needed sunshine and wisdom to the Bar 20 for almost six years.

Babs Hard inundated me with some of the most important memories of this book. Paula Huggins was equally forthcoming with her recall of events. Monica Payne was remarkably generous with pictures and recollections. Ken Presley made the Bar 20's history his personal campaign during a time when he was undergoing several painful eye operations. Without him, this book would still be floundering as a half-baked notion.

Eames Yates of Colorado, Eames Yates of New York, Suzel de la Maisoneuve Yates, Hayden Yates, Margaret Yates comprise a family that continue to leave me in awe. I owe each one of them for their very telling reflections on their antecedents. All helped this project with essential research and with photographs.

On many occasions, Bill and Pam Bryan, long-time friends, were generous with their many insights about the people and byways of Montana.

Wonderful friends, Susan and Roy O'Connor, provided Kathryn and me with an exhilarating two-week escape that allowed me to dedicate myself to this book with renewed enthusiasm.

My agent, Flip Brophy of Sterling Lord Literistic, helped guide *Yonder*. Gerry McCauley, an outstanding agent, supported me as a friend, in spite of my fecklessness. Patrice Silverstein rigorously edited my prose and Kevin Mulroy, my editor at the National Geographic Society, made this book possible, guiding it with dedication, foresight, and unwavering commitment.

I owe much to my sister, Hilary Heminway for the style, warmth, and tenacity she contributes to our small corner of Montana. My brother, Jay Heminway, silently stays with us through thick and thin, sharing, no doubt, our late father's sometimes blind commitment to his kids' folly. My nieces, Annabel and Tobin, and my nephew, Alexander, have all given me insights to the West I might otherwise have missed. I am privileged to be a member of such an embracing, colorful, and laughter-addicted family.

My wife, Kathryn, has generously shared her first year of marriage with this book. She has patiently let me work round the clock, and she has always been eager to offer gentle and wise counsel. Without her, this book would have been meaningless.